CAMBRIDGE STUDIES IN PHILOSOPHY

Mind and meaning

CAMBRIDGE STUDIES IN PHILOSOPHY

General editor D. H. MELLOR

Advisory editors J. E. J. ALTHAM, SIMON BLACKBURN, DANIEL DENNETT,
MARTIN HOLLIS, FRANK JACKSON, JONATHAN LEAR,
T. J. SMILEY, BARRY STROUD

Mind and meaning

Brian Loar
*Associate Professor, School of
Philosophy, University of Southern California*

Cambridge University Press
CAMBRIDGE
LONDON   NEW YORK   NEW ROCHELLE
MELBOURNE   SYDNEY

Published by the Press Syndicate of the University of Cambridge
The Pitt Building, Trumpington Street, Cambridge CB2 1RP
32 East 57th Street, New York, NY 10022, USA
296 Beaconsfield Parade, Middle Park, Melbourne 3206, Australia

First published 1981

Printed in Great Britain at the University Press, Cambridge

British Library Cataloguing in Publication Data
Loar, Brian
Mind and meaning. – (Cambridge studies in philosophy)
1. Intellect 2. Psycholinguistics
I. Title
128'.2   BF431   81–6121

ISBN 0 521 22959 6

Contents

vii

viii

ix

Acknowledgements

I am glad to express here admiring gratitude to Sanda Alcalay, whose encouragement and support made the project easier than it would otherwise have been. For more than seventeen years, I have been greatly influenced by innumerable conversations with Stephen Schiffer, both about general method and about many of the issues of this book, for which I am most grateful. In recent years conversations with Hartry Field have had a great influence on my thoughts on belief and truth. Stephen Stich's challenging scepticism was a helpful spur to the project.

Introduction

The attention that philosophers have lavished on propositional attitudes in the last hundred years has been thoroughly appropriate; there are few concepts whose explication would yield greater philosophical dividends than those of belief, desire and their content. In these opening pages I shall mention three concerns that make that true – namely, meaning, the mental, and truth.

MEANING

The theory of meaning is ostensibly about spoken and written language, and not thought or belief or intention. But it has become evident that it is not independent of the theory of propositional attitudes, or something closely related. The pragmatic concepts of a person's or population's language, or the reference of an expression as used by a person or population, will on any current account have something to do with belief. Beyond that there is a great diversity of theory. For some, meaning is a matter of the role of language in speech, while for others it is a property of language in thought. Among the former there are reductionists, who would explicate semantic concepts via propositional attitudes (e.g. Gricean intentions, beliefs, mutual knowledge), and anti-reductionists, whose position is that the concepts of belief and meaning play coordinate roles in rational psychology.

The account of chapter 9 accommodates both language of thought and communication-theoretic intuitions about semantic properties. And it is determinedly *reductionist* in two senses. First, the basis of all semantic properties is belief and desire; and thus it resembles Gricean reductionism: the meaning of linguistic items concerns the content of certain propositional attitudes. But the account is not exclusively communication-theoretic; for the theory of belief can serve as the basis of the semantic theory of "the language of thought" (rather the reverse of the usual view). Secondly, the account is reductionist in presupposing an explication of belief and desire themselves which does not rely on propositions or semantic concepts. Propositional attitudes can then serve non-circularly as the basis of meaning.

That belief and desire and their content can be explicated without presupposing anything about natural-language semantics will, to many, be implausible; the idea runs the risk of suggesting a picture of thought without language, with language a mere vehicle of communication. Perhaps this will help: even if belief were a linguistic state, those properties of beliefs which constitute their propositional content can be reconstructed independently of their linguistic aspects, especially connections with spoken language. The theory of propositional attitudes abstracts from overt language or its inner connections. This may be too analytical for some tastes, not enough about what beliefs and desires *are* — viz. perhaps linguistic states. But how better to pursue that than by settling how any state, linguistic or non-linguistic, must relate to behavior and perception to be the belief that p or the desire that q?

The reduction of meaning to belief and intention would leave many questions in the theory of meaning untouched, e.g. about reference, the relation of meaning to verification and empirical content, equivalence in meaning, logical form, the nature of truth — all of which are as troublesome as ever. A principal complaint against the proposed reduction has been, I think, that it purports to answer such questions. So a Gricean theory may appear to be attempting to clarify equivalence in meaning in terms of equivalence of beliefs.

But of course the reduction doesn't answer the basic questions; rather it suggests what they are. Nor does it block progress on them, since nothing in the reduction suggests that propositional content is not in turn explicable. Some may have reasoned thus: "If semantical properties are explicable in terms of propositional attitudes, the latter must be non-linguistic, and therefore relations to propositions. But propositions hypostasize precisely what needs to be explicated, and so the reduction obscures the problematic concepts of the theory of meaning." But, as I shall argue, propositions are eliminable; their roles can be played by unproblematic entities. If we resist being mesmerized by propositions and concentrate on propositional attitudes, sensible reconstructions are forthcoming, with no implication that we are platonic intellects whose mental lives consist in grasping essences. This all implies that much of the "theory of meaning" has not been about *meaning* but about the *content* of propositional attitudes.

2

An obvious incentive for an explication of propositional attitudes is to meet Brentano's claim that the intentionality of a mental state precludes its being physical, something those physicalists who think there are beliefs and desires must dispute. But that requires explicating propositional attitude-ascriptions so that they are satisfiable by purely physical systems, entirely by virtue of physical properties.

TRUTH AND CORRESPONDENCE

Realism in epistemology and metaphysics presupposes that thoughts or sentences have objective properties that determinately constitute their truth conditions. This is why, despite Quine's naturalism and anti-reductionism about the interpretation of scientific theories, his overall framework can seem anti-realist. For Quine's attack on the naturalistic acceptability of semantic properties, including *inter*linguistic truth conditions and reference, attacks the objective basis of truth as correspondence. The *intra*linguistic truth predicate, the disquotation device, preserves nothing about the contingent representational properties of language or thought. Much of the interest in causal theories of reference is due to their pointing the way back towards a correspondence of thought and the world. But reference is not enough; some naturalistic account of the truth conditions of beliefs and utterances is required to re-establish correspondence on a firm footing.

This is not to deny that there can be a substantive account of truth without propositional attitudes. For sentential attitudes, which on some accounts are introduced independently of propositional attitudes, may suffice. But for reasons that emerge in 7.7, taking propositional attitudes as the bearers of truth yields the most rounded accommodation of classical intuitions, for it accounts both for substantive correspondence intuitions and for certain strong redundancy intuitions. On other accounts those two functions are allotted to distinct devices, one intralinguistic, 'true', and the other interlinguistic, 'true in L'.

THE EARMARKS OF PROPOSITIONAL ATTITUDES

Much of the animus against intensionalism, and enthusiasm for reference over meaning, was due not just to the ontological dubiousness of intensions, but also to the idea that no scientific good sense can be made of states with the classical earmarks of propositional attitudes. It will be useful at the outset to list those features.

First, propositional attitudes are *intentional*: no extensional equivalence of s and s' is sufficient for $\ulcorner x$ believes that $s\urcorner$ and $\ulcorner x$ believes that $s'\urcorner$ to ascribe the same belief.

Secondly, beliefs have *evidential independence of content*, which can be explained by contrast with the Quinean theory. From the evident observation that beliefs do not *epistemically* "face reality one by one", that is, that we take into account potentially everything else we believe in arriving at a particular judgment, Quine takes the further step, in effect, of identifying the content or meaning of s, for person x, with s's evidential connections – its conditioned connections in x to other sentences and to sensory stimuli. Classically, however, propositional content is individuated independently of such evidential connections. While determining a belief's truth requires taking into account other propositions, under what circumstances it corresponds to reality is independent of what counts as evidence for it.

Thirdly, beliefs, individuated intentionally, are interpersonally ascribable; there is such a thing as *intersubjective synonymy*. This is not independent of the last feature, since it implies it; for, as no two persons ever are in precisely the same evidential situation, if content were a matter of evidential connections no two persons would ever have the same belief. But this is nevertheless a distinct feature, since it implies that there is an objective criterion for interpersonal synonymy.

My account will be *holistic*, in that the content of a belief is a matter of its functional role in a system of beliefs and desires. Now functional role is relative to a given system of generalizations connecting inner states, input and output. If those generalizations that define the functional roles of beliefs and desires can apply equally to two persons, independently of their evidential connections, then that holism of content is quite different from the Quinean holism.

Fourthly, beliefs and desires are true and false, fulfilled and unfulfilled. The truth conditions of a belief are linked to the first three features – i.e. intentionality, evidential independence and interpersonal ascribability.

Fifthly, beliefs and desires are not as such necessarily linguistic states – i.e. states which involve relations to sentences of a public language. It must be emphasized that this is quite compatible with explicating 'x believes that s' as asserting a relation to a sentence of the *ascriber's* language. (Thus the following is not a good argument:

4

beliefs are not linguistic states as such; belief-ascriptions are relational; therefore belief-ascriptions assert relations to something non-linguistic – e.g. propositions.)

Now this fifth condition is independent of the first four. For some theories of propositional attitudes attribute to them the first four features but also make them linguistic. The epitome is Carnap's theory, that belief is a disposition to assert a sentence, and that we describe the belief by producing a sentence of ours as being intensionally isomorphic to that sentence. (On Carnap's theory the possibility of interpersonal synonymy is simply taken for granted.) So we may think of the version on which beliefs are not necessarily linguistic as the pure classical theory.

I shall be attempting to show that these five features, or close reconstructions of them can be exemplified within a naturalistic framework without propositions or irreducibly intensional properties. Quine's demand for an eliminative explication of intensionality is not too strong. For any theory that would fully vindicate propositions, by showing their use to be appropriate in psychology, would thereby, by accounting for the physical bases of these five features, show how to eliminate propositions from psychology while preserving intentionality.

1

Propositional attitudes in the theory of mind

The principal concerns of this book are in the foundations of "the theory of meaning" – questions about the contents of beliefs, about truth conditions, and about linguistic meaning. Evidently a theory of belief must raise issues in the philosophy of mind, about the general status of ascriptions of mental states, about their physicalist reduction, and about the explication of the sentences that ascribe them. In this chapter I present a case for a theory that is realist about beliefs and their content (i.e. not instrumentalist), and that is functionalist, physicalist and reductionist.

1.1 THE BELIEF–DESIRE THEORY

Behaviorists had two tendencies in explicating belief: on one, the criterion of belief is linguistic behavior – what is or would be said; on the other, what matters is general behavior, the real test of belief being action and not avowal. The other particular philosophical questions a theorist was facing tended to determine the approach. The avowal theory was attractive for the analysis of intentionality and opaque contexts, the action-oriented theory for the analysis of acceptance, or subjective probability in decision theory, or sincere assertion. But both theories collapse for the same reason: what a person would do or say depends not merely on what he believes, but also on his desires and aims. The point is quite conclusive, for desire raises the reverse problem: what a person does or says indicates what he wants or aims at only given what he believes.

But the reduction of behaviorism to a vicious circle has been fruitful. For it has suggested accounting for belief and desire in terms of their *joint role* in predicting and explaining behavior. That joint role can be represented, in one form of a person x's *reasons* for an action A, as follows:

6

x desires that q;

x believes that if p then x's doing A will lead to q;

x believes that p.

Now, not every such combination leads to deciding to do A, because the desire may be overriden by another. But every account of an agent's reasons involves something like it; moreover, it shows how *any* belief that p and desire that q can lead to action by way of a conditional instrumental belief. This explanatory dovetailing of belief and desire evidently is no accident.

A revised behaviorist idea now might occur to one; namely, that it is those belief–desire combinations that are the relevant dispositions to behavior. But the idea is singularly unproductive. It yields no explication of belief- or desire-ascriptions separately, and we do manage them in partial ignorance of a person's other attitudes. Moreover, to have such a combination of attitudes is not *eo ipso* to be disposed to do A, again because of overriding desires. (Perhaps in some sense of 'disposition', 'tendency', or 'inclination' that combination is usually sufficient for a "disposition", etc. to do A. That concept, however, would have to be accounted for, not in terms of straightforward behaviorist counterfactuals, but within the context of some functional system.)

What then might the joint explanatory role of beliefs and desires amount to? Presumably it is our mastery of some system or *theory* that accounts for our understanding attitude-ascriptions, one that incorporates the explanatory pattern referred to two paragraphs ago. Although the answer to the following question is obvious, perhaps it is not a bad way to launch our investigation. Could our mastery of that pattern alone, as a general theory of behavior, account for our understanding attitude-sentences? Does it exhaust the relevant theoretical roles of belief and desire? Of course the answer is no; for no belief or desire is thereby distinguished from any other belief or desire. And evidently our mastery of attitude-ascriptions must lie in part in our understanding the difference between the beliefs that Edward is eating an avocado and that Jane is dancing the *bossa nova*.

So the theory, whatever it is, must appropriately distinguish distinct beliefs and desires – must imply something different about the belief that p and about the belief that q for all distinct p and q. If a theory lacked that property, our mastery of it could not possibly explain our mastery of 'x believes that p'. This point has not been prominent in recent discussion of belief as a theoretical concept. Even given the global *indeterminacy* of a system of ascribing beliefs and desires, within the system something must individuate distinct beliefs. Thus however arbitrary the choice of a translation scheme might be, its whole point is to generate a useful difference between 'means s_1' and 'means s_2'. So with belief. This point may be lost in discussions of general constraints like the Principle of Charity, which enjoins us to maximize truth and plausibility in ascribing beliefs. Such principles (for an important discussion of which see Davidson, 1972, and Lewis, 1972) do not as such contribute to the intrasystematic individuation of content. If attitude-ascriptions are explainable in terms of their role in some theory, something far more specific has to be introduced.

The thought naturally occurs that some special relation between beliefs and *linguistic* behavior, which is not via the practical syllogism, may individuate beliefs. While the practical syllogism relation between a belief and an action equally holds between any other belief and that same action, perhaps an independent relation which obtains between each belief and a certain utterance-type and between no other belief and that utterance-type, can be counted as fundamental. That would then individuate the contents of beliefs and desires, while their role in the practical syllogism makes them "beliefs" and "desires".

Now I do not doubt that there is an important relation that obtains, for a given person, between each belief and some utterance-type and no other belief and that utterance-type (except when the latter is ambiguous). But I do doubt that it can usefully be introduced as part of the foundational theory of belief. One such relation is specified in 9.1, but it requires an independent theory of belief. The idea is that a certain utterance-type, or internal linguistic state, can have a functional role for a certain person which makes it the belief that p. But the account of that functional role presupposes a theory that generates independently a unique systematic role for the belief that p.

My reason for denying a connection between belief and linguistic behavior that individuates content is elementary. If the behavior is described purely *syntactically*, the connection is not interlinguistically or even generally interpersonally ascribable; for sentences are connected with different beliefs for speakers of different languages or idiolects. If the behavior is described *semantically*, say as 'utterance of a sentence that means p', something either inside or outside the theory must distinguish 'means p' and 'means q'. If it is inside the theory our problem remains; if outside, the theory does not fully account for the content of beliefs, for its principal source would lie elsewhere.

8

Thus it seems the only salient relation our commonsense theory implies between x's belief that p and the sentence that expresses that belief in x's idiolect is the one generated by the practical syllogism: x's uttering s could be explained in terms of x's desire to communicate p, and x's belief that uttering s will secure that result. But that relation could obtain between any other belief and the utterance of s, and so our commonsense theory relates linguistic behavior to belief in the manner of behavior in general.

Systematic connections between beliefs, desires, and behavior do not then account for content on their own. It seems we must at least turn to connections with perception. What these connections are and how they contribute to the individuation of content is discussed in chapter 4. Let me simply register here the relevance of *input* generalizations connecting perceptual circumstances and some beliefs. Finally, there are also *a priori* rationality constraints that operate together with the input generalizations to secure the distinctness of distinct beliefs (cf. 4.5 and 4.7). The hypothesis is that our mastery of attitude-ascriptions involves a certain theory that consists at least in:

(a) input generalizations relating perceptual circumstances to beliefs,

(b) internal constraints of rationality on beliefs, and

(c) output generalizations relating beliefs and desires to actions.

1.2 INTERPRETATIONS OF THE BELIEF–DESIRE THEORY

To say that our mastery of a certain theory explains our understanding attitude-ascriptions is hardly enough; for that raises the general question of theory interpretation. It is far from obvious that there is a unique correct device of theory interpretation, of explaining the meaning of the theoretical terms of T in terms of their occurrence in T. For theories are artifacts, constructed for purposes that differ in ways that affect their interpretation. Some theories perhaps should be taken instrumentally, e.g. parts of economics: while others, say in cognitive psychology, may best be interpreted in a realist vein.[1] The literature suggests three schemes for interpreting attitude-ascriptions – namely, instrumentalism, functionalism, and a certain sort of anti-reductionism. While the first and third of these unfortunately are not often distinguished, they ought to be.

---

[1] Perhaps there is a unique best kind of *realist* interpretation of a theory, but that isn't obvious. Functional interpretation may not be appropriate for theories that are not functional in the sense of chapter 3, e.g. theories in physics.

The instrumentalist account treats the belief–desire system simply as a device for systematizing perceptual–behavioral facts. Attitude-ascriptions would not then have *truth* conditions; they would be evaluated purely in terms of their contributions to the systematizing effort. Later I offer reasons for looking for a realist interpretation; but notice that if one accepted both the Brentanian thesis of the incompatibility of the existence of intentional states and physicalism, and physicalism, the only sense to be made of attitude-ascriptions would be instrumentalist.

Functional theories are theories of how states of an individual are related to each other, to input and to output, causally, transitionally, and so on. So to interpret the system of beliefs and desires as a functional theory is to explicate an ascription of an attitude to x in terms of x's being in a state that realizes a functional role associated by the system with that form of ascription. A functionalist interpretation is a *realist* interpretation: the theoretical terms of a functionally interpreted theory *denote* (in the cases that normally interest us) *internal* states of the individual. These are either non-functional states that realize the functional roles, or the functional states themselves, according to how one sets up the interpretation.

A functional interpretation of a theory is *explicative*: it assigns to each sentence containing a theoretical term of the theory an equivalent sentence, free of theoretical terms, that somehow captures a functional role. And indeed it seems to me (quite at variance with the intuitions of many, I think) that any plausible account of the belief–desire theory that is both realist and physicalist will generate an explicative treatment. Consider the denotational scheme of realist theory interpretation suggested by Putnam (1975). In psychological theories, the only plausible denotations for theoretical terms, as Putnam has pointed out, are functional states. Now, what is the criterion of denotation? The most natural suggestion is that the theoretical terms of psychology denote those functional states which would explain the success of the theory. But they, it would seem, are the states determined by those interconnections in the organism which mirror the connec-tions that the theory generates among its terms. For, if there is no approximately similar system in the organism, why say that those terms *denote* any functional states at all? The upshot is that one can read off the criterion of denotation of the theory's terms from the theory itself, and that means that functional theories have expli-cative truth conditions, of the kind described in chapter 3 or 4.3. A realist–functionalist interpretation is perforce an explicative interpretation.

Some may deny that the instrumentalist and functionalist interpretations exhaust the possibilities. While I find it difficult to make sense of a third position, let me attempt notionally to describe what I shall call simply the anti-reductionist theory, as follows.

The belief–desire theory (it is said) is not to be accounted for instrumentally; it is a *bona fide* system of description and objective explanation. Yet the functionalist account is too strong; our common-sense psychological theories are not about our internal physical organization. The instrumentalist–functionalist dichotomy stems from an over-simplified conception of objective truth conditions. There are different levels of objective explanation, each determined by theories at its own level. Belief–desire explanation in particular need not be answerable to any other level. The understanding it produces is *sui generis*, determined by its own interpretative explanations and no less objective for that. The meaning of 'believes' and 'desires' is given by that system; our understanding of attitude-sentences is just our mastery of that system.

The important thing about the anti-reductionist theory is that it takes the concepts of belief and desire to depend on the belief–desire theory; it is a sort of *implicit definition* theory. Now there is an important distinction among such theories. The question is this: as regards philosophical explanation, do the concepts of behavior and perceptual circumstances have *explanatory priority*? Is it by virtue of the belief–desire theory's being anchored in those unproblematic concepts that our mastery of the theory generates understanding of the concepts of belief and desire? I have nothing to say about theories that deny this – that regard the concepts of behavior and of mental states as on a par. Clearly, the concepts of physical behavior and the relevant sorts of physical perceptual circumstances are not themselves determined by their role in anything as narrow as the belief–desire theory; the whole physical object framework would need to be invoked. And I assume that a theory of mental states is a theory of an *isolable* part of what there is, so that we can in principle describe the rest of the world without it, but not *it* without the rest of the world. On that basis I offer the following argument.

Let us call any condition that marks off creatures that have beliefs and desires from creatures that lack them a *demarcation condition*. Now presumably whatever determines the meaning of belief- and desire-ascriptions, e.g. a belief–desire theory of the form (a)–(c), ought to determine a demarcation condition. There are two ways in which it might do that – by virtue of what it says taken at face value, or as interpreted in a certain way. Both the functionalist and instrumentalist interpretations (as we shall see) do determine demarcation conditions. What needs first to be pointed out is that (a)–(c) do not *explicitly* determine one.

Generalizations of sorts (b) and (c) would merely say that *if x* has certain propositional attitudes, etc., then *x* has or lacks certain other attitudes, or performs certain actions. Nor would (a) yield a sufficient condition for having attitudes; for while its antecedent might itself lack mention of attitudes, it would say that if *x* satisfies such and such perceptual conditions, then *x* has such and such beliefs *provided that the theory as a whole applies to x*. So generalizations (a)–(c) do not explicitly say when they collectively apply to *x*. This shows that learning them without applying some device of interpretation or evaluation would not put one in possession of a condition that distinguishes creatures with attitudes from creatures without them; and that means that the mere mastery of them is not sufficient for having the concepts of belief and desire. The point is not epistemological – it is not that the theory would not generate its own day-to-day evidential conditions. The point rather is that (a)–(c) would not explicitly say anything that would, given all facts about cactuses, preclude them from having beliefs.

It seems that the only extension of the theory that could determine a demarcation condition would say something like: creatures have beliefs and desires if they *behave* thus and so, for more conditions like (a)–(c) will not help. But apart from an instrumentalist account, where the behavior is described simply in terms of its susceptibility to systematization by (a)–(c), there is no reason to be hopeful. The most one might expect is *sufficient* conditions, that is, descriptions of *x*'s behavior, and counterfactuals relating it to *x*'s perceptual circumstances, that would incline one to ascribe beliefs and desires to *x*. But such conditions would be far too specific to be *necessary* for *x*'s having attitudes. The class of behavioral repertories that would instrumentally warrant ascribing beliefs and desires is open-ended; all any two of them may have in common is that they could thus be rationalized.

Might the implicit definition theorist suggest some general meta-theoretic principle, by virtue of which the theory determines a demarcation condition? What might it be? That the theory successfully systematizes *x*'s behavior does not imply that the theory is *true* of *x*;

that is not in general a good inference. The systematizing success of the theory does not imply that x is *denoted* by any term of the theory, like 'believes p'. If the import of the theory is then taken to be that x's behavior can be systematized thus, we have simply the instrumentalist interpretation. And that the theory determines a demarcation condition by determining how the internal states of x are organized is just the functionalist account. The implicit definition theory leaves it a mystery what constitutes the difference between having beliefs and lacking them.

Does the argument beg the question? Evidently, I am insisting on a demarcation condition that is free of the concepts of belief and desire; but the anti-reductionist in effect denies that the line can be drawn without using those concepts. The argument, however, is not directed against every possible anti-reductionist position, but against any on which mastery of the concepts stems from mastery of the theory, and the other terms of the theory have an independent conceptual role. What would such an account amount to if it did not also hold the belief–desire theory to determine a demarcation condition? Suppose you were presented with the theory *de novo*, with prior understanding of all its terms save 'believes', 'desires', etc. Would you *thereby* have any idea, without further interpretation of the theory, of the difference between creatures with and without beliefs? Clearly not. Now, suppose it were said that the demarcation condition has to *emerge* in one's attempts to apply the theory – in other words, that one has to discover empirically which creatures the theory applies to. The following two situations seem to be covered by that: first, the theory successfully and non-trivially systematizes the behavior of such and such creatures; secondly, that success also indicates that certain states of those creatures are systematically organized as the theory says beliefs and desires are. Accepting the theory as applying to those creatures on the former basis is instrumentalism, and on the latter functionalism.

A functionalist interpretation of the belief–desire theory yields a demarcation condition quite straightforwardly: x has beliefs and desires provided that x is functionally organized in such and such way and x actually is in some of the states defined by that functional organization. What this amounts to cannot be explained in one paragraph; in fact it takes most of chapters 3 and 4 to do the job. But the functional interpretation assigns to attitude-sentences truth conditions that are expressible without using the problematic terms of (a)–(c). It thereby shows why, although the theory explicitly yields no demarcation criterion, it implicitly does so. For while in its unexplicated version the

13

theory has the conditional form outlined above, its functional explication gives it a different logical form – namely that of an existential quantification over states.[2] For it to apply to x is for some of x's states to be functionally organized as the theory, thus explicated, says.

From the instrumentalist perspective, belief–desire-*ascriptions* do not have truth conditions; a plausible demarcation condition emerges nevertheless. A first approximation is that a creature has beliefs and desires just in case its behavior and perceptual circumstances can successfully by systematized by ascriptions that conform to (a)–(c). (Naturally further generalizations will be required as well, since (a)–(c) do not provide an adequate epistemic basis on which to ascribe beliefs and desires to a new creature. An account of those further generalizations is given in 6.3.) Now that is too weak: the behavior of a pencil, of anything whatever, can be systematized in terms of beliefs and desires. Some condition of non-triviality would have to be added, possibly this: attributing beliefs and desires to x should, in the absence of an independent scientific account of x, be indispensable to finding useful systematic patterns in x's behavior; *and* a full range of propositional content should have non-otiose employment.

Is there some reason for preferring the functionalist–realist interpretation to the instrumentalist one? Several lines probably will occur to those who are inclined to be realists here, which have much to do with my own inclination towards a functionalist–realist position, but which may not polemically be successful against the instrumentalist. One is simple: we think of beliefs and desires as among the real *causes* of behavior and not just as devices for systematizing it. The instrumentalist may reply, however, that 'cause' itself is used instrumentally in such contexts. Another is this. One reason for not attributing beliefs and desires to amoebae is that the physical mechanisms that account for their behavior are too simple, and exhibit none of the structure of explanations in terms of reasons. Similarly, if it were to turn out that the physical mechanisms that completely explain human behavior at no level exhibited the structure of beliefs and desires, then something we had all along believed, viz. that beliefs and desires were among the causes of behavior, would turn out to be false. Naturally we would continue to use the belief–desire framework to systematize behavior, but that should then at the theoretical level have the air of

---

[2] That the theory implies existential quantifications over first-order states doesn't become fully apparent until the end of 4.2.

fictionalizing and contrivance. The trouble with this argument is that the instrumentalist can simply say that he does not intuitively discern any commitment, by the normal pre-philosophical use of the theory, to anything that would be falsified by the absence of structural analogues at the physical level. So while in some way both of these considerations may appear to some, as they do to me, to provide reasons for working out a functionalist position, they are not thereby reasons for the otherwise unconverted. What might be more persuasive, *in partibus infidelium*, is a specific, detailed, functionalist theory.

1.3 PSYCHOPHYSICAL CORRELATIONS AND REDUCTION

The requirement of correlations between *types* of mental states and types of physical states has in recent years been widely rejected by physicalists in favor of the weaker and apparently more plausible requirement of token–token identities – in other words, of particular dateable mental states or events with particular dateable physical states or events. That rejection is evidently correct if the requirement on physicalism is that mental states should be correlated with the same physical states in all individuals. But there are weaker correlation theories, and I see the reasons for rejecting them as more than correspondingly weak. In particular there is the theory that, to each of z's possible mental states at t, there corresponds one or more of z's possible physical states at t, such that z would at t be in that mental state iff z were at t in the (or a) corresponding physical state. As it happens the functionalist theory of chapter 4 implies that there are psychophysical type–type correlations relativized to individuals at times – or implies that if there are such states as beliefs and desires there are such correlations. In this section I make a preliminary case for this weak correlationist physicalism, and consider its bearing on the issue of psychophysical reduction.

First argument for psychophysical correlations

This really is an argument for a certain conditional – namely, if there are token–token identities of propositional attitudes and physical states then there are such relativized type–type correlations. It might be noted here that the token–token theory itself follows from two innocuous premises – namely, that beliefs and desires are among the causes of bodily movements, and that physical events have only physical causes.

Suppose x's belief at t that emeralds are green is identical with x's physical state(-token) B. That means that B has a certain property – namely, being a belief that emeralds are green. Now what is it about B – that physical state – that constitutes its having that property? We may safely say this: it must satisfy the predicate 'x is a belief that emeralds are green'. Here another assumption comes into play – namely, that the satisfaction conditions of 'x is a belief that p' are somehow determined by its *systematic role* in the belief–desire theory. But then presumably B's satisfying that predicate must be by virtue of some systematic role of B itself, and what could that be except its counterfactual causal interactions and associations with other states with complementary systematic roles? Now I suggest that role of B's can perspicuously be spelled out only as follows: B is of a type that has a certain position in a *system of state-types* of z's that are interrelated at t by certain counterfactual relations.

That B's systematic properties cannot be accounted for more economically may be seen by considering a certain weaker, and somewhat notional, competitor. On the type–type format just sketched, B's systematic role is a *second-order property*[3] – that is, a property which B has by virtue of having certain first-order properties that satisfy certain conditions: that is what implies the (mental) type – (first-order) type correlation. Now, suppose we try to identify B's systematic potential with some *first-order* counterfactual property. B's systematic role consists in part in its possible interactions with other attitudes, e.g. desires, to yield yet further attitudes or actions. This is all counterfactual, of course, and for B to be a belief that p these other attitudes need not exist; rather what needs to be true is that *were* certain state-tokens of such and such kinds – those other attitude-kinds – to occur, then they would combine with B to such and such effect. How, though, do we specify those "such and such kinds"? Given that the meanings of 'x believes that p' and 'x desires that q' depend on their systematic roles, then we should be able to *abstract* those systematic roles without using the terms 'believes' and 'desires', for otherwise, identifying their meaning with their systematic role would be without substance. But such an abstraction of roles cannot be done in terms of first-order counterfactual properties. Suppose the relevant role of B consists in part in how it would interact with a desire that q in certain circumstances to yield a decision. At the level of first-order properties there is no way, *except circularly*, of abstracting the systematic role of the desire that q;

---

[3] There are two sorts of second-order property involved here, namely second-order properties of persons, and second-order properties of belief-tokens.

for one would have in turn to employ the concept of belief. This is the very circularity problem that refutes analytical behaviorism, except that here the putative counterfactual properties are of physical state-tokens and not whole organisms.

The solution is to move up a level and quantify over first-order types. One may then say: there are state-types of z at t that are counterfactually organized thus and so.

The argument has been as follows. For the token–token identity, the physical token B must satisfy the predicate 'x is a belief that p'. That means that B must have a systematic role at t that corresponds to the position of that predicate in the belief–desire theory. But the only way of accounting for that systematic role is to identify it with a certain second-order property – one whose obtaining entails type–type correlations relativized to a person at a time.

The nominalization 'believing that p' is, I suggest, most appropriately used to denote the relevant second-order property. So if a mental state(-type) is whatever is denoted by such nominalizations, mental states are identical with second-order state-types and not first-order physical state-types. A non-identity *correlation* between mental state-types $M_1, \ldots, M_n$ and first-order physical state-types $P_1, \ldots, P_n$ may take this form: z is in M_i by virtue of being in some first-order state that has the systematic role involved in M_i, and P_i is that first-order state. On the other hand, one might use the locution 'z's belief that p at t' to refer to the first-order state that for z has such and such systematic role at t; if one uses the term 'mental states' to mean the *denotata* of such nominalizations (as opposed to those of the form 'believing that p') then one could appropriately say that mental states are identical with first-order physical states. But one had then better keep the former sense of 'mental state' as well, if one wants to be able to say that different creatures can be in the same mental state.

The second argument for psychophysical correlations

Here token–token identities are not presupposed. The claim is that if beliefs and desires are among the causes of behavior then there must be type–type psychophysical correlations for persons at times. The argument proceeds on this assumption: no explanatory theory, be it folk or scientific, is immune from the possibility of overthrow by virtue of *explanatory irrelevance*.

Suppose sophisticated advances in information-processing models in psychology permit far more fine-grained explanations of human action than commonsense belief–desire psychology. Suppose moreover that neurophysiological knowledge makes it probable that the functional system described by the information-processing theory is realized by the human central nervous system. Suppose also that the states and structures the theory invokes are systematically linked to other important parts of psychology about which commonsense psychology has little to say – for example, how memory works. Naturally the integration of action-explanations into such a larger framework would tend to confirm those explanations.

Consider, against this background, the status of explanations of actions in terms of beliefs and desires, and therefore the question of the very existence of beliefs and desires. Someone might argue: the new theory shows that the belief–desire theory is explanatorily irrelevant, and therefore not to be counted as true of humans. There would be, it seems to me, only one interesting counter to such an assertion – namely, that the belief–desire theory, when interpreted functionally, respresents, however crudely and partially, some discernible structure at some (perhaps rather general) level of the functional organization which makes the new theory true. That aspect of the new functional organization to which the belief–desire theory corresponds need not be especially *salient*, independently of prior interest in the structure of the belief–desire theory.

On this vindication of the belief–desire theory, given that the new theory implies first-order states (say neurophysiological states) with certain functional roles, the existence of relativized type–type psychophysical correlations would follow directly. But there are, after all, fairly strong reasons to suppose that such explanations are ultimately forthcoming – that we are in the situation described. The argument has been that the only way to avoid the overthrow of the theory that we have beliefs and desires, on grounds of explanatory irrelevance, is to find a vindication of it within the new functional theory. But that would indirectly imply psychophysical correlations, relativized to persons at times.

Naturally the anti-reductionist reaction is not likely to be favorable. But what might an alternative reply be to a revisionist scientist's claim that there are no beliefs and desires on the grounds of explanatory irrelevance? (This would allow one's remaining strongly attached to the belief–desire theory construed instrumentally.) Suppose one were to insist that no scientific results could count against the proposition that human beings have beliefs and desires. The question arises: could *anything* count against that proposition? It is difficult to identify any candidates apart from competing scientific explanations and the resistance of behavior to systematizing by the belief–desire theory. So to reject the relevance of the former is to hold that the only thing that could falsify the general ascription of beliefs and desires is behavior. Now on that basis I see only two possible accounts of the status of the belief–desire theory. The first is that its truth *logically follows* from its systematizing success; but that is instrumentalism, with a somewhat perverse use of 'true'. The second is this: the belief–desire theory is to be realistically interpreted, i.e. its truth does not logically follow from its systematizing success; but it is related to the perceptual–behavioral data as theories in physics are related to the observational facts, i.e. they exhaust the evidence. Now this is a dogmatic dualism of a quite extraordinary sort; it could not be refuted by any degree of success in scientific explanations of behavior, however exhaustive. What is worse is that, given the argument about the demarcation condition, it is far from clear that it has a coherent interpretation.

The requirement of psychophysical correlations relativized to times is rather a weak reductive constraint. That the belief–desire theory would be vindicated only by an isomorphism with part of some more detailed scientific theory indicates, however, that in practice vindicating the theory would require a stronger reduction. For any new evidence, apart from the instrumental success of the theory, that Jones's neurophysical state-types are at a given time functionally organized thus and so would *in practice* also be evidence that those very states are somewhat enduringly, but not unchangeably, organized thus in Jones and also to some extent in others.

The advantage of the weak formulation, however, is that it does not require us to pronounce *a priori* on what sort of fit between the belief–desire theory and the structure of theoretical psychology would prompt scientists or philosophers to regard belief–desire psychology as having successfully been reduced. This point deserves expansion. That the belief–desire theory is instrumentally successful does not entail its truth in any chunky non-trivial sense. Developed theories of the brain's connections with behavior may ultimately explain why the belief–desire theory has been successful, but not just any theory that explains the success of another theory thereby generates a reduction of that other theory. There is a difference between a theory's *explaining away the success of* another theory, and *vindicating* it, and these relations are matters of degree. The point here is that to say where scientists and philosophers would draw the line may not be possible in advance of a substantive theory. The requirement of type–type correlations relativized to persons and times might perhaps be seen as the bottom line of vindication, simply because nothing weaker appears to capture a suitable matching of counterfactual structures, except of course some qualification about the correlations *approximately* holding.

1.4 PSYCHOPHYSICAL LAWS AND PSYCHOPHYSICAL REDUCTION

In this section I turn to Davidson's argument (1970, 1973) against there being psychophysical laws – for, as he puts it, the anomalousness of the mental. Actually the issue is not psychophysical laws as such. They are implausible on independent grounds; but they are also irrelevant to functionalist reduction. Davidson's specific argument is what concerns me; for if it worked against psychophysical laws it would also establish the far stronger conclusion that there can be no functionalist reduction. Davidson quite clearly endorses this further conclusion: "complete understanding of the workings of the body and brain would not constitute knowledge of thought and action" (1973, p. 715). And again: "There is no important sense in which psychology can be reduced to the physical sciences" (*ibid.*, p. 722).

The key premise is something I have no quarrel with – what Davidson calls the *constitutive force of rationality* in the ascription of beliefs and desires. We cannot make sense of patterns of attitude-ascriptions that do not satisfy certain constraints on logical consistency, and on the relative cogency of the explanations of behavior which those ascriptions yield. Davidson's argument on this basis proceeds as follows.

Consider a psychophysical generalization G which employs non-disjunctive unified physical predicates and predicates ascribing attitudes. One could never have reason, Davidson claims, to accept G as *strictly* true and projectible. It would always remain possible to discover a person whose behavior would be most cogently rationalized by denying that the person has, say, some belief which G, given the physical facts, implies that he has, or vice versa. And if one could never have reason to accept G as strictly true and projectible, then G can't be a law.

Why would the evidence for G never rule out such a possibility? Davidson's reason is this: the mental and physical schemes have "disparate commitments", the former to the constraints of rationality

20

and the latter to nothing comparable. The idea seems to be that one could never have strong evidence that a certain physical state-type is projectibly correlated with a certain belief, since nothing in the relation of that physical state to *other* physical states is comparable to the rationality-relations that belief has to other beliefs and desires. For nothing in physical theory resembles rationality. Davidson writes, "These conditions (of coherence, rationality, and consistency) have no echo in physical theory." Consequently one could never find a *principle* in the correlation, but would always have to regard it as accidental. (Similar considerations could be given with regard to psychophysical generalizations that assert something more complex than correlations between one mental predicate and one physical predicate.)

The argument rests on the claim that the constraints of rationality "have no echo in physical theory". Naturally if that were true (and if "physical theory" is interpreted broadly enough to include the physical facts a functional system rests upon) then a functionalist theory of attitudes would, given the constitutive force of rationality, be wrong; for the functional interpretation of a predicate gives it satisfaction conditions that can be met entirely on the basis of physical facts. But, as we shall see, the very possibility of a functional interpretation shows that claim to be false.

Before proceeding with the functionalist reply, two preliminary points. First, there is a quite independent reason for doubting that there are any psychophysical laws of at least one sort that Davidson appears to have in mind – namely, those that assert one–one correlations between specific propositional attitudes and structural (first-order) as opposed to functional (second-order) physical states. For it seems highly unlikely that one neural state is in all of us reserved for being, say, the belief that rhubarb is nourishing. The functional role of a physical state may depend upon contingencies of development that vary from person to person, because of differences in the order in which things are learned, or in how they are learned, for example, by seeing, by inferring, or by being told. This is not to deny that two states of different people, both of which are the belief that p, have something physical in common, which they have in common with everyone else's belief that p. But on a functionalist theory that is a second-order property. Perhaps the laws relate mental properties to second-order properties? That isn't what normally has been meant by psychophysical laws; and those correlations between second-order states and attitudes would not be a matter of *law* but of *explication*. This is no *a priori* argument against psychophysical laws, as Davidson's purports to be; the point depends on general empirical considerations. And it is quite compatible with functionalist reduction.

The second preliminary point is this. Perhaps when one is considering Davidson's *a priori* argument a certain empirical point could be quietly operative. Our theory of rationality has developed independently of physical theory, and its ramifications are complex. It would be surprising if there turned out to be a correspondence between its structure, the demands of its constraints and principles, and the structure of some physical system. Consequently, if presented with any possible pairing of the psychological and physical properties of a person one might feel that the disparate commitments of the two theories could quite easily yield counterexamples.

This of course is not Davidson's argument; and it is not persuasive. If sense can be made of a physical embodiment of rationality (thereby undercutting the *a priori* argument), the tendency of empirical considerations would be in the opposite direction. It would be surprising if there were no such correspondence, person by person, given that the staggering success of the belief–desire theory requires a physical explanation.

Now to the main question, posed first under an innocuous guise. Can a functionalist theory, that each attitude-sentence ascribes a second-order property expressible in a physical vocabulary, recognize the constitutive force of rationality? Of course it can, and must. Let us anticipate in a rough and general way the functional interpretation of attitude-ascriptions of chapter 4. The idea is that each predicate of the form 'z believes that p' (for variable z and specific p) ascribes a distinct functional state, which is determined by the predicate's role in a theory that includes constraints on rationality (as well as certain perceptual input conditions, and output conditions to decision and behavior). The theory is counterfactual in form, and what is required of first-order state-types if they are to have the right functional roles is that they stand to each other, to input and to output, in those counterfactual relations of causation, transition and co-occurrence that the theory requires. In particular, a system of physical state-types satisfies the constraints on rationality provided they are all related counterfactually as the theory says the beliefs to which they correspond ought rationally to be related.

This must be sayable in a physical vocabulary, and the question arises how we can get round propositions to achieve that happy result. But that needn't concern us here (cf. 7.2). The important question is whether, regardless of whether propositions are referred to, the constraints on rationality correspond structurally to purely physical constraints on physical states. And there is no impediment to that. For physical state-types x and y to be related as the theory says the belief that p & q and the belief that $\sim p$ are counterfactually related is, in part, for it to be the case that if x were to occur then y would not occur. The rationality constraints generate a vast network of such counterfactual relations among physical states, ultimately with the effect of describing a system of physical state types whose counterfactual interrelations mirror the relevant logical relations among beliefs and desires.

When Davidson writes that there is no echo of the rationality constraints in physical theory, and speaks of the disparate commitments of the mental and the physical, there is the suggestion of something like the following argument. In the formulation of the *laws* of the physical sciences there is nothing that resembles the constraints of rationality. Therefore no reduction of rational psychology to physical science is possible, since reduction requires a subsumption of the laws of one theory under the laws of the other. Perhaps there is an important kind of inter-subject reduction that is law–law in the classic sense. But it is quite unmotivated to infer from the absence of a psychophysical reduction of *that* kind, that "complete understanding of the workings of the body and brain would not constitute knowledge of thought and action". For *functionalist reduction is not law–law reduction*, which can be seen as follows.

The functional organization of the physical states of a person results from many contingencies of physiology of basically two kinds. First, even those structural features of the anatomy of the brain that are genetically determined are not a matter of *law*, for any "laws" of genetics would be quite conditional in form. Secondly, as has already been pointed out, the psychological functional roles of brain states may well be a matter of developmental contingencies. So, that a system of physical states is organized functionally according to the constraints of rationality would be a quite non-nomological fact. Nothing like the constraints of rationality shows up in physical *theory*; but counterfactual constraints that are isomorphic to rationality constraints may show up in the physical *facts*.

How can contingent facts about a physical system amount to rationality, whose ingredients are far from contingent? It is *a priori* that

23

if certain states are to be counted as beliefs and desires they must satisfy the constraints of rationality. But that they do satisfy them can be as contingent as you like; if they fail to do so they are not beliefs and desires. It is a fallacy to argue that, since rationality has constitutive force, a physical system would have to conform to rationality non-contingently for its workings to constitute the workings of a mind.

I have been taking the key arguable point in Davidson's argument for the irreducibility of the mental to be that nothing in physical theory corresponds to rationality. But others may have located the crucial point elsewhere – namely in the claim that rationality has constitutive force in rational psychology, which implies a certain *unrevisability* for psychology. For it is possible to read Davidson's argument thus: there can't be psychophysical laws, because no psychophysical generalizations can be indefinitely revisable, or "homonomic", which is a key feature of scientific laws. The requirement of rationality is an impediment to revisability in certain directions. Although I do not think this is Davidson's main argument, it deserves discussion. First, we must distinguish revisability and revisability without change of subject matter. That rationality is constitutive in psychology rules out the indefinite revisability of psychophysical generalizations without change of subject matter, without their ceasing to be about beliefs and desires. But is that sort of revisability really a constraint on being a law? It would also rule out inter-subject laws connecting narrower and broader theoretical frameworks, when the initial constraints of one framework are so entrenched in our semantics that their revision counts as a change of subject matter. Accepting a generalization as indefinitely revisable without change of subject matter is not a necessary condition of accepting it as both true and projectible. Suppose basic theoretical physical concepts and certain laws governing them were as entrenched in common sense as rational psychology; the laws of physics would not then be indefinitely revisable without "changing the subject". But we could still regard them as true and as projectible. Secondly, the functionalist reply to Davidson does not deny the constitutive force of rationality or his claim that psychophysical generalizations are not revisable without changing the subject. On the contrary, the functional theory I envisage takes that as quite central. And thirdly, the argument from unrevisability has a far less interesting conclusion than the one which seems to be Davidson's basic point; for it would show at most that there are no psychophysical laws. That would not imply that psychophysical *reduction* is not on the cards, for functionalist reduction requires, not psychophysical laws, but psychophysical type–type correlations relativized to individuals at times. So the non-existence of laws is compatible with our being able to read off, from a person's physical organization and state-tokens, a whole mental life.

This discussion has faced only obliquely a certain *epistemological* point in Davidson's argument – namely, that we would never be in a position confidently to regard a psychophysical correlation as lacking exceptions that are required by consistency and cogent rationalization. On a functional reduction the problem is not to verify one by one correlations between single mental and physical properties. Functionalist reduction is rather holistic. What is essential is whether a whole system of physical states exhibits a certain overall counterfactual structure. Moreover, functionalism does not imply that we could ever in practice discover or master all psychophysical correlations for a person at a time; perhaps the brain's workings are too complex for any of us to have a total grasp of them. What is essential is evidence that there are such correlations, even though it is not evidence for specific correlations. Finally, reducibility is more a metaphysical than an epistemological matter. The key question regarding the rationality constraints is whether truth conditions for attitude-sentences can take them as constitutive, and at the same time describe circumstances of physical organization that would appropriately satisfy them. But given the truth conditions, the epistemology falls into place. It is quite the wrong approach to consider unexplicated psychophysical generalizations, and to wonder about getting evidence for their strict truth and projectibility: the overwhelmingly intimidating difficulty of the empirical question could seem an *a priori* impediment. The fundamental point is that there is no incoherence in the idea that certain physical states meet the demands of rationality.

2

Explicating attitude-ascriptions

Whether intentionality corresponds to objective and determinate features of our psychology and its extramental connections depends on what naturalistic sense can be made of propositional attitude-ascriptions, sentences of the form '*x* believes that *s*'. Not every current theory of belief focuses on ascriptions of belief. For some, that would smack of a concern for philosophical analysis, a supposedly discredited enterprise; but there is also something more specific. A naturalistic explication of '*x* believes *s*' is possible only if interpersonal non-extensional synonymy is possible. But it may be thought that the latter has been shown by Quinean arguments not to make naturalistic sense, and hence that trying to explicate attitude-ascriptions is pointless. (This would still allow scope for saying what beliefs are.)

In 2.5 I discuss a certain sort of theoretical activity, conservative explication, which appears inevitable and sensible regardless of one's views about analyticity. As for interpersonal synonymy, I shall be proposing, *pace* Quine, a physicalist conservative explication of attitude-ascriptions. Concentrating on attitude-sentences is inevitable; the content of beliefs is whatever that-clauses ascribe. To account for intentional forms of psychological explanation is to account for a certain sort of theoretical discourse. This is not to say that, were a naturalistic conservative explication of attitude-ascriptions not forthcoming, no more radically eliminative reconstruction could go part of the way towards answering the question. Explication is a matter of degree.

2.1 BELIEFS AS RELATIONS

I take belief-ascriptions to be *relational*; that is, sentences of the form '*x* believes that *s*' have the form B(*x*, that-*s*), where the that-clause as a whole is a singular term (or, as on Davidson's theory (1969), 'that' is a singular term, referring to the utterance of the rest). This does not imply that if a belief is a physical state its underlying physical structure is somehow relational – e.g. to an internal "sentence". That might be true, but it is not implied by calling belief-ascriptions "relational". For the reference of a that-clause may be quite *extrinsic* to those natural facts about x which constitute the belief.

What justifies the relational assumption? Consider first these two arguments. (1) Attitude-ascriptions have their meaning from the belief–desire theory, and so they must logically interact with it appropriately. It consists of generalizations, with variables in place of that-clauses. But, assuming first-order variables (on which more shortly), the relational construal follows. (2) To explicate attitude-ascriptions is to point to natural properties which could make attitude-ascriptions *true* of us, to assign them truth conditions of a certain sort. That, it seems, requires the devices of a Tarski-type truth theory, which means finding logical structure in 'believes that…'; each such predicate must be logically complex. But, since '…' is not truth-functional, and given the first-order assumption, that-clauses are either complex names (of sentences or propositions), or demonstratives referring to the utterance of '…', or sequences of names (which would permit taking the that-clause to name the sequence of the things thus named).

Now consider this reply to the first argument. "We could take those generalizations to be *axiom schemata*; the 'p' in 'x believes that p' is not a variable, and universal quantifiers '$(\forall p)$' '$(\forall q)$' may be dropped without loss. The relevant interaction of the theory and a particular attitude-ascription is just a matter of the ascription's relations to all other instances of the schemata. The systematic connections between that belief and other beliefs and desires will thereby be captured."

This can be reinforced by the following reply to the second argument. "Why can't 'believes that…' be non-complex? That infinitely many predicates have to be accommodated is not obvious, for if ordinary mortals are capable only of beliefs of finite complexity, the set of belief-ascriptions to be accounted for is finite. Then every such (superficially complex) predicate can be a non-complex theoretical term whose meaning is determined by the "theory" that results from conjoining all instances of the axiom schemata. There exists a lucid device for generating explicit definitions of theoretical terms on the basis of how they occur in a theory – namely, David Lewis's modification of Ramsey's method." (To be discussed in chapter 3; Lewis, 1970.)

Apart from a denial of the first-order assumption, this conjunction of replies constitutes, as far as I know, the only way of avoiding the thesis that belief-ascriptions are relational. Is it a reasonable theory? Well, it is rather artificial; its main attraction would be its avoiding the relational interpretation if that were desirable. Otherwise it is unattractive. According to it, when we seem to be generalizing about beliefs and desires, we are really talking about belief- and desire-ascriptions. Moreover, all the *structure* in our generalizations about beliefs and desires becomes an accident of the syntax of those simple theoretical predicates 'x believes that...'. But surely it can't be an accident that persons who believe that s_1 and s_2 tend not to believe also that not s_1; there must be a principle. And the implied account of our *mastery* of the concepts of belief and desire is odd; for the meaning of 'x believes that snow is white' is supposed to depend upon a vast conjunction of schema instances. Now, the second part of the theory, which treats each predicate of the form 'x believes that...' in terms of its role in a theory interpreted *à la* Ramsey, is on the right track; but on the account of chapter 4, normal intuitions about generalizations about beliefs are preserved, within a relational framework. Perhaps it is bound to be inconclusive to argue in the abstract for a relational theory without a specific proposal. But given the first-order assumption it is the intuitive way of treating generalizations about beliefs and the problem of systematic truth conditions for belief-ascriptions.

As for the first-order assumption, let me say this. Alternative ways of generalizing, substitutional and higher-order quantification, make perfectly good sense; but by my lights that is because their semantics is in a first-order metalanguage. Higher-order quantification is supposed by some to be ontologically conservative – that is, to avoid commitment to properties or propositions as entities. But naturally that is not so if one assumes a first-order semantic metalanguage which is not ontologically neutral. Thus in the current context there seems to me no advantage in proceeding on other than a first-order basis.

Classically there are two types of relational theory of belief-ascriptions: they assert relations to propositions, or to sentences or utterances. In the latter case, the relation depends on what the sentence or utterance *means*, in the mouth or language of the ascriber; so I shall call such theories semantic-relation theories. Now I am going to argue that, given the constraint of physicalism, neither sort of theory is attractive. That may be surprising, for what further possibility is there? The answer is that on my account that-clauses name linguistic entities

28

(in the ascriber's and not the believer's language), but their independent semantic properties are not invoked. The theory is a sentential theory, but not a semantic-relation theory.

2.2 THE PROPOSITIONAL THEORY

It is a bad argument for propositions that, because beliefs are not intrinsically linguistic states, belief-ascriptions must assert relations to non-linguistic items. To describe a non-linguistic state of γ's via its relation to something linguistic of ours is perfectly possible. Similarly, that we can ascribe beliefs to speakers of other languages without mentioning their sentences does not imply that we refer to something non-linguistic.

More cogent arguments for the propositional view are based on negative logico-semantical reflections upon semantic-relation analyses, coupled with the unsurprising assumption that the only alternative is the propositional theory. The centerpiece is Church's argument against Carnap's sentential analysis (Church, 1950; Carnap, 1947). Suppose 'Columbus believed that the earth is round' asserts a relation between Columbus and some sentence of ours that depends upon what we mean by that sentence: 'Columbus believes something equivalent to 'the earth is round' as we use it'. Had we meant by that what we now mean by 'smoking causes cancer', the truth-value of 'Columbus believed that the earth is round' would have been affected. As Columbus did not believe that smoking causes cancer, the sentence 'Columbus believed that the earth is round' would have been false on that analysis. But clearly (the argument proceeds) it would not thereby have been false: whether Columbus believed that the earth is round is quite independent of what we English speakers mean by 'the earth is round'. The belief-sentence has different possible world truth conditions than the semantic-relation analysis gives it. Now the argument depends only upon the analysis invoking contingent semantic properties. So Davidson's theory (1969) that, on an utterance of that belief-sentence, one refers to one's own *utterance u* of 'the earth is round', and asserts a relation between Columbus and u that depends in part on what u means (evidently a contingent property of u), falls within the scope of the argument.

The interesting upshot of the argument seems to be that it is the meaning of 'the earth is round', and not the sentence, that should be carried through other possible worlds in determining the truth conditions of 'Columbus believes that the earth is round'. But a "meaning" *qua* entity is a proposition.

Another argument is this. If s is literally ambiguous, so is $\ulcorner x$ believes that $s \urcorner$. But on the semantic-relation theory exactly one relation is involved, and one sentence s; so there is no room for ambiguity. The propositional theory handles it nicely: if s is ambiguous in sense, then $\ulcorner$that $s \urcorner$ is ambiguous in reference.

The form of both arguments is: the propositional theory accounts for the semantic facts about belief-sentences; semantic-relation theories do not; there are no further theories that do; so belief-sentences assert relations to propositions.

Now, it is not true that they are the only two relational theories available. A theory that takes belief-sentences to assert relations to linguistic entities, but not by virtue of contingent semantic facts about them, is straightforwardly immune to Church's argument and the ambiguity argument (as I show at the end of 7.2.) Moreover, there are replies to the Church argument at the logico-semantical level.[1] But, most importantly, those arguments are not motivated at a certain foundational level. For if one has one's eye on problems about explicating semantic concepts, about the compatibility of intentionality and physicalism, or about the vindication of truth as correspondence, a certain amount of regimentation and reconstruction might well seem justified if we could then get an otherwise satisfactory theory that preserved the basic structure of belief–desire psychology.

An argument for the propositional analysis that would be more to the point would be that propositions are needed to capture intentional explanations of behavior. Suppose there were a persuasive argument of this kind: how should a physicalist react? It would remain an open question whether intentionality is compatible with physicalism (as Brentano denied it was). So a physicalist could not accept the propositional theory on the basis simply of that argument, for it would remain to be shown that such relations to propositions can be accounted for within a physicalist framework.

My reason for rejecting propositions, put baldly, is this: to explain the contributions of propositions to the explanation of behavior is to

---

[1] Invoke a trans-world equivalence-relation: let w_a indexically denote the actual world. Then, let 'x believes that s' have the form '$B(x, s, w_a)$'. Its truth conditions, in a possible world w', depend on a trans-world relation between Columbus, as he is in w', and s, insofar as s means what it means in w_a – i.e. in the real world and not in w'. The explication is committed to the real world, and not to other possible worlds, which are invoked only at the meta-level, in considering whether the explication satisfies Church's intensional standards of explication, as it seems to.

show how to eliminate them. The point does not involve a verificationist–reductionist formula such as: 'to justify invoking A's (electrons, physical objects, mental states) is thereby to show how to eliminate them' – not a very happy principle. The difference is this. I am presupposing, and not arguing for, the adequacy of a physicalist framework. (By that I do not mean one that by definition excludes propositions; some physicalists believe in other possible worlds.) A compatibilist about physicalism and the existence of beliefs would then deem it necessary to show what physical facts about x would constitute x's having the belief-relation to a proposition. Now I suggest that that would be to show *either* that one could separately, independently of propositions, specify the relevant physical features; *or* that a person's physical properties are somehow *structurally isomorphic* to some systematic framework that can be specified by mentioning propositions, their logical interconnections, etc. But in the latter case, it is difficult to avoid conjecturing a framework of more mundane entities than propositions and relations on them, suitably structurally isomorphic to the propositional framework. The second strategy is the one I shall pursue (cf. 7.2). Since I can think of no way, apart from those two, in which the relevant relations to propositions can be physically grounded, it seems to me that a physicalist, even one who is independently prepared to accept possible worlds, ought not to regard beliefs as, irreducibly, relations to propositions.

2.3 SEMANTIC RELATION THEORIES

The classical alternative has been to regard the that-clause as referring to a sentence or utterance of the ascriber that is equivalent in meaning or content to the belief. On some theories, Pierre's belief involves Pierre's accepting a sentence of his own, which we characterize only indirectly by producing something of ours as equivalent in meaning to it: a propositional attitude-ascription indirectly describes a sentential attitude. But there is a more general idea, for one can envisage a theory on which beliefs are not necessarily linguistic, not sentential attitudes, but can still, in some way to be clarified, be described as equivalent in content to something linguistic. On either theory, regardless of whether the that-clause refers to a sentence, a sentential complex (an open sentence paired with a sequence of referents) or an utterance, the relation asserted by 'Pierre believes that s' obtains in part by virtue of what s means. Hence such theories may be called semantic-relation theories.

Linguistic items have meaning only relative to a language, a speaker, or a population of speakers. This is evident for sentence-types, which could mean different things in different languages or populations. Equally obviously, an actual utterance's meaning depends on the utterer's intentions, the population's conventions, or the rules of the language. So, a semantic-relation theory must rely on some notion of meaning-relative-to-a-language, or person or population. That is, the relation asserted by 'x believes that s' is such that one of its terms is a sentence or utterance, and another, implicit term is a language, person or population, and its obtaining depends in part on the meaning of the one in the other. Now I want to eliminate immediately one of those possibilities – namely, that *languages* are usefully invoked at this point.

In chapter 9 there is an account of what a language is; but it presupposes the theory of attitude-ascriptions developed in this book. Otherwise there are, I think, only two notions of a language that might be relevant. On both a language is something involving a set of sentences as interpreted in a certain way. On the first, to interpret sentences is to assign propositional meanings, and a language is a function from sentences to meanings (Lewis, 1976). But that yields no real alternative to the propositional theory and we may dispense with it forthwith.

On the second, to interpret is to assign truth conditions in the form 's is true iff...'. A language is then the set of sentences, $\mathcal{S}$, *as* interpreted thus – that is, as interpreted by a truth theory $\mathcal{T}$ which implies truth conditions for each sentence in $\mathcal{S}$. So a language could be identified with the pair $\langle \mathcal{S}, \mathcal{T} \rangle$. What sort of entity is $\mathcal{T}$? It is a *theory*, a certain set of sentences. But reference to a set of sentences $\mathcal{T}$, if it interprets $\mathcal{S}$, must be to $\mathcal{T}$ under a certain interpretation of $\mathcal{T}$ itself. Suppose $\mathcal{T}$ implies 's is true iff electrons have negative charge'; the meaning that equivalence assigns to s would depend on what the right-hand side means. Now we are here referring to or *mentioning* $\mathcal{T}$ and not *using* it – that is, referring to a set of entities whose intrinsic properties are syntactic and not semantic. Initially, in interpreting 'x believes that s', mere reference to the syntactic entity s is not taken to determine how s is to be taken; that requires further, implicit, reference to a language or population or person. But then the mere reference to the syntactic entity $\mathcal{T}$ is not enough to determine its meaning and hence not the meaning of s. We must invoke something further that interprets $\mathcal{T}$. Unless we arbitrarily now bring in reference to a person or population, we are launched on a series of implicit references to an infinite hierarchy of truth theories – and all on our original utterance of 'x believes that s'! Of course, those references must be cumulatively ineffectual, since they are always to purely syntactic entities. (I hope it is evident that this is not an argument that we can never ascribe truth conditions without launching a self-defeating regress – of course we can, but by *using* $\mathcal{T}$, not by mentioning it.)

If reference to $\mathcal{T}$ did not also require reference to something further that interprets it, then neither should the original reference to s: if an interpretation for $\mathcal{T}$ could simply be taken for granted, then so for s. But 'x believes that s' does not then refer to s as meaning what it does relative to a *language*, which is *contra hypothesem*.

If we are to persist in the apparently inevitable intuition that meaning is always meaning-relative-to-something, the semantic-relation theory must presuppose some *pragmatic* notion, of meaning-relative-to-a-person or population. One such theory is that in uttering 'x believes that s' the speaker refers to that very utterance of s (Davidson, 1969), either with an implicit direct reference to himself ('insofar as that utterance of s means what it means in my mouth') or a quantification over speakers ('insofar as that utterance of s means what it means in the mouth of whoever uttered it'). Another theory is that 'x believes that s' refers to a sentence (or sentential complex), with an implicit direct reference to the speaker ('insofar as s means what it means for me') or to a specific population of speakers.

Now the point is not that the pragmatic concept of meaning for a person or population cannot be explicated within a physicalist framework; on the contrary. Rather it is that the only promising explication requires an *independent* explication of propositional attitude-ascriptions. What my sentences and utterances mean involves relations to my beliefs and, perhaps, communicative intentions; short of that, the prospects for a reductionist account of the relevant pragmatic concepts are bleak. That will be no surprise to many, but let us get the reasons out in the open.

Semantic-relation theories take the truth of 'x believes that s' to depend on our sentence or my utterance of s's equivalence in meaning or content to something of x's, some linguistic or non-linguistic state $s^\star$: '$s^\star$ has for x the same content or meaning as s has for us – M($s^\star$, x, s, us)'. Thus the general form of semantic-relation theories is: 'x believes that s' is to be explicated as 'for some $s^\star$, B*(x, $s^\star$) and M($s^\star$, x, s, us)'. The question now is whether M is to be explicated in terms of some more fundamental pragmatic semantic concept. Short of

33

bringing in propositional attitudes, there seem to be only two candidates for semantic concepts more fundamental than equivalence in meaning – namely, something *intentional*, in the form '*s* means that *p* for us', or something *extensional*, in the form '*s* is, for us, true iff...'.

Now, '*s* means that *p* for us' is no help here, given the classical treatments of that-clauses; either '*p*' ranges over propositions, or we need a semantic-relation analysis of '*s* means that *p*' itself, which leads to a vicious regress.

Could the equivalence of meaning of $s^\star$ and s be captured by facts of the form '$s^\star$ is true for x iff...' and '*s* is true for us iff...'? Certainly not in that form; for then any materially equivalent $s^\star$ and s' would count as equivalent in meaning, which would mean that in '*x* believes that *s*', we could substitute, *salva veritate*, any s' that has the same truth-value as s.[2] But the intuitive idea is that equivalence in meaning is equivalence in truth conditions, and perhaps there is a more sophisticated way of capturing that. Why not say that $s^\star$ and s are equivalent in meaning, relative to x and to us respectively, just in case the correct truth *theory* $\mathcal{T}^\star$ of x and the correct truth theory $\mathcal{T}$ of us are such that:

there is a sentence s' in both $\mathcal{T}^\star$ and $\mathcal{T}$ such that

(1) $\mathcal{T}^\star$ implies $\ulcorner \bar{s}^\star$ is true iff $s' \urcorner$, and

(2) $\mathcal{T}$ implies $\ulcorner \bar{s}$ is true iff $s' \urcorner$

(the bars over '$s^\star$' and 's' indicate that their proper *subtituends* in that context are structural descriptions of sentences rather than the sentences themselves).

Now our correct truth theory $\mathcal{T}$ of ourselves is *homophonic*: any s' that satisfies the above condition is either s itself or something strongly equivalent to s. But then a far more direct explication of $\ulcorner x$ believes that $s \urcorner$ follows from that account of equivalence in meaning:

'*x* believes that *s*'

is to be explained as:

'$(\exists s^\star)$ B* $(x, s^\star)$ and the correct truth theory

$\mathcal{T}^\star$ of x implies $\ulcorner \bar{s}^\star$ is true iff $s' \urcorner$'.

In other words, the function of a belief-ascription on x is to give the truth conditions that the correct truth theory of x assigns to what x holds true.

---

[2] For precisely this reason, we cannot explicate $\ulcorner x$ believes that $s \urcorner$ as: $\ulcorner (\exists s^\star)$ B$^\star(x, s^\star)$ and $s^\star$ is, for x, true iff $s \urcorner$. As stated, the correctness of the choice of s requires only that it be materially equivalent to $s^\star$. Moreover '*s*' does not occur in that formula as a first-order variable, since it occupies a sentential position; but then that formula can't explicate '*x* believes that *s*', in which '*s*' is a first-order variable. Both problems suggest the next theory discussed in the text.

Now there is something fishy here; for this last proposal adverts to no *pragmatic* semantic property of *our* sentence *s*. (How could this happen if it is equivalent to the preceding pragmatic semantic-relation theory? The answer lies in the equivalence of ⌜on the correct truth theory $\mathcal{T}$ of us, the sentence *s* is true⌝ and *s* itself.) But the theory has, in any case, to be turned into a pragmatic theory if it is to be adequate – what *we* mean by $\mathcal{T}^\star$ has somehow to be relied upon, for the following reason.

Earlier, in connection with languages, in the form $\langle \mathcal{S}, \mathcal{T} \rangle$, it was seen that the mere reference to a body of sentences $\mathcal{T}$ was insufficient. What $\mathcal{T}$ means relative to something further had to be invoked. Similarly here. For it is crucial that $\mathcal{T}^\star$ should be the correct truth theory for *x*, and the notion of correctness is in part semantic: uninterpreted theories are not correct or incorrect. Consequently there must be some notion of what $\mathcal{T}^\star$ means relative to something further, and, as introducing higher level truth theories is now quite pointless, that would amount to this: 'relative to what we mean by $\mathcal{T}^\star$'. So we have:

'*x* believes that *s*'

is to be explicated as:

'$(\exists s^\star)\ B^\star(x, s^\star)$ and (for any $\mathcal{T}^\star$) if $\mathcal{T}^\star$ is the correct truth theory for *x*, relative to what *we* mean by $\mathcal{T}^\star$, then $\mathcal{T}^\star$ implies ⌜$s^\star$ is true iff *s*⌝'.

Notice that, if you drop the quantifier '$(\exists s^\star)$', what is left has the form: $M^\star(s^\star, x, s, us)$. Now it is incredible that this is the fundamental pragmatic semantic concept; that is, not in its turn to be unpacked via the more elementary concept of pragmatic equivalence in meaning: $M(s^\star, x, s, us)$. In any case, if $M^\star$ were taken as unanalyzable in further semantic terms, the apparent quantification over $\mathcal{T}^\star$ turns out to be just so much syntax, the whole construction to be understood as a baroque way of writing '$s^\star$ means for *x* what *s* means for us'; for the essential information conveyed is this: *s* is that sentence of ours which, relative to what we mean by ($\mathcal{T}^\star$ and hence by) *s*, captures what *x*'s sentence $s^\star$ means.

The point of the rather complex argument I have given is that, in the present context of explicating belief-ascriptions, the attempt to avoid taking pragmatic equivalence in meaning as the fundamental semantic concept by invoking truth theories fails. So the final question about semantic-relation theories is whether there is a reductionist explication of pragmatic equivalence in meaning, that is, apart from the explication that becomes available on the basis of an independent account of propositional attitudes.

Equivalence in meaning

Pragmatic equivalence in meaning may be given the canonical form ⌜s^* means for x the same as s means for y⌝, where s^* is either linguistic or non-linguistic (an internal state perhaps), s a sentence or utterance, and y a person or population. Can this concept be accounted for without relying on any further concept of propositional content or meaning? The first suggestion to be considered is that the concept gets its identity from its role in the explanation of behavior. The idea is this. To explain Pierre's behavior we must know his *reasons*. Now, suppose we knew all his sentential attitudes – all the sentences he accepts as true and desires to be true; would we thereby know his reasons? That could hardly be so without some account of what his sentences *mean*. But, on certain ways of matching them with our sentences Pierre begins to make sense to us. So perhaps the concept of equivalence in meaning gets its identity from its explanatory role: it enables his sentential attitudes to count for us as his reasons.

Let me indulge in a parody. If I am trying to understand why Pierre looks groggy, stumbles about, and speaks incoherently, it can be explanatory to point out that his state is *equivalent in degree of drunkenness* to what mine would be after five double scotches. This shows that we can take the concept 'equivalent in degree of drunkenness' to be foundational in the theory of intoxicated behavior; it gets its identity from that explanatory role. Now, while analogies that we count as explanatory do rely on equivalence-relations in that way, it is obvious, as I think the example makes clear, that their explanatory value depends on an independent grasp of the basic reference case – depends in that example on my knowing or guessing what it is like to have drunk so many whiskies. My understanding of that equivalence-relation is simply my grasp of 'his state affects him like this, like that, etc.'.

Some explanations account for the concepts thereby employed, and some *presuppose* an independent understanding of them. The former happens when the explanatory context introduces the concept as 'the state, relation, etc. that has such and such causal etc. role', where that role is somehow specified. But in the whiskey example the equivalence-relation is not supposed to have any causal role; it is appealed to extrinsically to characterize something, an internal state of our subject, that has the explanatory causal role. Similarly for invoking equivalence in meaning in explaining another's behavior. Suppose certain linguistic states are among the causes of a person's behavior. Instead of characterizing them directly as having certain causal roles, we might characterize them as equivalent in meaning to certain states of ours; and that presupposes a separate understanding of equivalence in meaning.

This leads naturally to another suggestion – namely, that pragmatic equivalence in meaning is a certain equivalence in explanatory or functional role. Perhaps the idea can be made more vivid as a proposal for explicating attitude sentences – something like:

'Pierre believes that snow is white'

is to be explicated as:

'For some s, Pierre accepts s, and the functional role of accepting s for Pierre is the same as the functional role of accepting 'snow is white' for us'

But functional role is always relative to a particular system of connections among input, output, and internal states; there is no concept of equivalence in functional role *tout court*. It is always relative to a specified functional system; two states, e.g. two physical states, may be functionally equivalent in one functional system but not in another. So the above condition should read: 'Pierre's holding-true s is functionally equivalent to my holding-true 'snow is white' in functional system F.' But a moment's reflection shows that to specify F essentially is to give the wherewithal for specifying all the particular functional roles which F generates. But that implies being able to specify the functional role of Pierre's holding-true s independently of its functional equivalence to my holding-true 'snow is white'. And that functional role would seem to be what elucidates 'Pierre believes that snow is white'; the content of Pierre's belief is the functional role of what he holds true. The details of *my* psychology drop out of the picture.

This may initially be somewhat puzzling, for what might a direct specification of such a functional role look like? Might it be something like 'Pierre believes that snow is white'? We shall see that indeed it might. The analysis I shall propose takes 'believes' to express a relation between Pierre and my sentences; but the relation does not depend upon the *functional role* or *meaning* which those sentences have for *me*.

I conclude that no semantic-relation theory of belief-sentences can be maintained, if, that is, we are to avoid irreducible pragmatic semantic concepts. On each way of explaining the theory we come to a dead end. If the basic concept is 'means that p', the theory is circular. If it is 'is true iff p', the conditions are either not sufficient or depend, in effect, on equivalence in meaning. If it is equivalence in meaning, then, given that it can't be accounted for by its explanatory role, the only way to explicate it would be in terms of equivalence in functional role. But that indirectly requires an independent specification of the functional role of Pierre's holdings-true, so that their equivalence to our sentences is beside the point. Semantic-relation theories are half-baked. They rely at bottom on taking interpersonal equivalence in meaning to be more basic than the specification of particular meanings. But while that has a nominalist appeal, it cannot be vindicated. If equivalence in meaning or content can be explained at all, that must be in terms of an independent account of the content of beliefs, and of derivative concepts of meaning.

2.4 BELIEFS AND DESIRES WITHOUT THAT-CLAUSES

Propositional and semantic-relation theories exhaust the hitherto available options for explaining belief- and desire-*ascriptions* – in other words, for explaining that-clauses. But there are other theories of what beliefs and desires *are*. Suppose they are essentially linguistic, that to believe or desire something is to stand in a certain relation to a sentence of one's own language, 'holding-true' or 'wanting-true' ('z holds-true s' does not mean 'z believes that s is true'; to hold-true s is not to have a metalinguistic belief about s). A common view nowadays explains those relations in terms of their systematic roles in explaining behavior. And, some recent theories take sentential attitudes as primary in rational psychology, de-emphasizing propositional attitude-ascriptions on the grounds that non-extensional interpersonal synonymy can't objectively be accounted for. Truth conditions and references are then assigned directly to sentences as the objects of sentential attitudes.

There are two such theories, interestingly different; and while their details do not matter to the main point, it will help to indicate their general form. Hartry Field (1978) has proposed that we regard beliefs and desires simply as internal representational states whose structure is that of a language. While Field allows the internal "sentences" of two persons to be alike in reference and extensional truth conditions (with predicates denoting properties and not sets), he is sceptical of any stronger interpersonal synonymy, and therefore of a determinate reading of propositional attitude-ascriptions.

Donald Davidson (1974) proposes a different reconstruction of rational psychology: sentential attitudes are basic, not as internal states, but as relations to the believer's public language sentences which we ascribe, in an instrumentalist spirit, in order to systematize behavior. Truth conditions are determined by a Tarski-type truth theory on the believer's language, and nothing like propositions come into the picture.[3]

The point I wish to make is that eliminating that-clauses in favor of just sentential attitudes and their extensional semantics carries away certain apparently basic features of rational psychology. The propositional attitude system contains resources for describing patterns of motivation, learning, reasoning, etc., at a *non-language-specific* level. That is, we have general conceptions of inductive and deductive tendencies, the role of the practical syllogism in motivation, as well as processes introduced by more specific psychological theories having to do, e.g., with cognitive dissonance or unconscious motivation and so on, whose description involves no mention of specific features of the subject's language. Evidently history and the social sciences depend essentially on such explanations and descriptions.

Conceived in general terms, such patterns are at a level of abstraction not to be found within a framework of sentential attitudes and extensional semantics; and, as I shall try to make clear, to supplement that framework suitably is to move towards a basis for propositional attitude-ascription. The point is not that this is *eo ipso* a defect in the sentential attitude framework; for it could turn out to be the most that can be vindicated. But it needs to be registered that a framework for psychological theorizing which lacks the resource of propositional attitudes is bound to be strikingly different from the one we operate with. Substituting sentential attitudes would be quite radically eliminative, even when the extensional semantics is taken into account.

Taking other creatures as subjects of ordinary rational psychology turns on whether we can describe such things as their motivation, in the pattern 'wants q, believes p, believes that if p then doing A results

---

[3] Nor do semantic-relations of the sort I have discussed. However, Davidson has in another paper (1969) proposed an account of propositional attitude-ascriptions that goes roughly like this: on an utterance of 'x believes that s' I assert that some state of x's stands in a certain semantic equivalence-relation to my utterance of s. Now if that state of x's is a sentential attitude, and if the semantic equivalence-relation is equivalence in what Tarski-type truth theories ascribe to my utterance and to x's state, the theories of the 1972 paper and of the 1969 paper fit together. In effect I have discussed that sort of account in the preceding section. But it is possible also to read the 1972 paper as a proposal of a sentential attitude theory in which propositional attitude-ascriptions have no essential role.

in q, does A'; or their generalizing from experience; or their reasoning via *modus ponens* or certain simple patterns of non-contradiction; and so on. But, evidently such description abstracts from the lexical and syntactic features of their sentences, that is surface features described in a formal syntax, 'e.g. as in 's consists of s_1 followed by 'and' followed by s_2'. We then have these questions. (1) Given that generalizations of those types abstract from syntactic details, are there still resources within a sentential-attitude framework for capturing them? (2) What about mimicking them language by language in generalizations that in effect are about the practical syllogism, *modus ponens*, etc., but are couched in the syntax now of Hans's language, now Pierre's language, now José's language, etc? Would that be a useful substitute for the more general framework?

As regards (1), perhaps we can generalize in terms of *truth conditions*. On the face of it, that would involve quantification and semantic description of a sort that goes beyond the resources of an ordinary truth theory. Thus, suppose we want to say that Pierre has just reasoned by *modus ponens*: he holds-true a sentence s_2 because he holds-true s_1 and a sentence s_3 which is a *conditional* of s_2 on s_1. The force of 'is a conditional', on the line being pursued, is semantic. But no such semantic predicate occurs in an ordinary Tarskian truth theory, and naturally it is not unproblematic here. If we try to define it in terms of s_3's being described in a certain way by the correct truth theory $T^\star$ of Pierre, we are back to the semantic-relation theories of 2.3: the truth theory $T^\star$ is itself being referred to as meaning something relative to something further. In any case, if we could unproblematically cash out the full array of semantic predicates of the form 'is a conditional', etc. (including 'is a *cat*-word' and so on for the non-logical words of Pierre's language), we would thereby have an effective account of that-clauses.

Something similar results from (what appears to be) the only other possible way of extending the sentential-attitude framework to capture those generalizations. Suppose one were to say that whether Pierre's sentence s_3 is conditional depends upon its *role in reasoning*, i.e. that it behaves functionally thus and so. Now if we could treat all details of Pierre's language in such terms, we could thereby construe that clauses – namely, as devices for ascribing functional roles to what the believer holds-true.

(2) What then about imitating those generalizations within each language? That would be fine, but the *functional* similarities between

'*et*', '*and*', '*und*', etc. would then somehow be captured, and provided the same thing happened across the board, we would again have a framework for explicating that-clauses.

This leaves two positions. First, the sentential-attitude framework eliminates those generalizations and forms of description. Then we have eliminated something very basic indeed, and we are left with a drastically truncated rational psychology, if indeed that term still applies.

Secondly, there is another more attractive possibility – a kind of compromise. Perhaps some interlinguistically ascribable functional roles can be captured by such logico-syntactic descriptions of sentential attitudes as 'is a conditional', while we cannot spell out interlinguistically or interpersonally ascribable functional roles for non-logical or non-structural components of sentences, like 'cat' (for whatever reasons). Then we could capture those generalizations but could not fully explicate that-clauses. This possibility has to be borne in mind; it would constitute in effect a partial explication of propositional attitude-ascriptions.

The generalized functional account suggests a new way of accounting for that-clauses: somehow they capture functional roles of sentential attitudes that are interpersonally ascribable, and subsumable under those generalizations that are virtually constitutive of our commonsense rational psychology.

2.5 PHILOSOPHICAL EXPLICATION

The functional theory of propositional attitudes of chapter 4 depends on a certain attitude towards philosophical explication on which it is both flexible and conservative. The following comments on the general subject of explication may clarify the constraints on the project.

An attempt at analytical explication may arouse two different negative reactions of principle. There is anti-reductionism: a thing is what it is and not another thing. And there is eliminativism: if a concept is philosophically troublesome, get rid of it and, if necessary, replace it with something more lucid, more rigorous, more scientific, more ontologically parsimonious. There is something simplistic in both extremes. To make a concept sacrosanct, not illuminable by reconstruction, may simply make it *uninteresting* in the light of ongoing theory; and, in any case, the drive towards explication may be irrepressible. On the other hand, philosophical explication does not have to be seen as Moorean analysis. There is an apparently ineliminable role for explication in philosophy and science; so it has to be at some level a naturalistically describable cognitive phenomenon. Let me explain why it is inevitable, and why it does not depend on any non-natural analyticity.

'Explication' covers a broad spectrum of philosophical constructions, and not just those that mimic Moorean analyses; they range from Quine's paradigm of Wiener's and Kuratowski's definitions of 'ordered pair', to philosophers' explications of 'x knows that p'. Not all explications have the same motivation, or the same ideal of what is to be preserved; indeed not all explications serve specifically philosophical purposes. It is the latter I shall be concerned with here.

Explication is *elimination*, according to Quine. And that must be the beginning of a naturalistic account, given the improbability of vindicating analysis as literally the unpacking of what already is there in meaning. The slogan could suggest what it does not entail – that all explications are conceptual overthrows. But explication is elimination with replacement; and the *conservativeness* of some replacements is the point to be made.

Quine (1960, pp. 257–62) emphasized puzzle-solving motivations for the replacement of troublesome concepts by others that preserve theoretically useful features. While puzzle-solving and theoretical utility are certainly important in many central cases, they are not what I wish to emphasize.

Consider what might be called an *explicative dilemma*, whose ingredients are as follows. (1) A theoretical framework A – for example, physical theory, extensional semantics, set theory, truth-functional constructions, quantificational constructions, or mechanistic biology. (2) An imperialist inclination to accept A as adequate for expressing all truths about a certain subject S. (3) A set of propositions B, within S, which are not in A, but which there is a strong inclination to accept; for example, propositions about beliefs and desires, or meaning, or numbers, or which are conditional, or modal, or about human autonomy.

Thus described, an explicative dilemma does not entail explicit inconsistency, since it involves strong inclinations and not outright acceptances; but perhaps some theorists' cognitive dilemmas involve outright inconsistency. Either way, an explicative set-up is unstable if faced up to. Given a classical notion of analysis, the inconsistency could be diagnosed as merely apparent: the propositions of B are deemed equivalent in meaning to truths of A. Otherwise there are two possible resolutions: overthrowing the imperialist pretensions of A, and giving up B. The point is that there is more than one way to give up B.

The first is ruthless revolution: pursue theories in A, and jettison B. But ruthless revolution is not always sensible for two reasons. First, there is the one that Quine has emphasized, the theoretical utility of B. Secondly, there is the matter of entrenched cognitive attachment to B – it is awfully difficult not to see people as having beliefs and desires or as making real choices, etc., quite apart from what those concepts contribute to ongoing theory. We simply accept certain things, and overthrowing them, even in the light of the imperialist theory, may be enormously difficult. There is then often ample incentive to seek a conciliation, and that comes in degrees.

Imagine two theorists early in the century who react to Russell's analysis of 'number' as "maximal set of conumerous sets", in these two ways. Both accept the replacement, but one feels his ontology has changed, while the second does not. Or imagine two philosophers who react to compatibilism about free choice (in terms of counterfactuals about wants and decisions) in the following ways. Both accept the replacement, but one takes his view of the human condition to have changed, and the other does not. My point is that the disagreement between these theorists need not be regarded as having a truth-value. For the latter member of each pair the replacement counts as a *conservative explication*, while for the former it is more or less radical. (There is still something factual in what they agree on. For the replacement to be correct, truths of B must give way to truths of A.)

The theorist for whom the explication is conservative may have achieved the happier resolution of the dilemma – not exactly because he hasn't had to change any beliefs, for that rests on the dubious concept of analysis. But his cognitive situation is *as though* he hasn't changed any beliefs. How can that be? I can suggest no more detailed account of the phenomenon of conservative explication; but it *occurs* and can serve as a cognitive resolution to what is perceived as a serious theoretical problem. An explicative dilemma is like a paradox; and why resolve paradoxes? There are two reasons: first, the cognitive discomfort may demand relief and, secondly, paradoxes can obscure the truth. So with explicative dilemmas. This suggests that one point of philosophical theorizing is cognitive therapy. But this is not the Wittgensteinian therapy of insights without theories; it suggests instead an important incentive to theory – even when conservative explication is not fully on the cards: some cognitive conciliation may be better than none.

3

Functional theories

Functional theories are theories of individuals, of how the states of an organism, or a machine, are causally or sequentially related. In cases that are normally of interest, those states are internal. While a functional theory says nothing of their composition or internal structure, it does far more than to summarize certain external input–output correlations. For a functional theory of *a* is falsified if *a*'s internal states are not causally or transitionally related as it requires. Such a theory does then commit itself to substantive claims about what is inside.

Those "states" are state-types and not state-tokens. So a functional theory of *a* does not describe the cause or effect of any particular dateable state or action. Rather it asserts that *a*'s *possible* states are counterfactually related to each other, input and output thus and so. 'Possible states' means (to restrict attention to physical things): state-types which *a* could be in, given *a*'s physical structure and composition.

That a functional theory asserts counterfactual relations among state-types is clear from its making sense to describe functionally a machine that has never been turned on. So explanations of *a*'s behavior in terms of *a*'s being in certain functional states are not part of a "functional theory" of *a*. They presuppose a functional theory of *a*, and are related to it somewhat as explaining a trail in a cloud chamber in terms of a positron's passage is related to a general theory of particles. A functional theory does not then say what is *going on* inside, not even in functional terms. This is related to the earlier point that token–token psychophysical identities presuppose type–type correlations. In what follows, the "belief–desire theory" is true of *a* at *t* if *a*'s possible state-types are organized functionally in a certain way at *t*. Whether *a* has a specific belief or desire is a further question, about whether *a* actually is in a state with a certain functional role.

Evidently the concept of functional organization ought to be relativized to times. An individual can cease to have a certain functional organization or, a quite different matter, it can have the same functional organization at t and at t', but by virtue of different underlying state-types. Thus, although type–type correlations are required by a functional account of mental predicates, the requirement is minimal. For a mental state-type M, all that is required for a to be in M at t is that *at t* a certain possible state-type has a certain counterfactual functional role, and a is in a state of that type.

This allows for maximal *plasticity* in a's wiring: a certain mental function can be switched from one neurophysiological state to another. No neurophysiological state-type is reserved for a certain mental role, and how it comes to have a particular role may be radically contingent, for how it *would* interact with others may change from moment to moment. All that is required for a to continue from t_1 to t_2 to have a certain functional organization, and therefore to be capable of a given functional state, is that at each time between t_1 and t_2 some states of a's are thus organized, and these need not be the same states throughout.

The states over which a functional theory quantifies are not themselves functional states. Suppose T is a functional theory of a physical thing a, some machine say. So the states which would make T true of a, by being suitably causally related,[1] would be physical state(-type)s, which we can think of as *properties* of a. They are *first-order* properties, properties of individuals, whose definitions do not quantify over other properties of individuals. Now if a first-order property or state φ is among those which makes T true of a, that is because φ satisfies a certain counterfactual causal condition − φ has a certain *functional role*. This "role" is a second-order property, a property of a first-order property. Now, because a is in a first-order state with a certain functional role, a itself may be said to have a second-order property in another sense of that term, on which it means 'property of having some first-order property that satisfies a given condition'. A *functional state* of an individual is just such a second-order state or property − being in a first-order state with a certain functional role. Functional states, then, are not the states a functional theory quantifies over, for the latter are first-order, and functional states are second-order.

---

[1] State-types stand in such counterfactual causal relations if their instantiations would stand in certain causal relations to each other.

What is it to interpret a theory as a functional theory? What logical form do we thereby ascribe to it? So far I have indicated only in a general way what a functional theory of *a* says, that *a*'s states have certain counterfactual roles. Now the question is *how* a functional theory expresses that.

The most lucid account of the structure of *some* functional theories, of how a theory's terms denote states via their functional roles, is a certain application of David Lewis's general account of theory interpretation (1970). But the model thereby generated turns out, as we shall see, not to be completely general. It captures only one (albeit central) type, and the belief–desire theory is not thereby accommodated as a functional theory. But a reasonably efficient way of reaching a more general conception of a functional theory is via that model. First Lewis's account of theoretical terms in general needs explanation.

Ramsey (1929) took a theory's empirical import to be isolated by marking off observational from theoretical predicates, and then existentially quantifying the latter, with the (second-order) quantifiers prefixed to the whole theory, to the conjunction of its postulates. Ramsey's idea is quite intuitive; for if *T*'s theoretical terms are explained via their role in *T*, then it is natural to regard the proposal of the theory as being like this: 'There is a property (call it 'being an electron'), and another property (call it 'being a neutron'), such that, etc.'. Ramsey's theory, thus stated, is *realist* about theoretical *properties*, but *eliminativist* about the *predicates* that express those properties, their import being expressed entirely in an observational and logical vocabulary (including the crucial notion of a property). A Ramsey interpretation then takes a theory to say there are properties or relations that are related to each other and to types of observables in such and such ways.

Lewis's account departs from Ramsey's. First, there is a useful syntactic revision of the theory before interpretation. Each theoretical predicate, '*x* is an electron' say, is converted into a *name*, prefixed by the instantiation-relation – '*x* has electronhood'. Secondly, the theoretical–observational distinction is dropped, in favor of one between those terms that are understood via their role in the theory, and those understood independently of the theory.

Thirdly, Lewis holds that a theory is not explained merely by existentially generalizing its theoretical terms. Let $T[t_1, \ldots, t_n]$ represent the occurrence of all *T*'s nominalized theoretical terms; and let

$T[x_1, \ldots, x_n]$ represent the substitution of distinct variables throughout. On Ramsey's account, T says that $T[x_1, \ldots, x_n]$ is realized by *some* sequence of properties, relations, etc. Lewis claims rather that normally a theory's proponent intends its theoretical terms to denote *uniquely*, and that therefore T is analytically equivalent to the assertion that $T[x_1, \ldots, x_n]$ is satisfied by a *unique* sequence of properties, etc. I shall put this by saying that T is equivalent to:

There are items (properties, relations) $x_1, \ldots, x_n$ which uniquely are such that $T[x_1, \ldots, x_n]$.

An important effect of the strong interpretation is the explicit definition of each theoretical term:

t_1 = the item x_1 for which there are $x_2, \ldots, x_n$ such that they all are uniquely such that $T[x_1, \ldots, x_n]$.
$$\vdots$$
t_n = the item x_n for which there are $x_1, \ldots, x_{n-1}$ such that they all are uniquely such that $T[x_1, \ldots, x_n]$.

So the term t_i means: 'that property, state, etc. which is the ith member of the unique sequence that realizes $T[x_1, \ldots, x_n]$'. This interprets theoretical terms not just as they occur within the theory, but also, say, in singular predications. (Ramsey's theory in this connection is awkward; cf. 3.4.)

Theoretical terms get their meaning from their role in T; but which are those? Lewis's answer is that a non-theoretical term is "one of our *original* terms, an *old* term we already understood before the new theory $T \ldots$ was proposed". Now this temporal criterion is not exactly right. For how relevant is it to interpreting attitude-sentences, for example, whether historically the concepts of belief and desire came later than the relevant concepts of physical environment and behavior, or whether children learn the one set before the other, rather than all together? What matters is that *now* the former concepts are relatively unproblematic, while those of belief and desire need elucidation. This is how it is with explication in general. Intuitions about the relative clarity of two sets of concepts, together with metaphysical assumptions (e.g. physicalism), determine what is worth explicating in terms of what. More archaic concepts might be explicated in terms of newer ones.[2] Of course, when a theory has *just* been proposed, the old terms will be the proper explicative basis.

---

[2] Indeed this often happens when sets and functions are involved in explication.

Suppose the belief–desire theory is universally quantified, the quantifier being over persons with postulates like: 'for any z, if z believes that p and q, then z believes that p', and so on. Nothing has been said about which expressions of the belief–desire theory, in what syntactic form, might be interpreted by the Ramsey–Lewis method, and we shall see there is a problem about that. The present point concerns merely the universal quantifier over the subjects of the theory: will applying Lewis's method to the theory in that form make it a functional theory in the intuitive sense?

The answer is no. For it would then have the form (dropping uniqueness for simplicity):

$$\exists x_1, \ldots, x_n \forall z \, T[z, x_1, \ldots, x_n].$$

This says that certain states $x_1, \ldots, x_n$ have a certain functional role for all persons. But that a functional theory is true of two things does not require them to have first-order states in common; and so there need be no states that have the relevant functional organization in all persons. The upshot is that functional theories are not in the basic case universally quantified. Rather, what gets interpreted are instantiations of the theory by particular things or perons. If we wish to speak of *the* belief–desire theory, rather than the Smith or Jones theory, that "theory" is an open sentence; henceforth I take functional theories to have such a free variable.

The Ramsey–Lewis method is then directly applied. If the original theory has the form:

$$T[z, t_1, \ldots, t_n]$$

then, ignoring uniqueness, the interpreted theory is:

$$\exists x_1, \ldots, x_n \, T[z, x_1, \ldots, x_n]$$

thus leaving it open that different individuals satisfy the theory by virtue of different first-order states having the relevant functional roles.

There is another possible way to apply the Ramsey–Lewis method to functional theories. The problem was that if the theory is universally quantified, the result of applying the method is an existential–universal proposition, which is too strong. Why not instead place the existential quantifiers inside the universal quantifier to get the weaker universal–existential proposition? That says that for each relevant thing or person some first-order states are functionally organized thus and so, not requiring creatures that share the functional organization to share first-order states. But this has the aesthetic defect of not being a direct application of the general method. More importantly, there is an independent reason to take some functional theories not to be universally quantified. Suppose a theory contains an input condition whose antecedent contains no theoretical terms. Some things may then satisfy the antecedent but not the functional theory. But on the universal–existential proposal they falsify the theory. For example, if an input law of a psychological theory contains an antecedent that lacks psychological terms, then an otherwise mindless mannikin that satisfies it, falsifies the theory. The general problem is not remedied by specifying the intended subjects; for the only discoverable relevant property they have in common may be the sharing of that functional organization. This is not to deny that there are interesting universal generalizations of the form: 'All members of species S instantiate the psychological theory T'. But that is not the basic form of a functional theory.

As I have already pointed out, a functional theory is also relativized to times, that is, contains a free variable over times; it is then satisfied by individual time-pairs. Earlier we saw that functional theories are counterfactual in form. The reason I gave was that a machine that has never run can have a certain functional organization. Another reason now is the relativization to times. So functional theories are not about merely *statistical* properties of states. But consider Lewis's proposal that the concept of a psychological state is of a state that *typically* has such and such causes and effects (Lewis, 1971, 1972). Without the relativizing to times, a psychological state can't be realized by different first-order states at different times. But if we do relativize to times, then 'mental state M (for x at t)' becomes: 'the state of x which at t typically has such and such causal role'. That 'typically' makes no sense. The problem evaporates if the theory in which 'M' occurs is counterfactual. For then 'M (for x at t)' means: 'that state which at t *would* play such and such role if...'.

This account allows for a's being in a certain functional state, even if the state that realizes it has a cause that is not among those mentioned in its definition. Suppose (what I doubt) that the commonsense concept of pain is in part the concept of that state of x which would at t be caused by burning, gouging, cutting; a's pain might still be caused by none of these, as an instance perhaps of causalgia, for it may be a state that *would* at t have been caused by burning, etc.

A theory's (a) containing free variables over individuals and times,

(b) asserting counterfactuals relating inner states, input and output, and (c) being interpretable by the Lewis method, with the theoretical terms denoting states by virtue of their functional roles – these would seem to be sufficient for its being a functional theory. But are they necessary? This is important because if they were, then, as we shall see, the belief–desire theory could not be interestingly construed as a functional theory.

There are two respects in which the model is not general enough. First, the unique realization requirement is too strong; and in the following section I shall suggest a way of liberalizing that. But that isn't the most important problem. For, secondly, those conditions contain a restriction so natural one barely notices it. I mean that the theoretical terms are construed as denoting the states to which the theory assigns functional roles. That does define an interesting class of functional theories, what we might call simple black box theories. But some theories that are, by a general and intuitive criterion, functional theories do not satisfy that condition. Even so, the Lewis method will still in its way be employed to explicate them; the belief–desire theory is among them.

3.4 THE MULTIPLE REALIZATION OF FUNCTIONAL THEORIES

The current concept of a functional theory appears to allow two physical states to have the same functional role, to realize the same functional state, to be functionally equivalent. A functional theory T can be multiply realized by sequences of z's states in such a way that T is to be counted as true of z. This is of course impossible on the recently given interpretation of functional theories. I shall present weaker conditions which still yield one of the principle benefits of Lewis' method – explicit definitions of functional terms.

(This section may be merely technical to those not interested in Ramseyfication as such; the reader will not lose the thread of the main account by passing directly to chapter 4. The central idea here is that a nominalized functional term denotes not a single first-order state by virtue of its functional role, but a set of states.)

Before considering multiple realization, it will be useful to consider an important way in which functional theories can be uniquely satisfied – namely, by *disjunctive* states. Suppose T contains both (1) 'if z were in t_i then p would result' and (2) 'if q were true then z would be in t_i'. Two underlying physical states a_i and b_i might interestingly correspond to the functional term t_i as follows: as regards (1), it might be that, if z were in a_i then p would result and, if z were in b_i then p would result; and as regards (2), sometimes if q were the case then z would be in a_i and sometimes if q were the case then z would be in b_i. One might be tempted to say that a_i and b_i were functionally equivalent and therefore T was multiply realized. But that would be wrong; neither a_i nor b_i actually satisfy (2), which is not statistically qualified. But the disjunctive state $[a_i \lor b_i]$ does satisfy both (2) and (1).

So disjunctive states can figure in cases that appear to involve multiple realization because of an ill-defined conception of functional realization. Characteristic of such cases is that the disjuncts of the disjunctive states do not realize the relevant functional states while they appear to do so because being in each of them implies being in a disjunctive state that does realize the functional state. Now let us see that disjunctive states cannot be invoked to forestall admitting multiple realizations.

Here are two examples of multiple realizations of functional theories. (1) Suppose T contains this clause: 'if z were in t_i and z were in t_j then q'. And suppose t_i occurs nowhere else in the theory. (An example in the belief–desire theory is the concept of *ability*: a decision leads to an action, only given the ability to do the action; the sole function of ability in that theory is to convert decision into action.) Now suppose several underlying states have the role of t_i, that is, they satisfy the condition on x_i that if z were in x_i and z were in t_j then q. Would we count the functional theory as thereby falsified? It appears not. Notice that the disjunction of those states also satisfies the condition; but it can't be invoked to preserve unique realization, for it and its disjuncts all satisfy the condition (cf. Lubow 1977). (2) Let T be a deterministic functional theory that contains 't_i causes t_j and t_j causes t_k', where that is the only occurrence of t_j in the theory. (This last proviso is not necessary for the general point, but it makes the case simpler.) Suppose underlying states x_i and x_k satisfy all the other conditions the theory imposes on t_i and t_k, and suppose there are states y_1 and y_2 such that x_i causes y_1, y_1 causes y_2, and y_2 causes x_k. Then, (1) x_i causes y_1 and, by transitivity, y_1 causes x_k, and (2) x_i causes y_2 (by transitivity) and y_2 causes x_k. So two sequences that differ in their jth places satisfy T. (This point is due to Neil Lubow, 1977.) If the functional theory were thereby counted as false the chance of true functional theories of organisms would be low, for sequentially linked states must underlie virtually all such theories that we are likely to produce.

We must then allow for multiple realization. At first, that might seem to imply that a functional theory $T[t_1, \ldots, t_n]$ is equivalent to its Ramsey sentence $\exists x_1, \ldots, x_n\, T[x_1, \ldots, x_n]$, which asserts that one or more sequences of states realize the theory. But this leads to considerable difficulty in interpreting functional terms one by one, as they occur outside the theory. What the difficulty is will emerge, the Ramsey version being in a certain respect too weak. But a certain stronger condition generates explicit definitions of functional terms while allowing for multiple realization. This I shall now present, and then give reasons for preferring it to the Ramsey theory.

If the predicate 'z is in t_i' of theory T expresses a second-order property of the sort usually suggested in this connection, then, for any first-order property in the ith place of a realization of T, having that property is sufficient for satisfying the functional predicate. Conversely, satisfying the ith functional predicate is sufficient for having some first-order property that is the ith member of some realization of T. These two conditions are direct consequences of a functional predicate's expressing the second-order property of having some first-order property that has the relevant functional role.

Those conditions are captured by taking t_i to denote the set of all and only ith members of realizations of T. That is expressed thus:

$$t_i = \text{def.} \{x_i : \exists x_1, \ldots, x_{i-1}, x_{i\ 1}, \ldots, x_n\, T[x_1, \ldots, x_n]\}.$$

This is equivalent to:

$$z \text{ is in } \quad t_i = \text{def.} \exists x_1, \ldots, x_n\, (T[x_1, \ldots, x_n] \quad \& \quad y \text{ is in } x_i)$$

or, if we retain the second-order quantification in terms of which Ramsey's theory originally was presented, P_i being the ith theoretical predicate of T, it is also equivalent to:

$$P_i z = \text{def.} \exists \varphi_1, \ldots, \varphi_n\, (T[\varphi_1, \ldots, \varphi_n] \quad \& \quad \varphi_i z).$$

In these last two forms, one might discern an intuitive account of how the theoretical terms of T are defined if T is equivalent to its Ramsey sentence: intuitive, but wrong.

Evidently, any interpretation of theoretical terms must account for their occurrence univocally, both within and without the theory if logical relations between the theory and independent predications of its predicates are to be maintained. On Lewis's theory that all goes smoothly: the results of substituting within T the Lewis interpretations of $t_1, \ldots, t_n$ is logically equivalent to the Lewis interpretation of T. But on my proposal there is a snag which requires an adjustment.

If within the theory each t_i is taken to denote a set of first-order states in the way presented, and impermissible equivocation is generated. For, as regards the satisfaction of the theory by a sequence of first-order states, each 'z is in x_i' is interpreted as expressing a relation between individuals and first-order states. But on the proposed interpretation each t_i is the name not of a first-order state but a *set* of first-order states, and then 'z is in x_i' expresses a relation between individuals and sets of first-order states. We can't have it both ways.

The problem is soluble. Think of each theory as having two variants as follows. The open sentence that results from substituting variables for theoretical terms can be thought of as having two interpretations. On the first, every predicate 'z is in x_i' is interpreted as meaning 'z is in some member of x_i', with 'x_i' ranging over *sets* of states; this is the *upper variant* of the theory. On the second interpretation, 'z is in x_i' is interpreted naturally, with 'x_i' ranging over states; this is the *lower variant* of the theory.

Now with regard to a sequence of states satisfying the theory, the lower variant is the relevant one. Then define each t_i of the original theory as 'the set of states which are ith members of sequences that satisfy the lower variant of T'. (The metalinquistic aspect of this formulation can be eliminated.) The theoretical terms, thus defined, can then be substituted for the variables in the *upper* variant of the theory with a fitting result. So the theory T is equivalent to T's upper variant. The lower variant is something the theory carries along with it; it is the lower variant that is, strictly speaking, satisfied or realized, multiply or uniquely, and not the theory itself. Identifying the theory with its upper variant means that (1) theoretical terms occur within and without the theory univocally, (2) multiple realization is accommodated, and (3) explicit definitions of the theoretical terms are generated in the non-theoretical vocabulary, thus explaining how a functional theory gives meaning to its theoretical terms.

Is a theory on this interpretation in general equivalent to its Ramsey sentence? Suppose T contains a conditional whose antecedent contains a conjunction of theoretical predicates:

(A) if z were in t_i and z were in t_j then z would be in t_k.

Suppose, also, the following conditions are satisfied:

(1) T is realized by *only* the two sequences $\langle \ldots, a_i, a_j, a_k, \ldots \rangle$ and $\langle \ldots, b_i, b_j, b_k, \ldots \rangle$;

(2) none of a_i, a_j, b_i, b_j are identical with each other;

(3) for every other n, $a_n = b_n$, in particular, $a_k = b_k$;

(4) t_j occurs nowhere else in T.

Evidently, the Ramsey sentence of T is true since T is realized. It follows from the proposed definition of theoretical terms that $t_i = \{a_i, b_i\}$ and $t_j = \{a_j, b_j\}$. But that, together with (A), (3) and (4), entails that the sequences $\langle \ldots, a_i, b_j, \ldots \rangle$ and $\langle \ldots, b_i, a_j, \ldots \rangle$ must also satisfy the theory, which is precluded by (1) and (2). So on the proposed interpretation T is false.

On the proposed interpretation of T, if T is true its Ramsey sentence is true; and, as we have just seen, the truth of the Ramsey sentence does not imply the truth of T on the proposed interpretation. On T's new interpretation T is logically stronger therefore than its Ramsey sentence.

Let us say that the sequences $\langle \ldots, a_i, a_j, \ldots \rangle$ and $\langle \ldots, b_i, b_j, \ldots \rangle$ are related to the sequences $\langle \ldots, a_i, b_j, \ldots \rangle$ and $\langle \ldots, b_i, a_j, \ldots \rangle$ by *recombination in the jth place*. The reason why the Ramsey sentence isn't strong enough to capture the theory that contains (A) is this: for it to be true on the proposed interpretation, the set of its realizations must be *closed under recombination* in the jth place.

That a theory is realized by several sequences does not guarantee that their ith members each interact with *all* jth members as the theory says t_i and t_j should interact; the Ramsey sentence may be true without such inter-realization interaction. But on the intuitive conception of a functional theory, if a certain first-order state realizes a certain functional state, being in the former state is sufficient for being in the latter. So if the theory says two functional states interact in a certain way, *all* combinations of the first-order states which realize those functional states must interact thus.

It could appear that the new interpretation of T can be captured thus: T is realized and the set of T's realizations is closed under recombination in all places. But there are theories that are true under the new interpretation whose realizations are not closed under recombination. Suppose, for example, that T contains

(B) if x is in t_i, then x is in t_j

and that t_i occurs nowhere else in the theory. And suppose $\langle \ldots, a_i, a_j, \ldots \rangle$ and $\langle \ldots, b_i, b_j, \ldots \rangle$ realize T, and that a_i, a_j, b_i, b_j are all distinct states. Does it follow from t_i's denoting $\{a_i, b_i\}$ that $\langle \ldots, a_i, b_j, \ldots \rangle$ and $\langle \ldots, b_i, a_j, \ldots \rangle$ realize T as well? Certainly not. All that is required is that if x is in some member of t_i, x is in some member of t_j, which is secured if only the former two sequences realize T. But it is not evident that any interesting functional theories contain a condition like

(B), given that t_i occurs nowhere else. This turns on the usual purposes of formulating functional theories, which might require that functional predicates occur either in the consequence of an input conditional, or in the antecedent of a conditional, conjoined with a functional predicate that satisfies the former clause or independently satisfies this clause. If it were a constraint on functional theories that every functional predicate be thus connected either directly or indirectly to both input and output, then, I suspect, t_i denotes the set of ith members of realizations of T if an only if the set of realizations of T is closed under recombination. In practice, we can assume closure under recombination to be necessary, since those theories for which it is not required are probably not among the interesting theories.

The question arises whether the proposed interpretation is too strong. Probably there is more than one concept of functional organization, on one of which all that is required is that the functional theory is realized by one or more sequences of states. But on that interpretation of a functional theory as a whole, the predicates do not express second-order properties; at least the natural account of which second-order properties are involved leads to the stronger interpretation, despite appearances. On the weak Ramsey interpretation of a whole theory, it is difficult to make sense of the theory's generating distinguishable functional states. This is not to deny that there may be some interest in an organism's multiply realizing a functional theory but not under recombination.

Functional theories may be constructed from two points of view. First, given a detailed knowledge of a machine's insides, we may wish to describe it at a more abstract functional level. That description could take the form of a functional theory interpreted in the weak Ramsey style. Of course what is crucial is not how much we *know* of internal structure, but whether the purpose of the theory is simply to describe overall functional organization. If so, the weak and strong interpretations merely yield different theories. But I doubt that those theories which it is interesting to interpret as functional theories have as their sole purpose to describe overall functional organization. Functional theories may also be constructed from an interest in prediction on the basis of partial information. Typically we construct and apply functional theories in ignorance of or abstraction from facts about internal make-up. I say 'abstraction from' to cover cases, say involving computers, in which the interest of a functional theory lies in the efficiency that results from ignoring compositional details. The motive for prediction may be theoretical or practical, say, to test a theory of overall functional organization, or to enable one to anticipate the subject's behavior. In any case, such prediction requires ascribing *particular* functional states from which other functional states or behavior may be inferred. This obvious observation has substantial consequences for interpreting functional theories.

For how are we to interpret ascriptions of particular functional states? On the normal view, z is in a certain functional state if and only if z's physical make-up *realizes* that functional state. But that seems to mean that 'z is in t_i' is equivalent to 'z is in the ith state of a sequence that satisfies the theory', and that leads to the stronger interpretation for theories that contain conditions like (A).

4

How to interpret ascriptions of beliefs and desires

4.1 INTERPRETING BELIEF-ASCRIPTIONS: PRELIMINARIES

There are problems about whether all mental states are conservatively explicable as functional states. I shall address only the question whether intentionality can be accounted for in functionalist terms, leaving it open whether experiential or phenomenal qualities of conscious states can thus be accounted for. Problems about the latter can be circumvented by filtering out from common sense psychological generalizations in which the only mental states are propositional attitudes. We would doubtless find it difficult to regard a creature as a person if only the propositional attitude part of our ordinary psychological theory applied. But the abstraction has a point: the only details of psychological theory needed for explicating the concept of propositional content in functionalist terms are such generalizations; if a machine satisfied the belief–desire theory on the interpretation I shall give it, it would be natural to ascribe to it states with propositional content regardless of any reluctance about ascribing conscious experiences.

Attitude-ascriptions are relational on their plainest reading. But that implies little about the nature of beliefs and desires, except that in ascribing them we refer via that-clauses to certain entities. It does not imply that a belief involves attending to a proposition, or a disposition to assert a sentence, or a relation to a "sentence in the language of thought", or any causal, dispositional or quasi-perceptual relation to something in the believer's natural environment. On the subsequent theory a that-clause refers to something quite extrinsic to the believer.

What then is the function of that reference? A propositional attitude-ascription describes a person's state in two dimensions: it places the state within a certain *system* − it captures the state's functional role, and it ascribes truth conditions. These are distinct matters, for functional role involves a state's lateral connection with other states, input and output, while truth conditions involve vertical relations with extra-mental things, properties, and states of affairs. Thus, *somehow* a that-clause's referent, whatever it is, captures the belief's functional role and its truth conditions. How it does the former will emerge gradually in this chapter.

In 2.2 I argued that beliefs are not irreducibly relations to propositions. But there is a problem about eliminating them at this point, for, given the hopelessness of semantic-relation theories, what might replace them? Once it is clear what propositions can contribute to attitude-ascriptions, suitable replacements will emerge, but for now let us retain them. Referring to a proposition somehow captures a functional role, and it obviously captures a truth condition.

What are propositions? On some theories they are sets of possible worlds: if p and q are logically equivalent, believing p is the same as believing q. But that has awkward consequences; if one believes that snow is white, one would also believe that snow is white and the real numbers are not denumerable, which provides too easy an access to mathematical facts. There are other problems. Robert Stalnaker has proposed an interesting way of explaining away the apparent absurdity of these consequences (Stalnaker, 1976), which would be a sound strategy given an independent reason to individuate beliefs thus. But I shall assume, with no argument other than its intuitiveness, that beliefs are individuated by a more fine-grained criterion than logical equivalence. Fine-grained propositions are constructions out of intensions (functions from possible world to extensions), and functions from intensions to intensions, at various levels of embedding, their structures being isomorphic to sentential structures. For an account of them, see footnote.[1]

The central point about fine-grained propositions is that, on the following theory, they are associated with *fine-grained functional roles* for beliefs, so that logically equivalent beliefs can have different functional roles.

---

[1] Let fine-grained propositions be constructed as follows. $\langle K, \langle a_1, \ldots, a_n \rangle \rangle$ is an *intensional structure* just in case either $a_1, \ldots, a_n$ are intensions and K is a function from intensions to intensions, or $a_1, \ldots, a_n$ are intensional structures and K is a function from intensions to intensions. Many such intensional structures, on this definition, will be unsuitable as objects of belief since no conditions on the *matching* of elements were given. But some will encapsulate exactly how the meanings of sentences (and their complex constituents) are determined by the meanings of their components: they are the fine-grained propositions we need. Each such intensional structure determines an *associated intension* as follows: $f(\langle K, \langle a_1, \ldots, a_n \rangle \rangle)$ is the associated intension of $\langle K, \langle a_1, \ldots, a_n \rangle \rangle$ iff it is the value of K for $\langle f(a_1), \ldots, f(a_n) \rangle$. In the limiting case, where a_i is an intension, $f(a_i) = a_i$. So if p is a fine-grained proposition, $f(p)$ is a set of possible worlds, or more precisely a function from possible worlds to truth-values.

I suggested earlier that a certain "belief–desire theory" can be interpreted functionally; it would contain input conditions from perceptual circumstances to beliefs, internal rationality constraints on beliefs, and output conditions from beliefs, desires and decisions to actions. So each sentence 'x believes (desires) that p' would express a functional state in that theory. Let me now be noncommittal about whether any commonsense generalizations constitute a functional theory that would individuate beliefs properly. The question I want to raise now is more abstract: how, *formally*, would 'x believes that p' (for specific p) be explicated as expressing a functional state of such a theory?

That propositional content determines functional role suggests this regimentation: each predicate 'x believes that p' is converted, by nominalizing, to: 'x has the belief that p', 'x has the desire that q', or, since a functional theory is relativized to persons and times, 'x has the belief that p for x at t'. When x and t are specified, 'the belief that p' could serve to designate a first-order state via its functional role. Then 'x has the belief that p' expresses a second-order state.

But the earlier model for interpreting a theory functionally does not enable us to capture this intuitive idea. I have so far characterized functional theories in two ways. The more general, and more vague, account was simply that a functional theory asserts that an individual has states which at a certain time are counterfactually related thus and so to each other, input and output, which says nothing about how the theory achieves that description.

On the more specific account of functional theories, existential quantifiers bind variables that are substituted for nominalizations which are *semantically simple* and are interpreted as denoting first-order states. But if the relevant nominalizations have the form 'the belief that...' and 'the desire that...', that technique of interpretation cannot be applied, for those expressions are not semantically simple. If we were artificially to treat them as semantically simple, and could put a motivated finite limit to their number, the resulting theory, with a distinct variable for each noun-phrase of those forms, would lack the shape of the original theory. The *systematic* description of functional roles is lost; interconnections of logical form are obliterated.

So if for each p 'the belief that p' captures a distinct functional role, it functions as a *complex name* of some state, or set of states. Those complex names are not interpreted by a direct Ramseyan quantification over first-order states, for that treats them as simple. We lack a model of how to interpret complex names of states functionally.

Before pursuing that question however I should like to discuss a suggestion of Lewis's about how to apply his general method to propositional attitudes (Lewis, 1972b, p. 256n). The relevant simple theoretical terms are just the relational 'believes', 'desires', etc. (This supposes that-clauses to be interpreted independently of the theory, as denoting propositions or sentences, say.) If those relational expressions are nominalized, we have: 'x is in the belief-relation to p', etc. If T[Bel, Des, Int] represents those nominalizations, in the belief–desire theory, its Lewis interpretation is:

There are relations r_1, r_2, r_3 which uniquely are such that T[r_1, r_2, r_3].

Now if those variables range over "first-order" relations there is a somewhat odd result. For suppose William is a purely physical entity, and that beliefs and desires are among the causes of his behavior. We then have to say that William's standing in a certain relation ('Bel') to a proposition is among the causes of his behavior and, moreover, because he is a purely physical entity, that relation is *physical*. But what might that physical relation to a proposition be?

Notice that taking the *relata* of propositional attitudes to be not propositions but sentences in the *ascriber's* language is no help: Harold's standing in such relations to my sentences is not in general among the causes of his behavior.[2]

There is a more important objection which goes beyond merely questioning a coherent reading for Lewis's proposal. His theory does not represent differences in propositional *content* as *functional* differences, for the only functional roles the theory would describe are those of the *relations* belief, desire and intention. Does this objection beg the question? Why require an adequate theory to represent differences in propositional content as functional differences, apart from my claim that there is a so far unspecified method of thus interpreting attitude-sentences? The point is that differences in propositional content make a *causal* difference, that is, on realist assumptions about beliefs and

---

[2] Here is a possible reply. "Temperatures are relations to numbers, and having a certain temperature can be a cause. It would not do to argue that temperatures aren't relations to numbers, thus: 'How could a relation to an abstract object be a cause?'" This is beside the point, for I am not saying you can't refer to physical causes via reference to propositions; I am saying that the relation to the proposition is not the cause.

desires. But physicalism implies that they are physical differences expressible in a physicalist language. It is clear then, from general motivations for functionalism, that unless differences in propositional content are functional differences they are not expressible in a physicalist language. (To characterize them physiologically would make them not interpersonally ascribable.) The upshot is that, if ascriptions of content are to be physicalistically vindicated, we cannot stop at functionally interpreting just the relations 'believes' and 'desires'.

This reinforces taking as a functional unit the second-order state expressed by the whole 'x believes that p', with nominalizations in the form 'the belief that p', etc., being the theory's means for designating first-order states via their functional roles. So the question is how such expressions thus denote. How does 'the belief that p' summarize a unique functional role?

If 'x has the belief that p for x at t' is now canonical, which are the theoretical terms of the theory? Propositional variables and names are not among them; propositions can be identified other than as the objects of belief, as constructions out of possible worlds and sets. The syntactical form of what remains is that of a *functor*: 'the belief that p for x at t'. Now although the Lewis method is not applied here in direct quantification over first-order states or relations, it is still our general device of theory interpretation. So, to pursue the Lewis strategy of nominalization, convert the functor 'the belief that...by...at...' into the function-name Bel, and let 'Bel[p, x, t]' represent the application of that function to those arguments; similarly for desire, Des, and intention, Int. That complex expression then is a description: 'the value of Bel for p, x, t'. And 'x believes at t that p' is re-expressed as 'x is in Bel[p, x, t]', which is to say: 'x is in the state which is the value of Bel for p, x, and t.'

Now this does not *interpret* anything; it merely tells us the logical form of our theoretical terms. They are to be interpreted in terms of their occurrence in the belief–desire theory, which we may represent thus:

T[Bel, Des, Int].

Although multiple realization must still be allowed for at a certain level, it is not relevant here, and we may apply the method directly:

There are functions f_1, f_2, f_3 that uniquely are such that $T[f_1, f_2, f_3]$.

This says that a triple of functions, whose arguments are propositions,

61

persons, and times, uniquely satisfies the conditions expressed by ' $T[x_1,$ $x_2, x_3]$ '. That, of course, would yield an explicit definition of 'Bel', to wit:

> The function f_1, such that there are functions f_2 and f_3, such that the three uniquely satisfy ' $T[x_1, x_2, x_3]$ '.

What are those functions? What are their *values*? For a first approximation, consider what we are taking 'the belief that p ' (for specific p) to denote, that is, first-order state-types, the sorts of things that have functional roles. If we now allow for multiple realization, the values of Bel, Des, and Int are sets of first-order states. *So, Bel maps a proposition, a person and a time onto the set* of that person's *state-types which then have the functional role a belief–desire theory somehow associates with that proposition.* How it does so is the key to the theory.

This yields an explication of attitude-sentences; each function-name is definable as 'the function satisfying such and such conditions (expressed by the theory)'. Then 'x believes that p at t' becomes 'x is at t in (some member of) Bel$[x, p, t]$'.

Of the two earlier characterizations of functional theories, the more specific is not satisfied here, that is, with quantifiers directly over the first-order states whose functional roles are thereby defined. Here the quantifiers range over functions, and it is not they that are being assigned functional roles, but rather their values. There is no puzzle about the functions' physical realizations as there was, in connection with relations, on the Lewis interpretation. These functions are functions-in-extension, quite extrinsic to whatever has the functional role. They *index* underlying states with propositions which, by virtue of their position in the theory, encode counterfactuals about that state. Perhaps this will help: certain logical relations among propositions, and correspondence relations between propositions and the world, mirror counterfactual relations among certain first-order states, and between some of them and extra-mental input conditions. So there is an isomorphism between the two networks. By virtue of its unique place in the logical network (which remains to be specified) a proposition can index a belief's unique functional role. It must be emphasized that the proposition is extrinsic to the underlying state.

Functional theories then have different forms. A simple black box theory, as described in 3.3, will not typically refer to extrinsic entities, relations among which correspond to functional relations among first-order states. What is essential to a functional theory is that it captures a network of functional relations; how it does so varies.

A final refinement about Bel, Des, and Int is necessary. That their values are sets of states, with certain functional roles, allows their value to be the null set. But the belief–desire theory could then be trivially satisfied by a rock. For we could take $Bel[p, z, t]$ to denote some state the rock is in, and, for every other q, $Bel[q, z, t]$ to denote the null set; it would follow that the rock believes that p. So we require that these functions not have the null set in their range. (The goal is not to account for the meaning of the English sentence 'x believes that p', but to explicate it conservatively. That 'Jones has the non-empty belief that p' is not natural English is beside the point.)

This condition, when conjoined with the functional theory of an individual y, entails existential generalizations over y's first-order states (like simple black box theories). Indeed, it is implied that for *every* p some state of y's has the functional role the theory assigns to the belief that p. This raises problems, for it is doubtful that some state of each believer corresponds relevantly to *every* proposition, because of finite brain capacity and conceptual gaps (cf. 4.10).

4.3 INTERPRETING BELIEF-ASCRIPTIONS: PROPOSITIONS AS INDICES OF SYSTEMATIC ROLES

When considering the that-clause in 'x believes that some trees bear fruit', it is easy to notice just its *referential* aspects – the truth conditions of the sentence 'some trees bear fruit', – and to ignore its placing the belief in an explanatory system. But belief-ascriptions do have implications about systematic role, which are in large part independent of truth conditions. So interpreting a that-clause requires a double decoding – into a systematic role and a truth condition. Or one may see things thus: truth conditions, propositions, are associated with systematic explanatory roles via principles built into the meaning of 'believes'.

Classical intuitions about *intentionality* conceal two factors that need distinguishing – namely, a belief's *individuation* conditions, and what it is *about*. Now, on my account, individuation conditions for beliefs are to be found in their systematic roles. This means that every aspect of a that-clause which intuitively makes a difference to a belief's content makes a difference to its systematic role. It does not mean there is some simple generalization about the role of all beliefs about, say, dogs, but rather that the generalizations that determine systematic roles for beliefs ought collectively to imply something different about any two beliefs.

It is part of my project to vindicate interpersonal synonymy – that a given belief, classically individuated, can be predicated of different persons on objectively determinate grounds regardless of its evidential differences for them. So it appears we must find interpersonally ascribable generalizations about beliefs – that is, those that are counterfactually true of everyone's beliefs, that collectively imply something unique about each belief individuated in the fine-grained way, and that belong to a commonsense theory (for, it would seem, that is what determines what a conservative explication must preserve).

It may seem unlikely that commonsense generalizations about beliefs could imply something unique about each. Mustn't they be quite general – in the form: 'for *all* p, for *all* q, etc., if x believes...'? But there is no problem. Certain propositions, to be called observational, are each associated with a distinct input condition, viz. that proposition's truth. How this is done interpersonally, so that different background beliefs don't get in the way, is dealt with in the next section. All other belief-types are counterfactually interrelated, some to observational beliefs, and the whole network is anchored at the periphery in a way that ensures each belief a unique place in the network (cf. 4.5).

(The internal systematic relations are of two sorts. Some involve logical form: 'it is not the case both that z believes that p & q and believes that $\sim p$', to be discussed in 4.5, and others have to do with non-logical constituents of beliefs – e.g. 'if z believes that a is north of b, then z doesn't believe that b is north of a'. Naturally these presuppose a certain representation of content, for one can have inconsistent beliefs, under different "modes of presentation". (More on this in 6.1.)

As I observed earlier, a proposition can index a belief's systematic role by having a unique place in a system (just described) of logical and "meaning" relations and extra-logical relations (between observational propositions and external conditions), for that system of intensional relations can mirror counterfactual relations among underlying states and between some of them and external conditions. Such intensional relations hold necessarily, but that does not preclude their informatively mirroring *contingent* counterfactual relations; rationality means conformity to necessary connections, but the conformity is itself contingent.

So far, I have left it open how this *systematic* role, implied for the belief that p by the commonsense constraints, is related to the *functional* role captured by 'Bel$[p, z, t]$'. As it happens they do not exactly coincide, which will be easier to clarify once we have laid out some of the constraints. The *desideratum* is then a set of commonsense constraints on beliefs weak enough to be interpersonally ascribable, and strong enough to imply something unique about each belief. They are *necessary* conditions for first-order states to be beliefs.

4.4 INPUT CONDITIONS AND OBSERVATIONAL BELIEFS

Perceptual input conditions are needed to secure uniqueness of systematic role because the internal constraints on beliefs do not individuate them. This is most obvious in connection with the logical constraints, for they determine uniqueness of systematic role only up to equivalence in logical form. Nor will it be enough to add "meaning" constraints, such as the one mentioned about 'north of'. Suppose two beliefs resemble each other except that 'red' occurs in one and 'orange' in the other. It seems most unlikely that there are any purely internal (non-observational) interpersonally ascribable contraints that distinguish such beliefs.

Adding connections between beliefs and wants, decisions and behavior will not secure uniqueness. This rests on the assumption that the relevant belief–desire theory is a theory of individuals, and not of individuals in combination with the whole world, and thus that the theory's output is bodily action and not the general effects of action: 'squeezed his right index finger' and not 'assassinated the heir to the throne'. The point is obvious, and connected with the point about the practical syllogism in 1.1. Consider this explanation of Harold's reaching out and grasping. "Harold wanted an apple; Harold believed that if he reached forth his hand thus, and grasped away, he would get an apple; hence he reached forth and grasped away." The result of substituting 'pear' for 'apple' is an equally good explanation, so the corresponding generalizations do not distinguish beliefs and wants that involve 'apple' from those that involve 'pear'. As I observed in 1.1, bringing in connections with linguistic behavior doesn't help.

But it is not just behavior and rationality constraints that we rely on in assigning content. For the apple does come into the picture, via perception and not action. There is nothing new in assigning a role to recognitional capacities in concept-ascription, and a recognitional capacity involves input, the effect of perception on belief. So the explanatory system must be connected to something *external* if suitable asymmetries among beliefs are to be found which, directly or indirectly, give each belief a unique role.

65

There clearly is no broad range of conditions of the form: *if z is in perceptual circumstance C, then z believes that p* which are universally and projectibly ascribable to human beings, whether C is a matter of sensory stimulation or of external factors with which a person is in perceptual contact. What beliefs are acquired in perception depends on interpersonally variable contingencies of learning. Because of this, it might appear that suitable input conditions should be conditional – that is, conditional upon already acquired beliefs, in this form:

If x believes $q_1, \ldots, q_n$ and is sensorily stimulated in manner S, x believes that p.

This is no help for the following reason. (1) Suppose $q_1, \ldots, q_n$ do not entail the proposition *if I am stimulated in manner S then p*. Then, what conclusion a person draws from $q_1, \ldots, q_n$ and the fact of S, depends upon substantive inferential dispositions. But the latter will not be universally true of humans, since they depend upon variable learning histories. So (2), suppose $q_1, \ldots, q_n$ do entail *if I am stimulated in manner S then p*. Since anything else in $q_1, \ldots, q_n$ is then otiose, we may take conditional input generalizations to have that proposition in their antecedent, thus:

If x is stimulated in way S and x believes 'if I am stimulated in way S and p,' then x believes that p.

The problem now is that this yields nothing *unique* about the belief that p, for, holding S constant, it could apply to every belief.

Taking perceptual beliefs to be about sensory stimulations does not help, e.g.

If x is stimulated in way S, then x believes 'I am being stimulated in way S'.

If this contributes to generating systematic uniqueness for all beliefs, beliefs about sensations must each have special relations to specific non-sensational beliefs, thus:

If x believes 'I am being stimulated in way S' and x believes $q_1, \ldots, q_n$, then x believes that p.

But the foregoing points (1) and (2), reapplied, show that this fails to secure either uniqueness or universality.

But do we need universality? My project is to make sense of the interpersonal ascribability of intentional content. If explicating intentional content in terms of functional role is inseparable from defining 'believes' in general, then the functional system that secures unique roles for beliefs must be ascribable universally, to every creature that has beliefs. But in the light of the foregoing considerations it seems

66

clear we must distinguish functionally defining propositional content from defining belief in general. While belief in general involves a certain kind of functional system, different functional systems may apply throughout the range of societies and species that have beliefs. Interpersonal ascribability requires sharing some such functional system, and, in particular, input conditions, for example among those who conventionally are deemed capable of the same beliefs as *us*.

The counterfactual properties that make a state the belief that p are the product of developmental learning contingencies. Suppose theoretical psychology yielded a functional theory of human being in general: the present point is that the functional system that defines interpersonally ascribable content is not at *that* level. We want a functional system somewhere in between universal human psychology and the personal evidential connections that define idiosyncratic conceptual roles (e.g. in Field's sense of conditional probabilities (1977)). That there is such a middling level of functional organization is not far-fetched, for members of the same society surely acquire many common structures of dispositions to belief. Learning a language alone must generate an extensive interpersonal belief-system.

The *recognitional abilities* we can ascribe to virtually any adult member of our society are numerous, involving types of artifacts, features of geography, kinds of flora and fauna, classifications of sounds as language, music, barking, laughing, and engine noise, not to speak of numbers, spatial and temporal relations, relative size, and shape. What generalizations, corresponding to these recognitional abilities, might serve as input conditions of an appropriate functional theory? It will be useful to approach them in several approximations.

Their general form is:

If z is in circumstances C, z believes that p.

Evidently, if that is interpersonally ascribable, the truth of p must be ordinarily ascertainable by any believer among us on the basis of mere observation, without requiring idiosyncratic collateral information − p must be like 'there goes a horse' and not 'there goes a veterinarian'. The apparently large class of such propositions I shall call "observational". While p's membership in that class turns on whether such a generalization about p is interpersonally ascribable, in principle those propositions must be specifiable independently of that condition. Given their finite number, we could presumably enumerate the predicates involved, and the logical forms; so that is, I think, no problem.

I shall be noncommittal now about whether these propositions are singular propositions (i.e. have perceptual objects built into them rather than contain descriptions), about tense, and about beliefs about oneself. These matters will be clarified in chapter 5.

Now p must vary with C, which is secured by letting the truth of p be part of C. (Observational beliefs are not guaranteed to be true; they are states whose functional roles are in part determined by p's truth being, with other conditions, counterfactually sufficient for them.) I assume we can spell out physical relations between z and objects and spatial regions whose features make p true, relations which are normally sufficient for z's being able to observe that p. Let us then say that z is observationally related to p at t, or $O(p, z, t)$; this presupposes that p is observational.

The perceptual input generalization, so far, is then:

(A) If p is true and $O(p, z, t)$, z believes at t that p.

We immediately face the problem of natural-kind concepts, which are not determined by observational properties. It is possible for lemons or tigers not to be recognizable as such, and from that a dilemma results: (1) Treat such concepts as not observational, with the result of so restricting that set that the set of interpersonally ascribable "theoretical" or meaning constraints may have to be unrealistically expanded if overall uniqueness is to be secured (but see the metalinguistic M-constraints of pp. 83–84). (2) Or retain them, thereby falsifying the input conditions. The way out, I suggest, is this. Qualify the "natural-kind" predicates in the antecedent: 'tiger' becomes 'normal tiger'. There are then two ways of construing such predicates in the consequent. First, regard them as natural-kind concepts; their place in our cognitive organization is determined then both by our ability to recognize their normal instances and by internal connections with other concepts. Secondly, regard them as observational concepts that are specially associated with natural-kind concepts, but not composites of simpler observational concepts – rather, they are *gestalt* observational concepts. The point is to allow to be as large as possible the class of observational propositions – i.e. those that have non-derivatively unique functional roles.

Now (A) is still too strong, for observable facts can stare one in the face, unnoticed through lack of attention. In our commonsense psychology we do employ the concept of attention in this connection. Mere general attentiveness is not enough: let us say that z is *p-attentive* if z is attending to those aspects of z's observational field that, given $O(p, z, t)$, are normally sufficient for z's perceiving that p. We then have:

68

(B) If p is true, $O(p, z, t)$ and z is p-attentive, z believes at t that p.

Of course, p-attentiveness is a futher functional state ($\text{Att}[p, z, t]$) whose functional role is determined by its interaction with input and belief. (An input condition can have a functional state in its antecedent in the form 'if z is in s_1 and p, then z is in s_2'.) Now the problem with introducing this functional state thus is that (B) is not strong enough to ensure that *any* pair of states having those functional roles is 'the belief that p' and 'p-attentiveness'. That is a general feature of the commonsense theory I am sketching; the problem gets a general solution in 4.6 Now let me simply observe that the point is to specify a commonsense theory which implies something about each belief which it implies about no other.

(B) is still too strong, for a normal observer can fail to accept the evidence of his senses. He can believe things not to be as they appear, when in fact they are. A non-scepticism condition is needed, and so let us speak of z's being *open* to p, with this result:

(C) If p is true, $O(p, z, t)$, z is p-attentive at t, and z is at t open to p, then z believes at t that p.

How is 'z is open to p' to be construed? There are two possibilities. First, it is definable; secondly it is a basic functional term of the theory on a par with 'p-attentive'. As regards the first, we take at face value an apparent observational fact p (i.e. when p is true, O holds, and we are p-attentive), unless countervailing beliefs *forestall* believing that p. This is not trivial, for many beliefs are not produced when other beliefs do not forestall them. So 'z is open to p' could be defined as 'z's other beliefs do not forestall z's believing that p'. (The resulting interpretation of (C) leaves it non-trivial.)

This won't do as it stands, for *unqualified counter-beliefs* may be absent while negative estimates of the probabilities make one suspicious. Since in this functional theory the cognitive attitude is not belief-to-a-degree, but straight-out acceptance, this creates a complication. I am sceptical of the psychological reality of degrees of belief defined as a probability measure, and even more sceptical that any specific decision function, such as maximizing expected utility, is generally ascribable. Perhaps a viable notion of subjective probability can be generated from comparative conditional probability: 'z believes that, given s, q is more likely than r', in some extension of this functional theory, thereby enabling us to define 'z is open to p' as 'z's subjective probabilities do not forestall z's believing that p.'

The second method is to treat 'z is open to p' as a basic functional term of the commonsense theory, and it is plausible that some such unified factor is operative in our normal dispositions to perceptual belief. Acquiring concepts like 'this is red, is a rabbit, is larger than that' seems to be in part to acquire dispositions to make the relevant judgments, in appropriate circumstances, provided one is *receptive* to p's being the case.

Suppose q is logically weaker than p, and that an ordinary believer would believe q on the basis of believing p; so, p might be 'there's a dog over there', and q 'there's an animal over there'. Then the belief that q satisfies (C) with p in the antecedent; so being in a state which satisfies (C) is not sufficient for believing that p. The resources are at hand for dealing with this. For every non-negative observational proposition p, let not-p also be observational. The input condition 'if not-p is true, etc., then z believes that not-p' will not in general hold of the belief that not-q (keeping the antecedent constant, that is), if not-q is stronger than not-p. Now suppose internal constraints on negation do adequately establish what it is for two beliefs to be negations of each other. The whole functional theory then implies something about the belief that there's a dog over there that it does not imply about the belief that there's an animal over there, viz. that it is functionally the negation of a belief whose input condition is that there is not a dog over there.

So the point has been to specify a unique functional condition for each observational belief; and since, in the antecedent, 'p is true' does not occur in the scope of 'believes', we help ourselves to it unproblematically. Relative to the independent enumeration of observational propositions (C) is a schema for as many input conditions as there are observational beliefs.

Does recognizing observational beliefs commit me to the observational–theoretical distinction of empiricist epistemology and theory of meaning that has come under heavy attack? It is probably incompatible with *something* in the recent literature to identify some beliefs as functionally observational. But let us be clear about what is not implied. It is not implied (1) that any beliefs are immune to counter-evidence, or even intrinsically credible, or (2) that acquiring observational concepts is *just* to acquire dispositions to produce such beliefs in the relevant perceptual circumstances; that also involves assimilating it into a theoretical framework. And (3) it is quite compatible with my account that what counts as *data* for scientific theories depends in part on our scientific theories. It is important to keep in mind the differences between explicating belief in general and characterizing a functional system that determines interpersonally ascribable belief content in a certain society. A radical revision of observational belief dispositions may block intentional synonymy across the revision. (The general distinction between functional role and truth conditions and reference would allow *reference* to be preserved across revision, even though *functional content* is not. The question of incommensurability for theories separated by conceptual revolution is doubtless affected by that distinction.)

4.5 UNIQUE SYSTEMATIC ROLES FOR NON-OBSERVATIONAL BELIEFS

The next step is to specify further conditions which secure systematic uniqueness for non-observational beliefs. The idea is to find interpersonally ascribable constraints on minimal rationality which imply, for each non-observational belief, a unique relation to a given n-tuple of observational beliefs. There are two classes: those concerning logical form (L-constraints), and those concerning non-observational predicates (M-constraints). The former, together with the input conditions, secure uniqueness for non-observational beliefs whose only non-logical constituents occur in observational propositions (A-type beliefs). I turn in 4.7 to the question of uniqueness for beliefs that have at least one non-observational component (B-type beliefs).

L-constraints, and uniqueness for A-type beliefs

I assume all beliefs are expressible in a first-order language with indexicals. For those who find this unrealistic, my account can count as a fragment of a fuller theory, which would contain constraints on non-first-order factors – modal operators, higher-order quantification, causal connectives.[3]

The L-constraints that follow are, as psychological assumptions, undemanding. Indeed, if any of them is not by and large true of z, beliefs of the relevant logical form seem not ascribable to z; the required rationality is so minimal that their approximate satisfaction is partially definitive of having the relevant beliefs. An interesting

---

[3] Naturally, the first-order restriction allows for expressing modalities, higher-order quantification in terms of first-order quantification over possible worlds, properties, propositions, etc.

by-product of their undemanding character is that they do not imply that the set of a person's beliefs is *deductively closed* – that is, that a person believes all the deductive consequences of his beliefs.

In what follows, person and time variables are omitted, and '$\Rightarrow$' is the counterfactual connective. So, 'Bp & $q \Rightarrow$ Bp, Bq' abbreviates 'if z were to believe that p & q at t, z would believe that p at t and z would believe that q at t'. These constraints are not supposed to be exceptionless; the whole theory is prefixed by 'in general'. Their consequents are negative, but I have appended to some, in square brackets, positive consequents which may not be too strong. The L-constraints are supposed collectively to imply something distinct about each logical form. Constraint (7b), on the existential quantifier, may seem out of place, but it plays a key role in chapter 4.

The L-constraints

(1a) Not B$\sim (p \lor \sim p)$

(1b) B$p \Rightarrow$ not B$\sim p$

(2a) Bp & $q \Rightarrow$ not B$\sim p$, not B$\sim q$ [Bp, Bq]

(2b) Bp *and* B$q \Rightarrow$ not B$\sim (p$ & $q)$

(3a) B$\sim p$ and B$\sim q \Rightarrow$ not B$p \lor q$ [B$p \lor q$ and B$\sim p \Rightarrow$ Bq]
                                                            [B$p \lor q$ and B$\sim q \Rightarrow$ Bp]

(3b) B$\sim (p \lor q) \Rightarrow$ not Bp, not Bq [B$\sim p$, B$\sim q$]

(4a) B$p \to q$ and B$p \Rightarrow$ not B$\sim q$ [Bq]

(4b) B$\sim (p \to q) \Rightarrow$ not B$\sim p$, not Bq [Bp, B$\sim q$]

(5a) B$t_1 = t_2$ and B$Ft_1 \Rightarrow$ not B$\sim Ft_2$ [BFt_2]

(5b) not B$(\exists x)(x \neq x)$ [B$(\forall x)(x = x)$]

(6)   B$\forall x Fx \Rightarrow$ not B$\sim Ft$

(7a) B$\sim \exists x Fx \Rightarrow$ not BFt

(7b) BFt and B$Gt \Rightarrow$ not B$\sim \exists x(Fx$ & $Gx)$

(8a) B$\exists x(Fx) \Rightarrow$ not B$\forall x \sim Fx$

(8b) B$\forall x Fx \Rightarrow$ not B$\exists x \sim Fx$.

These are quite minimal; it is hard to see how one could ascribe beliefs that exhibited widespread exceptions. They do not require that one is even rudimentarily proficient at making *inferences* (except for those in square brackets, which are perhaps then dubious). Each connective, apart from the quantifiers, has two conditions parallel to introduction and elimination rules for natural deduction except that they require one *not* to believe a certain thing – the negation of what the rules infer. The reason for including both will become clear when we turn to truth conditions in 8.3; it secures that the functional system

72

is, while minimally demanding, still strong enough to impose certain restrictions on assigning truth conditions.

As I have noted, these constraints do not imply deductive closure for a person's beliefs. There is no constraint like: 'if x were to believe p, x would believe p or q'; or 'if x were to believe $\forall x F x$, x would believe Fa', both of which introduce new subject matter. No constraints correspond to certain other ways of securing completeness, e.g. associative rules like: 'p or q and r or s' implies 'r and p or r and q or s and p or s and q'. We can make sense of z's believing the former without the latter because z may satisfy the L-constraints on conjunction and disjunction, which do not yield the associative rule.

Certain observational beliefs, the "simple atomic", are usefully demarcated at this point: they contain only one occurrence of a predicate, i.e. a property or relation-in-intension, and have the form [that is F], [this is R to that] etc. ('that' and 'this' are indexicals to be accounted for in chapter 5). Simple atomic beliefs are the foundation of the uniqueness of A-type beliefs, those whose only non-logical constituents occur in simple atomic observational beliefs.

Now the input conditions and L-constraints together imply something unique about each belief, which is not to say something is uniquely *true* of each belief, but, more weakly, they imply something about each belief that they imply about no other. The significance of this will emerge in the next section. Let us see that the weak uniqueness property holds.

A-type propositions have different degrees of complexity. Simple atomic propositions are of degree O; their negations, other direct truth functions, and quantifications of them are of degree 1, etc. The theory implies something unique about each belief of degree O, and, by the L-constraints, for any belief B of degree $n+1$, the theory implies connections with a set of beliefs of degree n that it implies between no other belief and that set. Thus suppose Bp & q is at level 1; (2a) relates it to B$\sim p$ and B$\sim q$, (also at level 1) which L-constraint (1) relates to Bp and Bq at level O. A glance at the other constraints shows that no other belief is related, by those indirect functional relations, to that pair of simple atomic beliefs. In general, the theory implies something unique about Bp & q (of degree $n+1$), or B$\exists x(\ldots x \ldots)$ etc., if it implies something unique about Bp and Bq (of degree n), or B$(\ldots t \ldots)$ etc., which is the inductive part of demonstrating systematic uniqueness for A-type beliefs.

The L-constraints are not deductive; they singly establish functional incompatibilities between beliefs, but *chains* of such functional relations may not do so. That a certain chain of functional relations obtains between an A-type belief and a set of observational beliefs, does not imply that the latter are deductive consequences of the former, or verification conditions or anything like that. Obviously A-type propositions do not in general imply their atomic constituents. The point is simply that, in the network of functional relations implied by input conditions and L-constraints, no two A-type beliefs have the same relations to a given set of observational beliefs.

The objects or indices of beliefs are fine-grained propositions. So, given the L-constraints, beliefs in logically equivalent propositions can have distinct functional roles. Suppose p is A-type and q is a logically true proposition: the belief that $p \& q$ is functionally related to the belief that q in a way that the belief that p is not, although p and $p \& q$ are logically equivalent. The intuition that the logical equivalence of s and s' is not sufficient for that of $\ulcorner x$ believes that $s \urcorner$ and $\ulcorner x$ believes that $s' \urcorner$ is thus vindicated and not explained away. (Cf. Stalnaker, 1976.) Now fine-grained propositions determine sets of possible worlds (see footnote, p. 58) and therefore contain all the information the latter contain; but, as indices of functional roles, they contain far more information – all that their structure implies.

4.6 UNIQUE FUNCTIONAL ROLES FOR BELIEFS

To specify a "belief–desire theory" is not to specify all principles and generalizations that enable us to ascribe beliefs to z from what we observe about z. To specify the latter fully would be a monumental task, requiring more than what is *prima facie* about beliefs and desires. In 6.3 I discuss the epistemology of attitude-ascription, in particular how the various generalizations we rely on are related to those I am suggesting in this chapter as constitutive, as determining what the functional organization must *be*, and not how we *know* about it.

The L-constraints and perceptual input conditions are minimal constraints on z's being functionally organized so as to have beliefs with certain logical structure and content. They are not all of the relevant constraints, but having them in hand permits raising a certain fundamental question about explicating belief-ascriptions in terms of functional role. The question concerns the relation between their conjointly implying something unique about each (A-type) belief, and

74

the idea that each belief-ascription is to be explicated as expressing a unique functional role.

That the enterprise is the conservative explication of attitude-ascriptions in functional terms certainly suggests that common sense ought to provide a functional theory adequate for capturing Bel and Des — that a *sufficient* condition of believing p is being in a state defined by a certain folk theory. Now, I am committed to this: the incorporation of these constraints is *necessary* for a functional theory adequately to define belief-ascriptions. But, I believe, no commonsense constraints constitute a functional theory strong enough to define Bel and Des. This raises a fundamental question about the project. But first let us see that these conditions are not sufficient.

The L-constraints and input conditions do imply something unique about each belief, something they imply about no other belief; but they do not imply about each belief something *uniquely true* of it. For, a *permutation* of the set of all beliefs (i.e. types) can, for a given person, satisfy all those counterfactual constraints just as well as the beliefs mentioned by them.

Let r be the proposition that Jones is a heavy smoker, and p that Jones will die of lung cancer, and suppose that if Smith believed r he would not believe $\sim p$. Now consider L-constraint (2 a): '$Bp \ \& \ q \Rightarrow B \sim p$'. The counterfactual relation which that asserts holds between Br and $B \sim p$; for it says merely that they would not occur together. Now Br may not satisfy the other conditions the constraints associate with $Bp \ \& \ q$ (for some specified q), but that can be managed. What is necessary, for Br to satisfy the remaining constraints on $Bp \ \& \ q$, is that it satisfy, first, the counterfactual condition expressed by '$Bp \ \& \ q \Rightarrow$ Not $B \sim q$', and secondly, the one expressed by '$Bp \ \& \ q \Rightarrow$ Not $B \sim (p \ \& \ q)$'. But they are easily satisfied in our example; as regards the first, we simply find some q such that if Smith believed r he would not believe $\sim q$; and, as for the second, Smith's belief that r presumably satisfies '$Br \Rightarrow$ Not $B \sim r$'. Thus, as regards Smith's cognitive organization, Br satisfies the conditions the theory so far requires of $Bp \ \& \ q$.

It will be well to discuss a natural response to this demonstration that the commonsense constraints do not individuate content. The counterfactual connections between Smith's belief that r and other beliefs will not be as *entrenched* as those for his belief that $p \ \& \ q$. Suppose Smith learned of an effective and available cure for lung cancer: that might sever the connection between his believing r and not believing $\sim p$; but nothing similar could apply to believing $p \ \& \ q$ and not believing $\sim p$; new information does not unravel rationality.

This suggests adding to the L-constraints a meta-constraint:

> For any q, the L-constraints would remain true of the whole set of z's beliefs, even if z believed q.

(This is not exactly right, for suppose $q = [\sim (p \lor \sim p)]$: believing it is inconsistent with the L-constraint (1a). So the meta-constraint is restricted to propositions q such that believing q satisfies the L-constraints.) Now this stability condition on rationality may seem reasonable; but it is too strong. For these constraints are about first-order states, and it seems possible for a malicious brain scientist to change Smith's wiring so that if, contrary to fact, Smith were in the underlying state that for him has the counterfactual role associated by the overall constraints with the belief that every tree has red leaves, his overall rationality would be destroyed; he would thereby cease to be capable of beliefs. But the meta-constraint is inconsistent with that possibility. So it is not easy to rule out such permutations of the set of our possible beliefs that satisfy the L-constraints as well as those mentioned by the constraints. There are other reasons for the non-sufficiency of the conditions.

(1) The L-constraints are not demanding: they are about certain states' not co-occurring. How could we show that no neural states which are not beliefs satisfy the relevant conditions? It would not be impressive to insist on specific counterexamples.

(2) There are permutations of beliefs on which logically equivalent beliefs are interchanged, such that z's beliefs on such a permutation would satisfy the L-constraints if z is logically astute enough, which threatens the fine-grained criterion of individuation.

(3) There are almost certainly permutations of psychological states that satisfy just as well the input conditions as the ones the theory covers. The roles of p-attentiveness and p-openness are there supposed, together with p's truth and the obtaining of $O(p, z, t)$, to lead to z's believing that p. But that states a, b and c satisfy that condition does not make them p-attentiveness, p-openness and the belief that p. Thus, let a be the belief that if p then q, and b the combined state of p-attentiveness and p-openness, and c the belief that q. It could happen that if p were true and $O(p, z, t)$, and z were in a and b, then z would be in c. Evidently there are also other ways those functional roles could be realized.

Apart from the foregoing, one suspects there are other possible

76

permutations of our beliefs (which do not preserve logical equivalence) which for a given person also satisfy the L-constraints.

To look to common sense for further constraints that make the conditions sufficient is fruitless, for further strengthenings threaten to undercut interpersonal ascribability. I shall now suggest how the commonsense constraints, and their unique implications (in the weak sense), have a key role that does not require them to be sufficient, that is, to exhaust the functional theory which defines Bel and Des, but that nevertheless allows *conservative* functional explications of 'believes that *p*' and 'desires that *q*'.

Suppose that, on a certain well-confirmed functional theory *T* about Smith, generated by theoretical psychology and neurophysiology, there is a striking, if only approximate, one–one projectible correlation between ordinary unproblematic well-confirmed *ascriptions* of beliefs to Smith and Smith's being in functional states defined by *T*. That correlation would not on its own warrant *identifying* specific beliefs with specific functional states. For consider this analogy. Suppose that, in the demonology of a certain people, specific demonic activities by specified demons are alleged to explain certain observable events, and that each such type of observable event does have a distinct unified, scientific explanation, in terms, say, of chemical or electromagnetic factors. That would vindicate *something* of the demon theory – namely, the insight that those event-types have unified causes; but it would not vindicate describing those causes *as demons*, for demons also must be the sorts of things that plot and strive, etc. Evidently a reductionist vindication of one framework in another must not only preserve ways of *individuating* states, etc.; it must also vindicate the *satisfaction* of the *predicates* of the one framework by the states, etc., of the other.

So the mere projectible correlation of *T*'s functional states with beliefs as ordinarily ascribed does not make those functional states of *T beliefs*. Suppose *T* also has this feature: the L-constraints and input conditions (and all other constraints to be specified) correspond, on that correlation, to counterfactuals implied by *T* that are defining conditions of *T*'s functional states, and which may not exhaust *T*. Suppose it turns out that for each person there is a theory *T'* on which such a correlation and the foregoing condition hold. Then, I suggest, the functional states of each such theory *T'*, as applied to a person *z*, should be counted as *z*'s beliefs and desires. For they satisfy the *full* complement of rationality constraints, recognitional abilities, and so on, imposed by common sense as necessary conditions of having beliefs and desires.

Their projectible correlation with ordinary ascriptions could mean, moreover, that they have the *causes* and *effects* we ordinarily ascribe to beliefs and desires, and when they turn out not to (e.g. where *a* seems to common sense to cause *b*, *T* might count them both as the common effects of *c*) we can take *T* to correct common sense. The truth of such functional theories would vindicate the supposition that there are such states as beliefs and desires.

The commonsense constraints determine, then, a *class* of functional theories of individuals; they are the *interpersonally ascribable core* of such theories. This is not to say that common sense thereby dictates to theoretical psychology. The picture is not of the former evaluating the latter, but the reverse: the concepts of belief and desire are shown not to have objective application if correct theoretical psychological theories do not vindicate them by satisfying the commonsense constraints.

The upshot is that it does not matter if permutations of our ordinary assignment of beliefs equally well satisfy the constraints. For the idea is not that any state that satisfies the commonsense constraints on the belief that *p is* the belief that *p*, but rather that the belief that *p* must satisfy them, and, if *z*'s functional states satisfy the correlation condition, and on that correlation satisfy the commonsense constraints, then they are to be counted as *z*'s beliefs and to have the corresponding contents.

Now this may be puzzling, for it could seem I am suggesting that common sense both does and does not supply sufficient conditions for having a given belief. Now, what common sense provides is a meta-constraint on a functional theory *T*'s adequately defining a unique functional condition for a state to be identified with a given belief. The commonsense constraints are not strong enough to define those functional states on their own. What then determines the meaning of 'Bel' and 'Des'? The point is that, because the relevant functional theory may vary in its further details from person to person, Bel and Des are, strictly, systematically ambiguous.

How does this permit conservative explications of 'believes' and 'desires'? If I were presented with such a true theory *T* of *z*, I would accept the predicate '*z* is at *t* in Bel$[p, z, t]$', that *T* defines, as a conservative explication of '*z* at *t* believes that *p*'. For that would by my lights show that there really is such a state as *z*'s belief that *p*. Conservative explication differs from classical analysis, for not all the explicating conditions need have been present antecedently in our commonsense beliefs. What is present are meta-conditions on the adequacy of any such explication. This suggests, contrary to what one might expect, that certain classical scientific reductions – e.g. of the gas laws within statistical mechanics – count as conservative explications in the sense of 2.5.

There is a general point to be made about common sense and functionalism in the philosophy of mind. One model has been that, in explicating a given mental predicate P as expressing a certain functional state, a certain entrenched subset of beliefs involving P make up a functional theory within which P is defined. I am suggesting a new model. Take certain commonsense conditions as necessary for P to be satisfied, and to determine necessary and sufficient meta-conditions for T to be a functional theory within which P can be explicated. T may then contain much that is not in common sense, and in general had better do so if it is to generate sufficient conditions for given mental states. (Some problems about whether phenomenal properties are functional properties may appear different within this version of functionalism.)

What might the rest of an adequate belief–desire theory T be like? One possibility is suggested by certain recent theories about conceptual role. Hartry Field (1977) takes the conceptual role of a sentence in z's language of thought to be determined by its subjective conditional probability given each of z's other sentences. The conceptual, and hence functional, role of each of z's beliefs would presumably be unique within that extended functional theory of z. Since conditional probabilities differ among persons, such functional systems, within which beliefs would have unique functional roles, would not be interpersonally ascribable; but the core of such functional theories (the constraints of rationality, etc.) would be.

But the general idea of such a broader functional theory does not require the part of the theory outside common sense to contain functional relations that correspond to cognitive intentional, or conceptual, relations. Moreover, as I hope is clear, my suggestion has no implications about the overall shape of theoretical psychology. Thus it does not imply that intentional models are to be employed in the functional *subsystems* of psychological theories. Nor does it imply that the proper research strategy is "top-down" – that is, proceeds from general functional theorizing to neurophysiological specifics. *How* it might be discovered that something in our functional organization corresponds to the commonsense constraints is completely open.

79

Theoretical psychology could *vindicate* commonsense psychology even if it were nowise guided by it, even if it did not take commonsense psychology seriously.

There is a large gap in the foregoing, having to do with vindicating ascriptions of propositions to particular functional states. This is related to what may have appeared as a discrepancy between my concern in 4.5 that the constraints should imply something unique (weak sense) about each belief, and then pointing out that they may not imply something uniquely true of each belief, that they do not add up to a functional theory within which $Bel[p, z, t]$ is explicated.

Why is it desirable that commonsense psychology should imply something unique about each belief? That does not enable commonsense to *distinguish* $Bel[p, z, t]$ and $Bel[q, z, t]$, which may have to wait upon science. The key lies in the general matter of vindication. As the demon example seems to show, a mere one–one correlation between the functional states of a well-confirmed psychological theory, and our well-confirmed belief-ascriptions, would not thereby make sense of ascribing predicates of the form 'is the belief that p'. The ideology of commonsense psychology would still need vindicating. Suppose the best we could do, by way of interpersonally ascribable commonsense constraints, were the L-constraints. Describing a functional state as the belief that rats eat cheese would then under-utilize the material in the that-clause, for its only aspect that would correspond to the constraints (the only aspect of the ascription which would be determined by interpersonally ascribable generalizations of common sense, and capable of being vindicated functionally) would be the *logical form* of the that-clause. No more detailed features of 'is a belief that rats eat cheese' could be vindicated in functional terms. But if the commonsense constraints determine something unique about each belief, every distinguishable aspect of a that-clause would correspond to some aspect of commonsense constraints on functional role. If, then, all the constraints are in fact satisfied by the theoretical psychology, every semantically active aspect of a that-clause is thereby vindicated, and thereby contributes something to the satisfaction of 'is a belief that p' by a given functional state. This would not be so if those constraints did not collectively imply something unique about each belief.

So although the constraints do not determine a unique functional role for each belief, the fact that they imply something about each belief which they imply about no other belief means that each distinct aspect of content encodes a distinct aspect of functional role. Each clause 'that

p' captures distinct necessary conditions for a functional state to be described as 'the belief that p'. The full sufficient conditions would be provided by a broader functional theory that defined $\text{Bel}[p, z, t]$ in accordance with the correlation condition.

There is an important consequence of taking Bel's explication to wait upon theoretical psychology, namely, it introduces flexibility into how we conceive the commonsense constraints. Suppose the input conditions were discovered to be too weak by virtue of there being some further condition on forming observational beliefs apart from those in (C) – i.e. O, p-openness, and p-attentiveness. To anticipate this possibility we could regard the antecedent as containing a place-holder. (This, as I shall suggest in 4.9, is a desirable move in specifying commonsense constraints on how belief and desire lead to action.) By relaxing the role of the commonsense constraints, to constrain functional theories rather than constitute them, their form can be more schematic. What is essential is only that if intentional individuation conditions are to be vindicated in functional terms, each aspect of a that-clause must correspond to an interpersonally ascribable constraint on functional role.

4.7 SYSTEMATIC ROLES FOR B-TYPE BELIEFS

So far, uniqueness of systematic role has been established only for A-type beliefs. Now B-type beliefs, whose indices contain non-observational concepts, constitute a dauntingly large class; to characterize their systematic roles would be roughly the same sort of task as the semantic description of a whole language. My purpose here is considerably more modest – namely to indicate in a general way the form of such a characterization of systematic role for B-type beliefs.

The idea is like Carnap's idea of meaning postulates (Carnap, 1947), that is, constraints on non-logical terms that are partially constitutive of their meaning, as in 'red is a color'. I shall call such constraints on beliefs "M-constraints". We can expect resistance to the notion of M-constraints, both on the Quinean ground of implying analyticity, and also in connection with the claim that terms do not necessarily change their meaning when theories containing them change. These raise different issues.

First, no notion of analyticity is *presupposed* here. Rather the idea is to *account for* interpersonal synonymy in terms of interpersonally ascribable constraints on functional roles. The M-constraints are constraints on a class of functional theories, whose satisfaction is an intuitively minimal condition for having such and such beliefs, where 'intuitively minimal' adverts to conservative explication. But both the relevant functional roles, and the methodological concept of conservative explication, have their place within a naturalistic framework.

Introducing M-constraints naturally does commit me to denying the second point in its strongest form. But it has a weaker, but still substantive, form compatible with the current point: to discard a theory that contains a certain term, in favor of a distinct theory that also contains it, is not thereby to change its *reference*. Functional role and reference are in general distinct, and it is quite possible for reference to remain the same while functional role changes.

The notion of M-constraints could suggest something far too strong – that a person's beliefs constitute a theory in which each non–observational concept can be defined *à la* Ramsey or Lewis (cf. 3.2). But it is no more required for non-observational concepts than for logical structures that the constraints imply something uniquely applicable to each. In general, the *desideratum* is interpersonally ascribable constraints that imply something about the functional role of each belief that they collectively imply about no other, which is a much weaker condition than Ramsey–Lewis definability. The full functional theory adequate for defining 'Bel$[p, z, t]$' is not comprehensively determined by commonsense constraints; M-constraints do not have to guarantee that any state which satisfies them is such and such belief.

M-constraints are not meant to be *verification conditions*. The requirement of systematic uniqueness implies that there are *functional* connections, perhaps indirect, between every non–observational belief and some set of observational beliefs, but these relations are not supposed to mirror confirmational relations. Thus the belief that $(p \rightarrow q) \lor r$ is related via L-constraints to the belief that p, but the latter does not count as evidence for the former. So with M-constraints. Suppose 'z believes that electrons are smaller than apples' is among them. Together with other constraints, it may establish a chain of functional relations between some belief about electrons and the observational belief that there is an apple before me. The latter is evidently not thereby implied to be among the verification conditions of the former.

Natural examples of M-constraints are those that establish entrenched properties of relations – e.g. the transitivity of *is north of* and the symmetry of *is next to*. And there are relations of contrariety (nothing is both red all over and green all over), of determinable–determinate (red is a color), of subkind to kind (iron is a metal). There must be enough of these to establish many distinctions in functional role among B-type beliefs. But probably systematic uniqueness is not thereby secured, because of pairs of concepts that exhibit symmetries – e.g. 'north', 'south'. So the M-constraints must imply interpersonally ascribable functional relations of B-type beliefs to observational beliefs.

Consider non-observational natural-kind concepts. Suppose Louis can't tell the difference between a beech and an elm, or aluminum and molybdenum (to use examples of Putnam's). What interpersonally ascribable constraints might functionally distinguish those beliefs of Louis's that we describe using 'beech' and those using 'elm'? I suggest taking such beliefs to be indirectly *metalinguistic*. Suppose we say, pointing to a tree, that Louis believes it to be an elm (he has taken someone else's word for it). One thing we might thereby be saying is that for some N, (1) Louis believes it is of the kind called N by the experts, and (2) the kind called N by the experts is *elm*. (This allows that Louis doesn't speak English.) A variation would be to substitute for the relation among N, *elm*(kind) and the experts, a causal relation among N, *elm* and the speakers of Louis's language. (These are in effect description theories that capitalize on the insights of anti-description theorists.) Now since the concept of such and such linguistic expression involves the notion of perceptual repeatables, asymmetrical functional relations of such beliefs and observational beliefs would thereby be secured. The problem now is how uniqueness of systematic role can be secured for the concepts 'is called', 'experts', 'caused'.

Because a metalinguistic account is an important ingredient of any workable theory of interpersonally ascribable belief content, it may be useful here to consider what might establish the functional roles of beliefs involving the semantic term '*x* is called *y* and *z*'. Naturally we do not ascribe to all believers the mastery of an explicative theory of semantic concepts (e.g. as in chapter 10) within which that relation can be defined. But consider this. Among English speakers there is an entrenched belief that sentences of the form '*N*'s are called *N* by us' are true. Now if we count them among the M-constraints, a unique systematic role would thereby be secured for *x is called y by z*, i.e. for beliefs of that form. The idea is not that the latter are all disquotational, but that there is no other relation whose disquotational role in beliefs of the former restricted class is projectibly interpersonally ascribable.

Now these constraints are of course not inter*linguistically* ascribable, for they involve having metalinguistic beliefs about English in the form: '*N*'s are called *N* by us' is true. For speakers of other languages, however, some beliefs are exactly structurally parallel to them, if, that is, they have thoughts involving the concept *x is called y by z*. That would enable us to ascribe that concept to them, in terms of its unique systematic role, as determined by structurally parallel conditions. We have, then, a broadened notion of M-constraint: the interlinguistically ascribable condition is not in terms of the specific *content* of those disquotational beliefs, but in terms of a *structure* in their content which seems expressible as a constraint on functional role.

If such beliefs are metalinguistic, then the combination of systematic uniqueness for semantic concepts, via disquotational beliefs, and the observational status of quotation descriptions of linguistic expressions, encourages the idea of M-constraints relating non-observational to observational beliefs and thereby securing systematic uniqueness for those B-type beliefs.

There is a certain important class of B-type beliefs such that, were the interpersonal ascribability of their functional roles secured, the general topic of interpersonal synonymy would be considerably affected. I mean beliefs that arise from applying the Ramsey–Lewis method of theory interpretation to theories that satisfy the following condition. The O-terms include observational terms (in our sense of figuring in the input conditions), a certain mathematical vocabulary, the concept '*causes*', and the predicates '*is a property*', '*is a relation*', etc. Now suppose, what seems safe, that we can establish suitable interpersonally ascribable constraints on these non-observational O-terms. Beliefs in such theories, Ramseyfied, are then interpersonally ascribable in the sense that our interpersonally ascribable functional organization makes it possible for each of us to have them. This means that, even without comprehensive M-constraints, "theoretical" beliefs of a large class are objectively interpersonally ascribable, i.e. their functional roles are.

Finally, let me compare this general approach to systematic unique-ness to positivist theories of meaning in terms of observational connections, and the generally anti-realist consequences of positivism. The difference is this. On a positivist theory, the meaning of a theoretical statement is constituted by its *a priori* connections with certain *epistemic* conditions. So on the simplest verificationist model, *S* is equivalent to a statement that such and such *perceptions* occur; or, on a more indirect model, learning the meaning of S requires learning that certain perceptions constitute *evidence* for S. But the connections that on my account relate non-observational beliefs functionally to observational beliefs do not establish *a priori* evidential connections between non-observational and observational beliefs. The M-constraints, as I conceive them, make it conceptually possible to be an anti-verification realist, in the sense that they allow one to think that *p* might be true even though we could never get evidence about *p*'s truth. Moreover, the grounds for ascribing *truth conditions* to beliefs are *external* to the functional system (cf. chapter 7), and so a functional theory of belief, including a special role for observational beliefs in establishing uniqueness, is consistent with a metaphysical realist conception of truth conditions. There is more than one theoretical–observational distinction; not every one of them is positivist or anti-realist. That some such distinction is entrenched in commonsense psychology appears to me philosophically unexceptionable.

4.8 TRUTH-CONDITIONS, AND THE DEFINITION OF 'BELIEVES'

A belief's functional role, and its truth conditions, are different matters, except for the case of observational beliefs. Now in some sense this must imply that functional role *does not determine* truth conditions – that capturing the former is not sufficient for capturing the latter. But then if we consider '*x* believes that *p*' to be *equivalent* to '*x* is in such and such functional state', that implies that functional role *is* sufficient for truth conditions, for the truth conditions of a belief are encapsulated in the proposition that is its object.

The inconsistency is merely apparent. That it is one thing to describe the functional role of a state and another to describe its truth conditions is compatible with a certain *conventional association* of truth conditions and functional roles being built into the meaning of 'believes'. As it happens, we choose to index certain functional roles with such packagings of truth conditions, propositions; but as regards their adequacy in indexing, our assignment of truth conditions to functional roles is *arbitrary*. That arbitrary association is conventionally encapsulated in '*x* believes that *p*', just as an arbitrary association of numbers with temperature states is encapsulated in 'the temperature of *y* is *n*° Fahrenheit'. Saying 'believes' in connection with a proposition is like saying 'Fahrenheit' in connection with a number. In explicating temperature ascriptions, we do not expect a justification of all specifics in the choice of numbers. Similarly with 'x believes that p'; the functional explication of 'Bel' does not *motivate* assignments of propositions to functional roles, which are nevertheless built into the meaning of 'Bel'. So there is a sense in which functional role does "determine" truth conditions – namely, conventionally; to ascribe a functional state using the verb 'believes' is to do so according to a certain conventional association of truth conditions and functional roles. That raises the separate problem whether that association can be shown on independent grounds not to be arbitrary, and there the analogy with temperature would end.

So the project has two stages: first to say how each belief is associated with a functional role; secondly, to explain why functional roles are assigned certain extra-mental conditions. In 7.2 we shall see how to filter out these two aspects of a belief in separate levels of description; but now, while we retain propositions, the two levels are inseparable.

Finally, let me suggest an alternative way of viewing the relation between the two levels. Regard the current project, which is to show how '$\text{Bel}[p, z, t]$' captures a certain functional state, as giving a certain *necessary* condition of believing that p. Accounting for truth conditions would then complete the project of providing *sufficient* conditions for a state's having a certain *content*, viz. being in a functional state with such and such associated (truth) conditions. This is not my preferred account of the two levels; why I prefer the earlier formulation becomes clearer in 7.3 and 7.4.

Perhaps these remarks will clarify the relation between the functional explication of $\text{Bel}[p_1, x_1, t]$, and Quinean indeterminacy. It is relative to an assignment of propositions that 'z believes that p' has a unique functional role, just as it is relative to an assignment of numbers that 'the temperature of $x = n°$ Fahrenheit' has its distinct import. The claim of *intrasystematic uniqueness* does not imply that those assignments of propositions of numbers to functional roles or temperatures are uniquely best. The determinacy of truth conditions cannot be resolved merely in terms of the psychological roles of beliefs; the question turns on a further interaction between functional states and extra-psychological reality.

4.9 WANTING, WILLING AND ACTING

The functional roles described so far do not suffice for explicating belief, for beliefs must systematically interact with desire to lead to decision and action. I shall use 'desire' and 'want' interchangeably for the generic pro-attitude; this is not mere terminology, for it implies that the more specific pro-attitudes, 'likes', 'wants', 'values', 'would like to', 'has as an ideal that', 'is in favor of', 'has a yen for', 'thinks it ought to be the case that', 'lusts after' are to be explicated in terms of wanting in general as a unified functional state. The contents of desires are a matter of their potential interaction with certain beliefs in leading to decisions. The uniqueness of their functional roles is inherited from that of beliefs, and so there is no need to introduce input conditions for desires; desires are not functionally specified in terms of their causes or terminating conditions, but solely in terms of interaction with beliefs.

Certain beliefs, of a type I shall call instrumental, have a special role: they have the form 'x believes that x's doing A would bring about p'. It is by virtue of their mediation that other beliefs influence action: the belief that q and the belief that [if q x's doing A would lead to p] lead to the instrumental belief that x's doing A would lead to p, which given the desire that p, *sometimes* leads to doing A. Thus all beliefs are states of an input–output system.

Formulating the output condition of the belief–desire theory has two stages: something connecting instrumental beliefs and desires with certain intentions or decisions, and something connecting intention to action. It will become clear that the two could be amalgamated, with intention cancelling out, thus suiting sceptical intuitions about volitions or intentions as distinguishable states. But there are advantages in introducing this third type of propositional attitude, which anyway seems inevitable on the following familiar grounds.

Suppose the desire that q wins out in a conflict of desires, and an intentional bodily movement results, a kick, say. Consider a case exactly like it except that something, not a mental state, prevents the kick. We would ascribe some propositional attitude other than desire with that bodily movement as its intentional object; the person decided, intended, or simply tried to kick. Moreover that state would be caused by a desire that q, and the belief that that action would bring about q. If that is true of a frustrated action, it is unmotivated to deny it of a successful action, to hold that the latter is caused simply by the belief and the desire without the intermediate state.

How should that state be described? 'Trying' is not the most appropriate word in the successful case (although, as Armstrong (1973) argues, this may be due more to implicatures than to the meaning of 'trying'). 'Deciding' isn't quite right either. The problem is not that decisions have to be conscious, but that decisions are events. Running a few miles is not a basic action that springs fully shaped from an initial decision, like the practiced playing of an *arpeggio*; but nor is it kept up by a series of decisions. Rather, one's running is the effect of one's more or less *continuously intending* to be running. So a better term for this third propositional attitude is intending.

There are two strategies for proceeding. The first involves specifying the functional role, not of intending in general, which covers both ulterior intentions behind actions and intentions in advance of action, but a kind of intending I shall call *willing*. Its objects are basic action types – bodily movements and mental acts. The general concept of intending would not then be defined directly by the functional theory, but indirectly in terms of believing, wanting and willing. The second strategy involves introducing the full notion of intending into the functional theory. There are problems, and I shall present it later mainly to clarify and to motivate the first strategy by contrast.

Certain actions are the primary *explananda* for belief- and desire-ascription – bodily movements, and intentional mental acts, which I shall not discuss. Consider a non-basic action like flying to Abu Dhabi. Although the intention to fly to Abu Dhabi occurs in its explanation, given enough information such an explanation can be factored into two components: (1) actions like boarding the plane and staying aboard, whose explanation contains the intention to fly to Abu Dhabi, certain beliefs and intentions to do those specific actions, and (2) independent facts, like the fact that the plane flew to Abu Dhabi. This division of explanatory labor ends with bodily movements, basic actions that are not thus explained by further actions and independent facts. Since the independent facts are not themselves explained by those intentions, save *per accidens*, the primary *explananda* of the belief–desire theory are bodily movements (or certain extended bodily movements, like pulling a trigger) described in "molar" terms. The intentions that explain them are present-tensed, self-ascriptive (in the sense of 5.3) and have those bodily movements as their objects. They are "willings".

What relates belief and desire to willing? There must be some generalization, ascribable to common sense if the functional analysis is to be carried through. Scepticism could arise arise now if one has too narrow an idea of a belief–desire–willing connection. Call a *complete decision theory* any generalization that predicts decisions, willings or states of indifference from the contents, and perhaps degrees of strength, of sets of beliefs and desires. Now common sense contains no complete decision theory. For obviously any adequate decision theory must take into account what a person thinks *might* be the case. For to any otherwise acceptable generalization about how unqualified belief affects decision, there are counterexamples in which, because of what z thinks might be so, z fails to will the relevant action. But then any decision theory, which says exhaustively how *degrees* of belief and utility determine decision, is hard to ascribe to common sense. Concepts of rough degrees of belief and desire do not yield a complete decision theory, while precise concepts of subjective probability are theoretical. Moreover, any particular decision theory, like maximizing expected utility, does not seem evidently part of common sense. (This is not meant to deny the usefulness in theoretical psychology of complete decision theories.)

There is a generalization relating beliefs and desires to willings, not a complete decision theory, but ascribable to common sense. The idea is that desires and instrumental beliefs lead to willings *when no competing desires override them*. That may sound vacuous; while it is not exciting, it is not empty either. What is it for one desire to override another? Suppose z desires that q and believes that z's doing A would lead to q. Suppose also z believes that doing A would or may also lead to not-p, and that z desires p. Now if the latter pair causes z not to decide to do A, then z's desire for p has *overridden* z's desire for q with regard to A. ·

A concept occurs here that we have not introduced functionally, namely, that z believes that doing A *may* lead to not-p; it would seem that degrees of belief have to be invoked after all. (The qualification, 'may lead to not-p', is needed; for one may refrain from an action, not because it would interfere with something else one wants, but because it *may*.) But there is perhaps a simpler way to get what we need than introducing degrees of belief. A way of "believing it *may* be the case that such and such" is by *not* believing that it is *not* the case that such and such. And so a way of "believing that A may lead to not-p" is not believing [not: doing A would bring about not-p]. This minimal concept is perhaps all we need to define *overriding* in the above context.[4]

So here is the belief–desire–willing condition:

---

[4] A more cautious device is this. Instead of invoking instrumental beliefs in the definition of overriding, define 'the desire that q overrides the desire that p with respect to A' simply as 'the desire that q causes z not to will to do A', without requiring it explicitly to have the negative effect via an instrumental belief.

If z desires q, believes doing A now leads to q, has no desire that overrides the desire that q with respect to A, and believes z-self able to do A, then z wills to do A now.

Some comments in order of increasing importance.

(1) The variable 'A' is virtually restricted to bodily movement types. But no independent definition of basic action is presupposed; for any bodily movement, if z believes it to be within z's power, then, given the other conditions, z wills it.

(2) Actually a further qualification is necessary. One normally has available several perhaps trivially different incompatible actions that equally implement the desire, among which one is indifferent. As stated, the generalization implies one does every such action; so we should have this: if a is the set of all actions of which the antecedent is true (for specific q), z does some action in a. The choice made by Buridan's ass, or a human in the same predicament, is not predicted by commonsense psychology. What we will is not always determined by our effective desires and beliefs – habit, conditioning and perhaps random neural firings may supplement them to determine one among several equally appropriate actions.

(3) The notion 'z believes z-self *able* to do A' occurs apparently ineliminably, which creates a complication. For ability is to be treated as functionally defined, in the condition, to be given, from willing to acting. So far I have avoided requiring *reflexive* attitudes in the theory, beliefs or desires about attitudes. For even if, as some have claimed, fully rational belief requires reflexive beliefs, the most promising explicative strategy would be first to specify a non-reflexive foundational level of cognitive and inclinational states with an otherwise full range of content. So, introducing 'believes z-self able to do A' muddies the waters. The natural move is to introduce a more primitive attitude towards A than the belief that one is able to do A: taking-A-to-be-in-one's-current-repertoire. Beliefs about ability arise with the reflexive awareness of circumstances in which willings are frustrated. The new primitive attitude is then functionally defined by its role in the theory.

(4) Finally, we come to the question whether the non-overriding clause makes the generalization trivial. The answer is, not at all; for its form is: 'if condition C were to obtain and a certain specified condition $C^\star$ did not cause not-E, then C would cause E'. That requires something substantial in how first-order states interact. The condition leaves it obscure, of course, what makes one desire override another,

in the way a complete decision theory does not. But this is all to the good, for that is obscure to common sense. Some have made much of the fact that desires do not unqualifiedly lead to decision, but are overridden by other desires with no apparent limit to the process being imposed by our commonsense theory, drawing conclusions as radical as the irreducibility of psychology (Davidson, 1970), the existence of a hitherto unacknowledged sort of explanation (Peacocke, 1979), and the existence of a new form of theoretical generalization (Grice, 1975b). These conclusions are, I think, based upon not seeing this as an instance of a broader and not awfully mysterious aspect of explanation. Consider forces. Certain of our general beliefs about physical objects can be expressed thus: if to an object in such and such circumstances a certain force is applied, it moves in a certain direction, unless a countervailing force prevents that. Again this is not trivial; but nor does it motivate any of the reactions just mentioned to what seems the same feature of the connection between wanting and willing. Moreover the analogy can be made even closer; for, it seems to me, it is only in a now unmotivated anti-mentalism, one which overlooks the functional interpretation of mental concepts, that it seems wrong to think of desires as like forces.

(5) As I earlier suggested, the perceptual input condition may contain a place-holder, for a condition supplied by the more comprehensive functional theories that define Bel, Des, and Int. This is important in the current context, and also in connection with intending, as I shall explain. If there is a place-holder in the antecedent of the belief–desire–willing condition, and a well-confirmed theoretical psychology implied something of that pattern for z's states, that would tend to vindicate ascribing beliefs and desires to z. A similar point is that if 'overriding' is not explicable in the way suggested, it may still be a basic functional relation within the more comprehensive theory, as with 'p-attentive', etc.

Finally there is the output condition of the belief–desire theory, which I suggest is simply this:

If z wills at t to do A now, z is able to do A at t, and no external condition prevents z from doing A at t, then z does A at t.

Introducing ability as distinct from freedom from external constraint is motivated by the functional theory's being of an individual and not a composite individual-plus-external environment. So 'z is able to do A now' is functionally defined: 'Able[[x does A now], z, t]' denotes the set of states sufficient at t for z's willing A to issue in A in the absence of external impediment. Naturally one might regard ability as explicitly definable via a counterfactual from willing to acting, but this functional definition prevents circularity. In general, if it is appropriate to explain F via its functional occurrence in 'if z were F and G, z would be H' and if F occurs nowhere else in the theory, then 'Fx' will naturally appear definable as 'if x were G, x would be H' especially if the truth of that counterfactual is independently evidence for being in functional state F.

If wanting and willing were our only inclinational and conative concepts, if we lacked the general concept of intention, then, to account for strategic behavior, we would have to rely on certain derived wants. When normally we would count z to intend to do A as a means to B we would have to count z as wanting to do A. That seems plausible; it does not imply the implausible stronger derived-want principle that, if one wants B and believes that doing A is a means to B, then one wants A at least to some small degree. All that is required is that in those cases in which we count z as intending to do a certain action we should count z as wanting to do that action.

While wanting can do some of the explanatory work of intending, something is evidently left out. But 'intends' is not easy to account for. Perhaps if we could define 'prefers' independently, in terms of some notion of 'overriding' related to, but obviously not the same as, that already defined, 'intends' could be defined thus: z intends to do A iff z wants to do A, z prefers doing A to not doing A, z believes that z will do A, and that belief is non-inferentially caused by that want and that preference (cf. Grice, 1971). Naturally we should want some explanation of why this construction has a unified role in commonsense psychology.

Could we introduce intending in general as a basic functional concept instead of willing? This would have to cover intending long in advance of the appropriate action. The condition which parallels the belief–desire–willing condition would be:

If z believes that doing A leads to q, and z wants q, and no other desire overrides the desire that q with respect to A, and z believes that z is able to do A, then z intends to do A.

This condition is not plausible, for it amounts to saying that if one believes one's desires on balance will be fulfilled by doing A then one forms the intention to do A. But there are reasons for doubting this. First, a person's current desires about the future may favor a given future action, while the person still adopts a wait-and-see attitude about the decision. In the willing condition, that is ruled out since, if the action is desired immediately, someone who didn't will it has not a want but something like a velleity, or really prefers inaction or another action. That account of not forming intentions towards more distant actions seems tendentious. Secondly, the antecedent of that condition doesn't require that z *believes* that z will do A. But my intuitions about intending rather favor taking intending to do A to imply believing that one will or might do A. This may partially explain the difference between wanting and intending. But not fully: for, to make a well known point, z can want what z believes will result from A and, knowing this, predict that he will decide to do A, without yet deciding to do A. So we add that the belief is *non-inferential* and caused by the relevant wants. But this is not sufficient because of deviant ways in which the non-inferential belief may be caused (e.g. by a brain manipulation).

Thus there are problems about explicating intending within commonsense psychology. But again a more comprehensive theoretical psychology may come to the rescue. For if functional states of z are suitably correlated with commonsense bases for ascribing intentions to z, and satisfy conditions something like the ones discussed, then no doubt we would count them as z's intentions. Thus common sense need not provide conditions on intending that yield a functional theory sufficient for explicating it.

There is a moral here regarding *deviant causal chains* (cf. Peacocke, 1979). *Causal* conditions that are supplied by common sense in explication, say, of memory or intentional action, etc., may be satisfied in odd ways, so that the concepts to be explicated are not satisfied. Deviant causal chains threaten the sufficiency of causal explications. Now the earlier suggestion about the relation between commonsense constraints and theoretical psychological theories removes this general threat to the conservative explication of mental and semantic concepts within a physicalist framework. That common sense does not supply everything is compatible with non-eliminative explication.

4.10 THE CLASS OF BELIEF–DESIRE THEORIES

The propositional variables that prefix conditions like the L-constraints are so far unrestricted; they range over the infinite set of all propositions. But on two plausible assumptions, that leads to an unacceptable result. Bel does not have the null set in its range; but then the belief–desire theory is true of z only if for *every* proposition p there is a first-order state that belongs to $\mathrm{Bel}[p, z, t]$, that has the functional role of the belief that p. On its own this does not entail infinitely many first-order states of z, for Bel might map infinitely many propositions onto finitely many states; finitely many first-order states could realize infinitely many functional states. But it would be amazing if that were so, for any pair of distinct beliefs of z would in fact always have different potential effects and causes; different first-order states would need to be involved. Indeed, one way for a creature to realize the belief–desire theory would be via first-order states which are structurally isomorphic to propositions and which then constitute something like the "language of thought" that Fodor (1975), Harman (1973), and Field (1978) have argued for. But then if the theory quantifies over infinitely many propositions, any creature with beliefs has infinitely many possible first-order states with the relevant causal roles. This means, of course, not infinitely many state-tokens, but infinitely many structurally possible states. But that, I take it, is not on, given the finite nature of the human central nervous system.

Another reason for not allowing unrestricted generalization over propositions is conceptual gaps – z's lacking a certain concept, of a quark, say. There may not be possible states of z's neurophysiology that are now uniquely suited as the physical basis for that concept, waiting to be triggered by a suitable learning process. It seems more likely that what neurophysiological state of z has the functional role of the belief that p depends upon how z acquired its concepts; if p contains a concept not already acquired by z, there may be no possible state-type of z's which now has the second-order property of being the belief that p.

An analogous point applies if p ranges over singular propositions which contain individuals as constituents. If Harry has had no cognitive contact with Ulugh Beg, no state of Harry's is set aside by nature to be Harry's internal name of Ulugh Beg; what state has that role would depend on how he achieved cognitive rapport with Ulugh Beg.

But our commonsense belief–desire theory does not seem to preclude that, for each person, only finitely many propositions are within that person's current cognitive and inclinational range, namely those whose constituent concepts and logical operations the person has mastered, *up to a certain level of complexity*. Such a set of propositions, a *propositional field*, will satisfy certain conditions: a sufficient variety of constituent concepts, and membership by all propositions resulting from those concepts by predication and iterations of truth-functional and quantificational operations, up to a certain level of complexity. Thus we may take a belief–desire theory of z to have propositional variables restricted to a finite propositional field. Or, *the* commonsense belief–desire theory may be prefixed by an existential quantifier over propositional fields. For any such field, Bel then has only finitely many first-order states as values.

Suppose a certain person z lacks one, isolated, recognitional ability that is in the scope of 'O' in the perceptual input condition. Since that condition is part of the very fabric of the belief–desire theory, it would then follow that z does not realize the theory and hence has no beliefs and desires. But this has more bark than bite, for a very similar set of functional conditions *is* true of z. Let us describe the general features of the "belief–desire theory", abstracting from the concepts it requires of believers. It employs propositional indices, certain cognitive states that are subject to L-constraints and, for a subset of those indices, certain inclinational states that interact with cognitive states to lead to certain conative states (willings). Now our imagined z realizes a functional theory that resembles in these and many more detailed ways the most complete possible version. Although, in a certain strict sense, the 'Bel' we apply to z and the one applied to the fully informed believer is ambiguous, our ordinary 'believes', applied interpersonally, reflects the shared features.

There is no reason not to extend the point to members of radically different cultures – to Kalahari bushmen or members of the Golden Horde. Functional theories that have those structural features were realized by them, and it is thus that they had beliefs and desires, while lacking our recognitional abilities and M-constraints, although doubtless not our minimal logic.

We can envisage theories that we would want to count as about propositional attitudes but do not have the sort of structure I have specified. Any variant of decision theory would be such, one which included maximizing expected utility or a minimax principle. The indexical account of the role of propositions in the belief–desire theory can be carried over to such a theory. Instead of defining a distinct systematic role for each belief and desire *tout court*, the theory would generate a unique systematic role, for each proposition and each degree of belief, for the belief in that proposition to that degree. No such theory could generate a *bona fide* theory of propositional attitudes unless it included an input law with a sufficient range of observational concepts to insure the requisite uniqueness of systematic role. In particular a theory whose only specification of input is in terms of sensory stimulation is doomed to failure, unless it attributes to the believer rather elaborate theories (M-constraints) that relate sensory stimulation to propositions about the world. Short of requiring such an epistemological extravaganza, there is, I think, no hope of explaining propositional content in terms of a sensational theory of input combined with a decision theory. Ascription of content is at that middling level of functional organization which presupposes quite contingent and culture-bound,[5] even if interpersonally ascribable, recognitional abilities.

[5] A general problem for functionalism has been raised by Ned Block (1978). Specifying input and output, in commonsense conditions, is bound to be too restricted to human features, too chauvinistic, as Block puts it. In other species, pain may not be caused by factors that cause human pain; and evidently pain and other mental states will cause different bodily movements in other species than in us. Hence commonsense functional theories will not capture the fully general concepts of non-species-specific mental states.

As regards input, let us keep in mind the distinction between those general features of functional theories that generate the most general concept of "belief" and the specific theory that defines beliefs with the contents that we are used to ascribing. Our normal ascription of specific content *is* chauvinistic, in that it presupposes (among other things) a certain range of recognitional abilities, that is, of relevant input conditions.

As regards output, the condition goes from 'x intends to do A' to 'x does A', but there is no chauvinistic restriction to human actions A. Notice also that the problem of output for states like pain would vanish if they were treated as causes of desires, and only indirectly then as causes of actions.

5

Beliefs about particulars

We need an account in functional terms of certain beliefs that are about particulars "indexically" and not under descriptions of them, for example beliefs about perceived particulars, tensed beliefs, and beliefs about oneself. There is a topic in the literature closely related to this topic, which needs at the outset to be firmly distinguished from it. I mean that of *de re* occurrences of singular terms ('I', 'now', 'that', 'he', 'the *F*', '*N*') in that-clauses in English, what they contribute to belief-ascriptions. I am not denying that it is an important topic: if my theory of beliefs about particulars fitted no good theory of *de re* terms in that-clauses, there would be a problem.

Suppose all beliefs about particulars were about them under descriptions; one still could *ascribe* such a belief *de re*, without using a description, simply by saying what or who it is about. So if you believe that the man standing in the corner is a botanist, I can say you believe Watson is a botanist, either with no implication about your conception of Watson, or with an implication only about the general *sort* of description involved.

In beliefs about perceived particulars, I shall suggest, there is something which, while not a description, functions like one, as the *mode of presentation* of *y* under which *x* believes *y* to be *F*. It corresponds to a functional fact about the belief. But, as on the description theory, it is not intended that whenever a belief about a perceived particular is *ascribed*, a specific mode of presentation is mentioned. You may mention the object, etc., the belief is about, without any implication about the mode of presentation, or with indication only of its general type. The topic I am pursuing is then *not* how the singular terms we use in ascribing beliefs *constrain* the modes of presentation involved. I am concerned with what figures in the content of such beliefs, and not how our ascriptions determine, indirectly, classes of such contents.

The theory of the latter which I find most attractive is Stephen Schiffer's (1977, 1978) (adjusted to include, as modes of presentation, not just descriptions, as on his account, but also the non-descriptive ones to be introduced). The idea is this. Take a sentence S of the form $\ulcorner x$ believes that $\ldots y \ldots \urcorner$, where the singular term y occurs *de re* (i.e. refers to a real object the belief is about). S implicitly refers to *types* of modes of presentation: 'there is a mode of presentation m, of *the contextually relevant type*, which determines y, and x believes that $\ldots m \ldots$'. With that interpretation of *de re* singular terms in that-clauses in mind, let us turn to modes of presentation and the aspects of functional role they correspond to.

5.1 BELIEFS ABOUT PERCEIVED PARTICULARS

The form 'Ft' appears in the L-constraints on quantification and identity; the question is what it is for a belief to have this form – to be about a particular. There are really two questions: how to represent such beliefs antecedently to a functional explication, and how then to explicate their content in terms of functional role. The clearest theory of beliefs about particulars has been the description theory, that beliefs are about particular things outside ourselves by containing definite descriptions true of those things. So my belief that Machu Picchu is in Peru is about those buildings by containing a description – say, 'the Andean city called 'Machu Picchu''; and my belief that that vase contains carnations is about the vase because my belief contains a description like 'the vase which is causing such and such sensations in me'. This theory, the *bête noire* of the "new theory of reference", must, to be interesting, allow (for reasons to be given) that some beliefs, about oneself or the present time or one's mental states, are about them by virtue of some non-descriptive relation to them.

My concern in this section is beliefs about perceived particulars. They include beliefs one forms about things while perceiving them, and a lot more. I look out of the window, spot a goat, and form the belief that the goat is capering. If I later discover that my chrysanthemums are no more, I may infer that the goat has eaten them. The latter belief is about the goat by virtue of my earlier perception, and not formed by perceiving the goat eat the chrysanthemums. So beliefs about perceived particulars are about them by virtue of perceptions that may or may not be causes of the rest of the belief's content. My reason for singling out these beliefs is that they are the least plausible candidates for the description theory of beliefs about things outside oneself, for reasons I turn to later. As regards other beliefs about particulars, say, containing proper names, I am more inclined towards the description theory.[1]

A standard alternative to the description theory of *sentences or utterances* of the form '*Ft*' is that they express singular propositions, propositions with built-in particulars. So 'that cat is fat' would express a proposition that has as one constituent the property fatness and as another the referent, say a certain cat. Transferred to *beliefs* about particulars, this theory would treat them as relations to such singular propositions, which may be represented as '$[F\alpha]$', or, in general, '$[F\alpha_1, \ldots, \alpha_n]$'. That is not just an intension, a function from possible worlds to truth-values; it has structure – think of it as a pair of a simple or complex entity F and the n-tuple $\langle \alpha_1, \ldots, \alpha_n \rangle$ of the particulars the belief is about.

Now singular propositions can't be the full content of such beliefs, for reasons well-known since Frege. These beliefs are about things under modes of presentation; what I believe is not specified without some indication of my perceptual contacts with those things. Suppose I see α, form the belief that α is F, and then see α again in other normal circumstances and, not identifying it as what I saw earlier, form the belief that α is not F. Although one belief is false, there is nothing irrational or out of the ordinary about my situation. But if singular propositions exhausted the content of my beliefs, and if a necessary condition of my having beliefs is that they usually satisfy elementary constraints on rationality (the L-constraints), then I could not normally have such pairs of beliefs. Since I can and do, singular propositions do not exhaust the content of beliefs about perceived particulars.

Notice that neither perceptual contact may yield a more intimate rapport with the object than the other; so there is no natural treatment of just one belief's content as a singular proposition. The point is not only about negation, but about all the L-constraints: if such beliefs were relations to singular propositions, then one could easily and often believe p and [if p then q] and not-q. Decision-making could also constantly be fundamentally irrational: one might often believe that doing A would bring about q and that doing A was within one's power, while wanting q, having no countervailing desires, and not deciding to do A.

Somehow perceptual circumstances must be represented in the belief's content. If content were always exhausted by possible-world

[1] For an illuminating defense of a more thoroughgoing description theory of beliefs about particulars see Schiffer, 1978.

truth conditions (or by the more fine-grained construction; cf. p. 58 n.), there would be only two ways to represent that extra element – as a definite description or individual concept of the perceived particular, and, more weakly, as a non-uniqueness property of it. The latter won't do: if we add to the singular proposition a non-uniqueness property the object is perceived as having – $\langle [F\alpha], \varphi \rangle$ – we do not escape the original difficulty. A person can perceive α to be φ on two occasions, and on one believe $\langle [\sim F\alpha], \varphi \rangle$ and on the other $\langle [F\alpha], \varphi \rangle$. There is no inconsistency, if the person does not reidentify α as the same φ.

Introducing definite descriptions would solve the formal problem; for it is irrational to believe that α, identified as the G, is F, while believing that α, identified as the G, is not F. But it does not follow from the inadequacy of the other accounts that the description theory is true; what follows is that either it is true or the content of beliefs about perceived particulars is not solely a matter of possible-world truth conditions or their compositional determinants.

I shall now sketch a non-description theory of beliefs about perceived particulars that satisfies the requirements imposed by the L-constraints. Then we may turn to the unique functional role of each such belief. The object is a theory which captures a natural way of individuating beliefs about perceived particulars so that they satisfy the L-constraints (whose sole possible inadequacy might be that the description theory gives a more exhaustively correct account of their content).

Let us call the elements of content referred to by $t_1, \ldots, t_n$, in belief-ascriptions of the form $B[Ft_1, \ldots, t_n]$ the belief's *subject indices*. Now, what we, the ascribers of a belief, refer to in indexing the belief's functional role is, on my account, extrinsic to the state, and so it is not necessary that an aspect of a belief's content be, so to speak, before the mind of the believer. The Fregean term 'mode of presentation' might suggest that, while 'subject index' does not. Apart from satisfying the L-constraints, what further requirements must the subject indices of beliefs about perceived particulars satisfy? They must presumably be items that we can be supposed normally to be referring to implicitly or existentially quantifying over when we ascribe such beliefs, and that can be associated (via input conditions as we shall see) with the functional roles that individuate those beliefs. (I say 'existentially quantifying over' to cover *de re* belief-ascriptions, as characterized on pp. 97–98. One can say that Jones believes something about Herbert, not indicating the subject index under which Jones believes it about

Herbert or when it is clear that Jones's belief is about Herbert *qua* perceived particular, with no further implication about how Jones has perceptually identified Herbert.)

What makes it possible, in the cases envisaged, to believe that α is F and also believe that α is not F, without thereby having internally inconsistent beliefs? A rough first answer is that α is differently perceptually identified. This suggests perhaps that the relevant element of content, or subject index, is a type of perceptual situation, where that includes α's perceptible properties and the believer's perceptual relations to α. But that won't do. However specific such a type P is, if P is a repeatable, a person can quite rationally believe α to be F, via a perception of type P, and also believe α to be not-F, via another perception of type P; for one might incorrectly, but not irrationally, fail to identify α on the first perception with α on the second. Perception-types are not the desired subject indices.

Evidently what emerges is that the subject index should include the perceptual event-*token* that is the source of the perceptual identification. A person may believe α to be F as seen on e_1 and believe α to be not F as seen on e_2; but he will not believe α to be F as seen on e_1 and α to be not-F as seen on e_1. Consider again my belief that the goat ate the chrysanthemums. I spotted the goat originally in perceptual event e, but it was not on e that my belief that the goat ate the chrysanthemums arose; subsequently I came to believe that about the goat as previously seen on e. It is *not* being said that my belief is 'the goat I perceived on e ate the chrysanthemums'; that is perhaps the description theory's version, but it is not what I am saying. We, the ascribers of the belief, extrinsically index a functional state, in part by referring to a perceptual event, which may have occurred earlier than the belief. The description version supposes the believer to refer to e, but on my theory it is we the ascribers who refer to e; if our ascription is correct the believer is referring to, his belief is about, the goat and not e.

What individuates a belief about a perceived particular, then, so that it satisfies the L-constraints, is (a) the particular the belief is about, (b) what is believed, and (c) a certain perceptual event-token. Henceforth I shall refer to this as the perceptual index theory. How is information (a)–(c) to be packaged as the *content* of a belief, as indexing its functional role and truth conditions? There are two natural candidates: z believes $[F, \langle\langle \alpha_1, e_1 \rangle, \ldots, \langle \alpha_n, e_n \rangle\rangle]$, and z believes $[F\alpha_1, \ldots, a_n / e_1, \ldots, e_n]$, where the latter represents the ordered pair of the singular proposition

$[F\alpha_1, \ldots, \alpha_n]$ and the n-tuple $\langle e_1, \ldots, e_n \rangle$ of perceptual indices. The two forms are intended to be interchangeable; the former is useful for representing the predicate-cum-singular-term format, $[Ft_n, \ldots, t_n]$, of the L-constraints, while the latter is more convenient in what follows.

The problem has been to represent the content of a belief about a perceived particular, without a definite description in such a way that it satisfies the L-constraints, e.g. 'B$p \Rightarrow$ not B $\sim p$'. What could make the belief that α is F and the belief that α is not F doxastically incompatible? The answer has been that they are about α by virtue of the same perception of α; that perceptual event-token is built into propositional content so that it satisfies the L-constraints. This is not to say that when we ascribe such beliefs we always refer directly to particular perceptual events, for we may be implicitly existentially quantifying over them.

So we have a way to represent the content of these beliefs antecedently to their functional explication; now the question is how to specify unique functional roles for them. The strategy is this: first to describe the functional role of a certain subclass of beliefs about perceived particulars – namely, the observational ones; and secondly to describe the functional roles of the rest of them in terms of a certain functional interaction with the observational ones.

The L-constraints do not on their own determine unique functional roles for beliefs; perceptual input conditions are also needed, that is, something that correlates aspects of the content of observational beliefs with aspects of the perceptual circumstances that normally give rise to them. That evidently is necessary in capturing the functional role of beliefs of the form $[F\alpha_1, \ldots, \alpha_n/e_1, \ldots, e_n]$. Earlier I pointed out that it is not required that every observational belief-*token* should arise because of perceptual circumstances of the relevant type; I may believe there is an apple in the bowl because I was told so and not because I observed it. The point is that the belief has that content because it is a state that *would* arise were I perceptually related to that fact in the right way.

Something like that is true of beliefs of the form $[F\alpha_1, \ldots, \alpha_n/e_1, \ldots, e_n]$. But what *functional conditions* on those beliefs do the perceptual event-tokens $e_1, \ldots, e_n$ correspond to? They are different from the input conditions corresponding to F, for the presence of perceptual event-tokens does not mean that such beliefs would occur if, somehow, those event-tokens reoccurred in conjunction with the right observational fact $Fx_1, \ldots, x_n$. Take the goat again. My belief under e that he ate my chrysanthemums (where the belief did not arise on e but later) is not to be characterized as a state that would occur if e were to recur and be relevantly involved in my seeing the goat eat the flowers; e is over and done with. It is in the index of that belief (type) rather, because that belief's (future) tokens would have it, that (past) event, among their causes.

So, as regards the predicative part of the belief, i.e. $Fx_1, \ldots, x_n$, the perceptual input conditions of 4.4 apply. A belief has the form $[F\alpha_1, \ldots, \alpha_n / e_1, \ldots, e_n]$ (for specific F and variable $\alpha_1, \ldots, \alpha_n, e_1, \ldots, e_n$) *only if* we have:

For all $\alpha_1, \ldots, \alpha_n$, if it were the case that $F\alpha_1, \ldots, \alpha_n$, and $O(z, [F\alpha_1, \ldots, \alpha_n])$ *etc.*, then, for some $e_1, \ldots, e_n$, it would be the case that z believes $[F\alpha_1, \ldots, \alpha_n / e_1, \ldots, e_n]$.

(The 'etc.' stands for the conditions of p-attentiveness and p-openness; cf. pp. 68–69.)

As regards the causal condition relevant to $e_1, \ldots, e_n$, it is notoriously difficult to find a commonsense causal condition that is non-circularly sufficient in such cases; but the handy methodology of 4.6 once again comes to the rescue. If a theoretical, non-commonsense, functional theory of z (which has the commonsense constraints as its core, and defines Bel, etc.) describes a causal relation, or class thereof, between perceptual events and belief-tokens, which intuitively are about their objects via those perceptual events, then those causal relations figure in the conservative explication of $\text{Bel}[F\alpha_1, \ldots, \alpha_n / e_1, \ldots, e_n], z, t]$. Naturally those relations will amount to z's *remembering* the objects $\alpha_1, \ldots, \alpha_n$.

The theory could seem to be a theory of *reference*, of the relation by virtue of which those beliefs are about $\alpha_1, \ldots, \alpha_n$. But what has been said about the functional role of the belief that $[F\alpha / e]$ leaves α quite idle, the functional role being determined simply by F and e. But on normal perceptions e, several particulars are perceived. So a refinement is needed. When I perceive α_1 and α_2 together, and form distinct beliefs about them, the perceptual input has suitably distinct aspects, each counting as an "event", a triple consisting of an n-tuple of particulars (e.g. α_i and my eye), a relation, and a time. Thus α_i is in part determined by building it into e_i, and e_i is individuated to accommodate pre-explicative individuation of such beliefs. But that is not sufficient to *uniquely* determine reference; thus it does not select the goat rather than the goat's visible surface as part of e. *As regards functional role*, this indeterminacy, I suggest, must stand. What picks out the goat rather than its surface, as the referent, lies in the theory of truth conditions (8.3) and reference (9.9); given the satisfaction conditions of 'F', the selection of the goat rather than its surface follows from the general maximizing of reliability for such beliefs.

What about non-observational beliefs about perceived particulars? What about their functional roles gives them subjects in common with observational beliefs? A certain L-constraint plays a crucial role here, namely, '$\mathrm{B}Ft$ and $\mathrm{B}Gt \Rightarrow$ Not $\mathrm{B} \sim \exists x Fx$ & Gx': if one believes t is F and believes t is G one does not believe that nothing is both F and G. Its importance lies in securing that beliefs whose indices share a subject index themselves share a subject; in particular, it implies that a non-observational belief $[Ga/e]$ interacts with the observational belief $[Fa/e]$ in a way that beliefs which do not share a subject with the latter belief do not.

Let us now turn to the description theory's account of beliefs about perceived particulars. Often my only individuating conceptions of perceived objects are of their being related uniquely to me, or to things I am directly aware of. (The question of beliefs about oneself is taken up in 5.3.) Moreover those conceptions often involve *psychological* and not spatiotemporal relations. Thus suppose I attend to a quite unprepossessing star, randomly chosen; there are no spatial relations, of which I have suitable information, that relate it and no other star to me. One description that involves a psychological relation might be this: 'the star I am attending to'. That does not yield a persuasive description theory: for what makes it true of an object that I am attending to it? A description account requires yet a further psychological relation, in a new description; while any other account prompts an unanswerable reply: if *attending* to an object doesn't have to be via some description of it, why does a *belief* about it have to be so?

The only suitable psychological relation, I think, is something like this: 'the object that is causing that aspect of my sensations (sense data, sensory field)'. How is *that aspect* to be captured? Not in purely qualitative terms, for wouldn't it sometimes be necessary to refer, say, to the *left* side of one's visual field? That can't be done purely qualitatively. Descriptive theorists thus, with Russell, have to allow aspects of sensations to be objects of beliefs *directly*, not under descriptions. But if beliefs can non-descriptively be about sense data, why not non-descriptively about physical objects? Metaphors of "directness" will not contribute much to the functional theory of content.

But there is another problem about description theory: it is implausible that we form beliefs about details of our sensations when there is an apparently exclusive devotion to external goings on. One wonders how we could be as successful as we are in registering the passing scene if our thoughts were as full as that description theory requires.

Perhaps a description theorist need not be dissuaded, for the model the objection implicitly suggests of beliefs about the sensory manifold may be the wrong one. We can of course abstract from the external correlates of our experiences and be psychophenomenological; but perhaps that is not what the description theorist needs. Another conception of our sensations is as *appearances*, whose psychological status is not being registered. If a child puts pressure on an eyeball and sees a blurred mess, he can be quite aware of how it looks, without conceptualizing it either in psychological terms, or as features of the external scene. That awareness of how it looks is perhaps a constant ingredient of perception and may be all the description theorist needs. But still the theory implies more structure in the content of beliefs than the perceptual index theory, without apparently any persuasive reasons for doing so; the perceptual index theory satisfies the Fregean requirement, and is less intellectualist.

Although inclined against the description theory for beliefs about perceived particulars, I find it more plausible for other beliefs; for example, those naturally expressed by using names, where metalinguistic descriptions seem generally available. Also, some beliefs are about particulars under complex *dossiers*, which may be mixed bags of perceptual indices and descriptions, and their functional roles can be viewed as amalgams of the functional roles associated with the dossier's components.

The point against the description theory of beliefs about perceived particulars has to do with psychological plausibility; it requires too much content. But the current anti-description-theory animus rests on less mundane grounds; commenting on them may serve to clarify what I take to be the real issue, by contrast.

First there are singular terms in modal statements. Many have been impressed by the fact that Aristotle could have turned out differently, could have lacked all his known biographical properties. This *is* an objection to a description theory that takes names in modal contexts to be equivalent to definite descriptions that have *narrower scope* than the modality. It is of course false that 'Aristotle might not have been a philosopher' is equivalent to 'Possibly: the philosopher who did such and such was no philosopher'. But what an absurd theory; evidently proper names normally occur with *wider* scope than the modalities in whose syntactic contexts they occur.[2] The description theorist should hold that proper names differ from overt descriptions in this respect: where often overt descriptions in modal contexts are scope-ambiguous, proper names are most naturally read (usually) as having widest scope; that is simply part of a sensible description theory.

The rigid designator theory of names is naturally associated with a particularist and "haecceitist" metaphysics: ordinary objects are ontologically basic, not constructions out of properties, and inhabit many possible worlds rather than merely having qualitative counterparts there. This metaphysical view I subscribe to, but it is quite compatible with the description theory. It has been a mistake, beginning with Russell and continuing through Kripke, to assimilate semantic and psychological questions, on which the description theory should turn, to metaphysical questions about whether objects are ontologically basic, or constructions out of properties, etc. Russell associated the description theory with the theory that objects are logical constructions, as I think did Strawson (1959) on the negative side, in his two-pronged semantic and metaphysical critique of Russell. In 'Naming and Necessity', Kripke associates his anti-description semantic theory with the metaphysical view that modal facts about objects are not about bundles of properties, that in assessing a modal statement containing a name, we carry the object and not its contingent real world properties through other possible worlds. But the two theories are quite distinct.

Secondly, metaphysics has perhaps come into the picture with regard to the nature of reference rather than referents. Some (not Kripke) may have been moved by the following line. "On the description theory, the relation between belief and object is via the *instantiation* by the object of a description. But that relation is platonic and non-natural, not one that belongs in a naturalistic account of mind–world relations. But if we make the relation causal we naturalize it." This is confused. (I have encountered mixed opinions on whether it is a straw man.) Some beliefs involve descriptions: does that mean that there is no naturalistic account

---

[2] I do not mean to beg questions about whether proper names have scope. On the rigid designator theory they have no scope, since that would imply that they must be evaluated at a certain stage in the evaluation of the truth conditions of the whole in which they occur; whereas on the rigid designator theory they can be evaluated at any stage in the overall evaluation. My point can be put in a way that everyone can agree to: they are existentially generalizable from outside, and so *if* they are held to be equivalent to expressions that do have scope they must be assigned widest scope.

of their relation to the objects that satisfy the descriptions? That is tantamount to denying that there is a naturalistic theory of a belief's being *true* of an object, for the instantiation of a description is just certain predicates' being true uniquely of the object. The upshot would be that, while we have a naturalistic theory of reference, we would have no such account of satisfaction, which makes the former rather uninteresting.

5.2 THE TENSES OF BELIEFS

A theory of content evidently must account for tenses. The literature on verificationism and on behaviorism, both pro and con, has quite rightly stressed the importance of the question what makes certain beliefs *past*-tensed. As with all questions about content on my theory, this involves both functional role and truth conditions, but here I shall discuss just functional role – of present and past tenses (the account of past-tensed beliefs yielding an account of future-tensed beliefs). If my general thesis about content and functional role is correct, the "belief–desire theory" must assign to the belief that p *was* the case a unique systematic role.

A present-tensed belief that p can be represented initially as [*Now* p], where p captures the rest of the propositional index including perceptual events – that is, a belief like [*Now* $F\alpha_1\alpha_2/e_1, e_2$] is subsumed under the form [*Now* p]. What entity this denotes can be discussed when we have the functional role. I shall take other tensed beliefs to employ quantification over times, a relation 'earlier-than', and the indexical 'now'. The belief that p was the case is the belief that some occurrence of p is earlier than now; the belief that p will be the case is the belief that now is earlier than some occurrence of p.

The present tense is the key to the past and future: let us then begin with its functional role. The natural starting place is present-tensed *observational* beliefs, and their input conditions, and a first approximation is this:

if p is true at t and $O(z, p, t)$ etc., then z believes [*Now* p] at t. But that is not adequate for assigning a unique interpersonally ascribable systematic role to present-tensed beliefs; it is true of them but also of others. Suppose I see Harold falling off his horse, and thereby believe that he is now falling. At the next moment I cease to believe that Harold is now falling: he has fallen. But surely I have also acquired another belief that I do not cease to believe once Harold has fallen. A rather dull example is that Harold is not among the unfallen. But there is a more interesting possibility. It seems that beliefs can be about particular times in much the same way as they are about perceived particulars, indexically and not under descriptions. This is especially interesting in connection with the present tense; for it would mean that a belief's being indexically about the present time does not *eo ipso* account for its being present-tensed. So let us consider this other indexical reference to times.

From beliefs that are indexically about perceived particulars it is a small step to beliefs that are indexically about perceived *events*. The same considerations against the description theory apply: the required psychological reflexiveness is equally implausible. Now, what is an event? I doubt there are pressing reasons to take events to be anything more basic than triples of particulars (including spatial positions), properties and times.[3] But reference to the particulars and property involved often will not individuate an event, and so, it seems, indexical reference to events presupposes indexical reference to times.

A belief's indexical reference to a time can be captured by the device suggested for indexing beliefs about perceived particulars – namely, a certain perceptual event. So the belief that the object α, as seen on e, was F at time t, as presented on perception e', is represented thus: $[F\alpha t/e, e']$. Naturally perceptual indices for objects and times will in some cases be identical.

To return to the input condition for the present tense, we can now see that another belief equally satisfies the one proposed, viz. the belief that $[p$ at $t/e]$, where e is the perceptual event involved. This is not the belief that $[Now\ p]$, despite its being about what happens to be the present time; for it is a belief that can *continue* even though I *cease* to believe that $Now\ p$. After Harold reaches the ground, I use the past tense – 'Harold was then falling'; but that is not a *new* belief; I acquired it while Harold was falling. This is not to say that there are two independent beliefs at t – that $[Now\ p]$ and that $[p$ at $t/e]$. Rather what is believed at t is something like $[p$ at t and $t = now/e]$.[4]

What is distinctive about genuinely present-tensed observational

---

[3] If one admits events as ontologically basic, that would probably be a reason for eliminating times as entities. Then the account of the functional role of tensed beliefs would be modified; that would be, I think, just an exercise. The point shortly to be made would then be: a belief's being present-tensed is not the same as its saying that such and such is simultaneous with e, where e is a present event.

[4] Another way to construct this index is to couple the particular and the perceptual index. That would convert this into $[p$ at $\langle t, e \rangle$ and $\langle t, e \rangle = now]$. If one has that belief at t one also believes, presumably, $[p$ at $\langle t, e \rangle]$, which is to say $[p$ at $t/e]$.

beliefs is that they are *unstable under observational change* in a way not true of beliefs that are merely about what happens to be the present time. I propose, then, the following input condition:

> If p were true at t and $O(z, p, t)$ etc. then z would believe at t that *Now p*, and if it then ceased to be the case at t' that p and it were also the case that $O(z, [not\ p], t')$ etc., then z would cease to believe that *Now p*.

The belief that $[p \text{ at } t/e]$ does not in general satisfy this condition.

What about non-observational present-tensed beliefs? Their functional role is described, as for non-observational beliefs about perceived particulars, using the L-constraint on two beliefs that have a subject or referent in common: '$B[Ft]$ and $B[Gt] \Rightarrow$ not $B[\sim \exists x Fx \ \& \ Gx]$'. If $B[Now\ p]$ is not observational, then, for any observational q, if z believes *Now p* and z believes *Now q*, then z doesn't believe that p and q are never true together. No aspect of propositional content other than the present tense is interpersonally ascribable as interacting with present-tensed observational beliefs thus.[5]

I turn to the question of what entity '$[Now\ p]$' stands for. If only the functional role of present-tensed beliefs were the issue, all we would need is the information contained in p together with something to mark the functional role of the present tense. Then building the present time t into the content of z's belief at t that *Now p* would be redundant. Now, p is (apart from perceptual indices) a propositional function with a time variable. So we could take present-tensed beliefs to be relations, not to full propositions (singular or general), but to propositional functions, if all that mattered were functional role; that the belief is present-tensed would then be marked by its object being such an entity. (I must emphasize that that would be so only by virtue of the relevant formulation of the conditions of the belief–desire theory, and therefore of the definition of 'Bel'.) There would not, on that way of marking the present tense, be *two* belief-relations, one for tensed beliefs and one for tenseless beliefs.[6] There would be one relation, defined by its role in the belief–desire theory; some of its *relata* would be propositional functions and some full propositions.

But the content of a belief is a matter not just of functional role but

---

[5] One qualification: if p is logically true, and simple, the belief that p satisfies the constraint regardless of its tense. There are various ways of eliminating this, but it is unimportant: what does it matter if every logically true belief has the present tense? Other tenses can be embedded.

[6] This is a mistake I made elsewhere (1976a) with regard to self-ascriptive beliefs. In suggesting that their object is a certain sort of one-place propositional function (see the following section) I took that to mean that there is a special self-ascriptive belief-relation.

also truth conditions. Naturally, z's belief at t that *Now–p* is true if and only if it is the case that p at t; and so we can build t into its index: $[p$ at $t]$, which is a singular proposition. (How truth conditions come into the picture is the topic of 7.3 and 7.4.)

Might $[p$ at $t]$ exhaust the content of present-tensed beliefs? Not if one accepts that beliefs can indexically be about times under perceptual indices without being present-tensed. Otherwise, that singular proposition would be adequate, for the only beliefs whose indices had the form $[p$ at $t]$ would be present-tensed beliefs, and thus '$[Now\ p]$' could variably denote such singular propositions. But, I take it, some beliefs are indexically about times via perceptual events; thus a belief's having the present time in its content is not sufficient for it to be present-tensed. So we should add a futher index that marks the present tense; why not the word 'now' itself? '$[Now\ p]$' can then variably denote $\langle[p$ at $t]$, 'now'$\rangle$, according to the time of the belief; when p contains perceptual events as indices of perceived particulars, '$[Now\ p]$' denotes something of the form $[F\alpha_1, \ldots, \alpha_n, t/e_1, \ldots, e_n,$ 'now'$]$.

Suppose Peter at t believes that *Now p*, and Harold at a distinct t' also believes that *Now p*. Do they have the same belief? In one important sense they do not, but in another they do – the truth conditions differ but the cognitive, or functional, states are the same. Something similar happens with self-ascriptive beliefs: if Peter and Harold each believe '*I am F*', in one sense they believe something different, but, in another, the same thing. This divergence of individuation for truth conditions and functional roles appears to be a feature uniquely of the sorts of beliefs that have (on some theories) been called "token-indexical". Both individuation conditions are captured in the complex index $[p$ at $t/$'now'$]$.

I should like to clarify the relation between my account and Reichenbach's token-reflexive theory of 'now'. Reichenbach's theory was about the meaning of utterances and not beliefs: '*Now p*' means 'p is true at the time of this (utterance-)token'. To make it about beliefs: z's belief at t that *Now p* is (the same as) z's belief at t that p is true at the time of this very belief-token. Now this is a description theory, one which of course relies on a further non-descriptive indexical, namely, 'this token'. Some anti-description theorists might dismiss Reichenbach's theory on the basis of '*now*' in modal contexts. Consider for example: 'if this very utterance had not occurred my mouth would now be closed'. It could seem that this couldn't be true on Reichenbach's theory, since it would mean: 'if this very utterance had not existed then my mouth would be closed at the time of this very utterance', which would at best lack a truth-value. But this is a weak argument: the token-reflexive theory should be understood as taking 'now', 'I', etc., as having widest scope. On that interpretation modal arguments against Reichenbach collapse.

But there is a reason for resisting the token-reflexive theory, more or less the same as the one against description theories of beliefs about perceived particulars: it requires tensed beliefs to be psychologically reflexive. Why suppose that z's belief that it is now raining is about z's own psychological state? There is no apparent reason why a belief can indexically be about itself and not directly indexically about the present time.

This is not to say one can't have an indexical belief about a psychological state, say a twinge. Its functional role is on the model of the perceptual index theory, with the odd twist that the very item that is the referent may also serve as the perceptual index.

The belief that p *was* the case I take to be the belief that p happens earlier than now. So what makes a belief about the past involves the functional role of the concept 'earlier than'. (Speaking of functional role for concepts rather than beliefs is a bit loose, but systematic differences in the latter are reflected in differences in the sub-propositional constituents of beliefs.)

The idea is to treat 'earlier than' as in part observational and in part "theoretical", subject to certain M-constraints in the sense of 4.7. It is I think obvious that the temporal element in beliefs is not generated by theoretical constraints alone; if we do not observe temporal relations, there is no way to have the concept of them. What about taking 'earlier than' as observational? The idea would be that if certain changes occur within a certain time, in the perceptual range of a standard observer, that observer acquires a belief that such a change has occurred. Using the indexicals to times recently introduced, we might have this input condition:

if p occurs at t_1, q occurs at t_2, t_1 is earlier than t_2 (modulo n), and z is observationally related to p via e_1 and to q via e_2, etc.,

z believes that $[p$ at t_1 and q at t_2 and t_1 is earlier than $t_2/e_1, e_2]$.

Actually we would still have to require that 'earlier than' is transitive, asymmetric and irreflexive, and so M-constraints to that effect are also in order.

The question is whether that input condition, and those formal constraints are sufficient to capture a suitable systematic role for 'earlier-than'. But there seems an intuitive difference between the abstract, theoretical concept we have of historical, geological and cosmological events ordered temporally, and what we observe in one event following another; different developmental stages of conceptual competence are involved. Perhaps once the more abstract concept has been acquired it supersedes the more primitive concept by becoming observational within the parameters of the input condition. But that implies that the first-order states that have the functional role of observational temporal beliefs are those that correspond to believing the last ice age to have occurred earlier than the Punic Wars. These are vague matters, and I hope we can avoid having to settle them, simply by treating fully general temporal ordering as "theoretical", while related in a natural way to a special observational temporal concept.

I assume there is a temporal concept appropriate for that perceptual input condition – 'observably earlier than'. It must be constrained to be asymmetric and irreflexive, but not transitive. So, how is the general 'earlier than' theoretically related to 'observably earlier than'? Temporal succession can be beyond observation both by being too drawn out and by being too brief. One approach then is to divide 'earlier than' into two theoretical relations: 'sub-observably earlier than' and 'super-observably earlier than'. The latter is the *ancestral* of 'observably earlier than' (if we take the former's extension to include the latter's). That is, if t_i is super-observably earlier than t_k, there is a chain of times from t_i to t_k, of each adjacent pair of which the first is observably earlier than the second. The relevant M-constraint can simply be that if one believes the antecedent one believes the consequent.

As regards 'sub-observably earlier than', how it is connected to 'observably earlier than' I shall not speculate about here, but 'super-observably earlier than' and the present tense together seem to account for the past and future tenses as they normally occur.

I should like to mention a second way in which the functional role of the past tense might be generated. The idea is this: if one believes that p obtains now, and then *retains* that belief, one believes that p obtained, that it *was* the case that p. The past tense is what memory introduces into our beliefs.

This constraint can be captured with the available apparatus, thus: if z believes $[p$ at t and $t = now/e]$, and time passes, and z continues to believe $[p$ at $t/e]$, then p believes $[p$ at t and t is past$/e]$. The concept 'earlier than' can then be introduced as follows: first, introduce the constraint that z believes that *Past p* if and only if z believes that p's date is earlier than now; secondly, impose the relevant formal properties on 'earlier than'; and thirdly require that everyone believe that there are or can be times than which now is earlier. The general concept of temporal order again may seem more abstract and "theoretical" than the concept of the past that arises from memory, and so the ancestral of the relation introduced by memory could be invoked.

The foregoing two methods are intended to capture the *systematic roles* of tensed beliefs. What determines their *truth conditions*, which is the question of philosophical importance, is a further matter.

5.3 BELIEFS ABOUT ONESELF

Even if the description theory of beliefs about perceived particulars were correct, not all beliefs about particulars could be by virtue of descriptions. There must be non-general aspects of content. Suppose, for example, that descriptions of perceived particulars had the form 'the object related perceptually thus and so to *me*'. Could the self-reference be accounted for by a description? Certainly not by a purely qualitative description, that involves no further non-descriptive reference to other particulars. That is, for no person z is there a purely qualitative predicate F, however complex, such that 'z believes z-self to be G' is equivalent to 'z believes that the F is G'. The latter is not necessary – a person can be amnesiac, in quite undistinguished surroundings, etc.; sensory deprivation examples make the point dramatically. But the lack of a qualitative self-description allows beliefs about oneself, for example, that one's right arm is extended. Moreover, no purely qualitative belief 'the F is G' is logically *sufficient* for believing oneself to be G; with such a belief it is always a further question whether one believes *oneself* to be G, because it is always a non-trivial question, for qualitative F, whether one is the F.

There are impure descriptions that could be adequate. So, if one has indexical beliefs about sensations, one's beliefs could be about oneself as the person to whom that sensation, that thought, that twinge belong, as on Russell's position (in his logical atomist and neutral monist periods). The considerations that counted against the description theory of beliefs about perceived particulars also count against this impure-description theory of beliefs about oneself. If I am cataloguing external facts about myself, need I be constantly, subconsciously even, checking my fleeting sensations so as to be able to refer to myself as their owner? The picture is more than a little absurd. There appears to be ample reason for taking beliefs about oneself generally not to be under any description, pure or impure.

Let us begin with a pre-analytic representation of self-ascriptive beliefs, before we raise the question of their functional role. Given the perceptual index theory of beliefs about perceived particulars, it is possible for me to have a belief about a particular that happens to be me, without recognizing myself, while the belief is not of me under a description. On that theory, I am then a constituent of a singular proposition that belongs to the content of my belief, and so that is not enough to make that belief self-ascriptive in the desired sense.[7] It may be tempting to suppose that sense to be unanalyzable, something we have an irreducible concept of; but that is not my view, for to specify, as I shall, a unique systematic role for self-ascriptive beliefs is in effect to explicate self-ascription. The full content of a self-ascriptive belief is given by saying: (a) that it is self-ascriptive, (b) who the believer is, and (c) what is believed about the believer. If we put aside aspects of content other than purely propositional content, like perceptual indices and the present-tense subject index 'now', (c) is a one-place propositional function. Then 'z believes z-self to be such and such' could be taken to express a certain relation B^* between z and a one-place propositional function. So if Harold believes himself to be hungry, what is true is 'B^*(Harold, [x is hungry])'.[8] The identity of the believer does not have to be built into the second term of the relation B^*, since it is identical with its first term.

This notation is not a theory; we can also *represent* other beliefs as relations to one-place propositional functions. So Harold's belief that the most prolific living poet lives in Baltimore can be *represented* as B^{**}(Harold, [x lives in Baltimore]), where the definite description is built into the relation B^{**}: '$B^{**}(z, F)$' = def 'z believes the most prolific living poet is F'. Evidently we need an account of what aspect of functional role makes beliefs self-ascriptive; and that, I venture to say, must have something to do with how they *arise*; an input condition must be specified.

I am identical with a certain organism, a four dimensional segment of the longer enduring particular that is my body. My self-ascriptive

---

[7] *Pace* Schiffer (1978).

[8] This is how I suggested representing self-ascriptive belief in 1976a. It has also been proposed by David Lewis (1979).

114

beliefs are about that organism, from a special point of view that is exceedingly familiar, from behind its eyes. When normal people in normal circumstances stand in certain perceptual relations to certain properties of a body, they identify that body as their own, and self-ascribe those properties. Now those perceptual relations are the basis of self-ascription, and of one's conception of oneself as a unified subject of predication. Beliefs about oneself go beyond those perceptual beliefs, but, I suggest, it is functional connections between non-observational self-ascriptive beliefs and observational ones that make the former self-ascriptive.

Certain sorts of visual contact and touching are prominent among self-perceptive relations; but external senses need not be involved – if one is prone, kneeling or standing with arms akimbo, one knows it. A possibly helpful way of reminding oneself of these relations is to consider, by contrast, those other perceptual relations to one's body that produce beliefs that are *not* self-ascriptive, where one does not automatically recognize oneself. Some relations between one's body and other things equally deserve to be included among the facts we register self-ascriptively.

So the unique systematic role of $B^\star$, of self-ascriptive belief, is founded in input conditions of this form: 'if z is self-perceptively related to the fact that Fz, etc., then $B^\star(z, F)$'. I am supposing that these self-perceptive relations can independently be specified. But there is another possibility; namely, that they are functionally defined, as with 'p-openness', etc.; one must keep in mind, in this connection, the account of 4.6.

There is an interesting contrast between self-ascriptive beliefs and beliefs about particulars under perceptual indices. It was pointed out that taking perception *types* as indices does not work, since one may believe α to be F and also to be not F under the same type of perceptual relation, given a false judgement of non-identity. But with self-perceptive relations it seems that cannot happen: if α believes under any self-perceptive relation type that α is F, α does not believe of α under that or any other self-perceptive relation that α is not F. Identifying something as oneself is secured by mere appearances.

Non-observational beliefs about oneself are self-ascriptive, I suggest, through sharing a subject with the observational ones, as secured by the now familiar L-constraint: 'BFt and $BGt \Rightarrow$ Not $B \sim \exists x Fx \, \& \, Gx$', or since we are using $B^\star$, of an extension of that constraint, namely, $B^\star(\alpha, F)$ and $B^\star(\alpha, G) \Rightarrow$ Not $B(\alpha, \sim \exists x Fx \, \& \, Gx)$. Beliefs about one's mental states, about one's past, etc., are beliefs about oneself by virtue of this functional relation to observational self-ascriptive beliefs. (Once again, this remark must be understood in the light of 4.6.)

There are familiar questions about the self that this account does not answer. It does not say what a person is, which may appear odd, since it purports to account for the *content* of self-ascriptive beliefs; surely, it seems, that must involve the concept of a person. But it is not clear that a self-ascriber must believe himself to be any certain sort of thing. (It is not even clear that a self-ascriber must attribute *thoughts* to himself, which would mean a rather limited sort of self-ascription; but it would provide a basis on which to explicate the more familiar sort.) Two self-ascribers need not *agree* on the rational grounds for self-ascription. Suppose two cobblers each have memories of former princely existences, where the rest of the story goes as usual, with interesting causal connections established between the earlier princes and the later cobblers, etc. Now suppose that both are apprised of the facts, exactly analogous in the two cases, and that one self-ascribes the quasi-remembered princely facts and the other does not. (It is hard to say who pulls off the more difficult feat.) They then don't agree on what a *person* is, but each has self-ascriptive beliefs.

There is also the matter of truth conditions for 'x is the same person as y'. That must be part of a general account of the *truth conditions* of self-ascriptive beliefs about the past; but it is not something we need in describing a systematic role for self-ascription. Indeed, the concept of self-ascription could be used in the analysis of 'x is a person' without circularity.

For reasons much like the ones about present-tensed beliefs, the believer ought to be built into the content of self-ascriptions. It is not that the use of $B^{\star}$ would leave us without an exact way of giving their truth conditions, but simply that, if content in general encapsulates truth conditions as well as functional role, we may as well standardize here. Suppose, again, that singular propositions were not involved in the content of any other beliefs. Then '$B(\alpha, [F\alpha])$' would be a perfect way to represent self-ascription. Not better than $B^{\star}$, of course; in no sense would there be only one relation involved on the former and two on the latter. It simply would not matter whether we indexed the functional role as '$B(\alpha, F)$' or as '$B(\alpha, [F\alpha])$'; on one the single belief-relation would have in its extension some pairs of persons and one-place propositional functions, and on the latter some pairs of persons and singular propositions. But if singular propositions are part

116

of the content of some non-self-ascriptive beliefs (on the perceptual index theory) we do need something more in the content of self-ascriptive beliefs, an arbitrary marker like the word 'I'. Harold's belief at t that he is now driving this car as perceived under e is then captured by

Bel[Harold, t, [Harold drives this car at t/'I', e, now]].

Its systematic role has been described.

As I earlier remarked, tensed beliefs can intuitively be individuated according to either functional role or truth conditions. They give different results. So if Harold and Herbert each believes he is getting bald, in a sense they believe the same thing; and if Herbert also believes about Harold that he is getting bald, then in another sense they believe the same thing. Now the interesting thing is that Harold and Herbert cannot both have one belief with the same content in *both* senses; only Harold can have a belief that is both self-ascriptive and about Harold. Given how the functional role is established, that is quite unproblematic. If there were some *single "proposition"* the belief in which counted as Harold's self-ascriptive belief that he is getting bald, then there would be a mystery – something Harold could never communicate. But there is no such proposition. There are two ways of individuating Harold's belief, hence two ways to give its "content", and each of these may separately apply to pairs of beliefs of Harold's and Herbert's. But they must be distinct pairs; no pair of beliefs of Harold's and Herbert's can be counted as the same in both dimensions. Self-ascription is as little a puzzle as self-shaving.

6

Objectively determinate beliefs and our knowledge of them

6.1 FUNCTIONAL ROLE AND THE DETERMINACY OF CONTENT

Quine's celebrated thesis of the indeterminacy of translation (1960, chapter 2) has a natural extension to the ascription of beliefs. If the translation of Pierre's utterances into mine is always underdetermined by the facts, inevitably any attribution of beliefs to Pierre is also underdetermined. The foregoing account of belief content in terms of functional role prompts the question whether it is in conflict with the indeterminacy thesis, and also what light it may throw from its independent perspective.

There are two levels to our discussion of indeterminacy. There is the question whether belief-ascriptions are underdetermined by the totality of physical fact and theory. Now on my explication of belief-ascriptions, the answer will be straightforwardly no. But there is a further possible indeterminacy – an arbitrariness in the assignment of propositions to functional roles, one that ought to be disconcerting to a believer in objective intentionality. But I shall argue in chapter 8 that when we consider natural constraints on assigning truth conditions that arbitrariness is largely eliminated. The upshot will be that there really is very little indeterminacy.

There is a certain facile argument for indeterminacy which gets a quick reply. For any stretch of x's behavior, there are always several incompatible ascriptions of beliefs and desires which would equally well explain that behavior. Therefore, the argument goes, it is arbitrary which of those belief and desire combinations we ascribe; hence indeterminacy. The gap in the argument is clear enough: it assumes the only constraints on ascribing attitudes are those germane to rationalizing behavior. But first, attitude-ascriptions make claims about functional organization that go beyond the mere systematizing of behavior; non-behavioral evidence for how x is internally functionally organized can be further evidence for some ascriptions over others.

Secondly, the argument ignores perceptual input connections, which also are to be counted in the evidence. Indeterminacy does not follow merely from the existence of incompatible rationalizations of behavior.[1]

Are attitude-ascriptions underdetermined by physical fact and theory? Consider the truth conditions my account gives to 'x believes that p at t' – viz. 'x is in (one of the states in) $Bel[p, x, t]$'. A necessary condition is that x's states are functionally organized in the way discussed in 4.6. Now whether x has such a functional organization is fully determined by physical fact and theory, assuming the latter implies all relevant counterfactuals about first order states. It is also necessary that x be in a first order state with a certain functional role, the one which the relevant psychological theory (cf. 4.6) uniquely associates with the belief that p. But if it is physically determinate whether x realizes such a functional system, it is physically determinate whether x is in a given state of that system.

Propositions are assigned to underlying states as indices of functional roles. *Even if that assignment is arbitrary*, it is still physically determinate whether x is in a state with the functional role with which p is associated by the definition of Bel.[2] Hence the truth or falsity of 'x is in $Bel[p, x, t]$' is determined by the totality of physical fact and theory.

But, surely that other assignments of propositions would be equally adequate in indexing those functional roles somehow affects determinacy. Suppose we change the perceptual input condition systematically as follows. So far it has this form:

If it were true that p and $O(z, p, t)$ etc., then it would be the case that z believes that p at t.

The proposition p indexes the functional state whose input condition it figures in. That is eminently natural, but if what matters is simply to index that functional role, other propositions are equally appropriate. So if f is a one–one function, other than identity, from observational propositions to observational propositions, a new input condition could be:

If it were true that p and $O(z, p, t)$ etc., then it would be the case that z "believes" that $f(p)$ at t.

Of course, when this is coupled with L-constraints, M-constraints, and the belief–desire–willing condition, all other functional roles get new indices as well. What we call the belief that there, in front of one, is

---

[1] Of course I am not suggesting that Quine has ever said it does.

[2] Compare temperature again: the arbitrariness of choosing the Fahrenheit indexing system is compatible with the physical determinacy of 'x's temperature $= n°$ Fahrenheit.'

a rosebush, might become the "belief" that there in front of one is a giant squid, and so on.

What is the significance of this? It is not incompatible with what I claimed about the determinacy of belief-ascriptions. For consider the class of all such theories, those that resemble the commonsense theory except for the transformed input law. They are *logically equivalent functional theories* – necessarily z satisfies all if z satisfies one. But do not attitude-ascriptions on one theory make claims that are incompatible with the ascriptions of the others? If, according to our normal theory, Jones believes that a certain thing is a rosebush, on another theory it might be correct to say that Jones believes that the thing is a giant squid. But the latter ascription is not inevitable, even though Jones is in the state that, on the second theory, is indexed by [that is a giant squid]; for we do not have to say that Jones *believes* that proposition. 'Believes', we can say, incorporates the *normal* assignment of propositions to functional states. Where f is the relevant function, we can call the new "cognitive" concept f-belief: Jones f-believes that that is a giant squid iff Jones believes it is a rosebush. So, it is definitive of Bel that normally if p is true at t and $O(x, p, t)$ etc., then x is in $\text{Bel}[p, x, t]$; and this secures that 'x believes that p' is physically determinate. The appearance of there being incompatible belief-ascriptions, which are equally supported, is explained away; the f-belief that q can be identical with the belief that p.

Quine has argued (1970a) that the logical fact of underdetermination of theories by observational data leads directly to the indeterminacy of any translation of non-observational sentences, as follows. Suppose theories T_1 and T_2, as expressed in our language, are incompatible, but each compatible with all the observation sentences $O_1, \ldots, O_n$ Pierre holds true, or rather with their translations into our language. Suppose Pierre assents to T_3, in his language. In translating T_3 all we have to go on is Pierre's behavior, whatever implies that he holds true $O_1, \ldots, O_n$. Translating T_3 as T_1 or T_2 is not decided by that behavioral evidence; since that is all we have, there is no fact of the matter as to which translation is correct. And, if that is right about translation, then, for incompatible non-observational beliefs p and q, equally supported by Pierre's observational beliefs, there would be no fact of the matter as to whether Pierre believes p or believes q.

I hope it is clear why that argument fails on the functional theory. If p and q are distinct, the relevant psychological theory of Peter assigns to beliefs in them distinct functional roles, and it is then physically determinate which belief Pierre has. Naturally the evidence for Pierre's over-all functional organization and for his actual functional states is going to be more varied and complicated than what he holds true – e.g. the syntactic structure of his theoretical pronouncements is relevant.

Now the determinacy that emerges on my theory is evidently incompatible with Quine's intended thesis, which implies that there are no objectively determinate differences conveyed by 'Pierre believes that p' and 'Pierre believes that q', whenever p and q are equally well supported by Pierre's observational beliefs. And the difference between my position and Quine's is just the difference between realism–functionalism about beliefs and behaviorism. On the latter there is no way of distinguishing evidentially equivalent beliefs; on the former, functional role is available. (*To this extent*, suggestions that Quine's behaviorism is essential to his thesis of indeterminacy are on the right track.)

But there is another, ultimately perhaps more important, question about determinacy that functionalism about beliefs does not resolve, regarding the assignment of propositions, or, as we might as well say, truth conditions, to functional roles. Truth conditions come into the essential specification of beliefs' functional roles in a limited way. In the perceptual input condition, it is the *truth* of the proposition p that is, given certain conditions, sufficient for the belief that p. In the willing–acting condition, z's being related by 'wills that' to the propositional function $[x$ does $A]$ is, given the ability condition, sufficient for that propositional function's being *true of z*. But with regard to internal functional connections truth conditions have no essential role, for the relevant structural relations among propositions, and the corresponding internal functional interconnections among beliefs, desires and willings, can be mirrored by structured relations among other indices (say, uninterpreted sentences) which are not thereby described as having truth conditions. Propositions are under-utilized in their indexing of functional states.

Their assignment is then arbitrary; lateral connections among beliefs, desires, observational input and behavioral output do not determine those vertical connections with the rest of the world that constitute truth conditions. And Quine's point has also been that assigning truth conditions to sentences (interlinguistically) or beliefs is not objectively determinate. Merely rejecting behaviorism is not sufficient to counter that.

Let me indicate here what I propose later in support of the determinacy of truth conditions (8.3) and of reference (9.9). Certain functional states, some beliefs, are *reliable indicators* of how things independently are – reliable, that is, relative to our normal assignment of truth conditions. The commonsense constraints that partially define beliefs' functional roles impose restrictions on the truth conditions that allow our beliefs to be reliable. For example, any such assignment of truth conditions should make our logical inferential procedures truth-preserving. These, and related constraints on input conditions and M-constraints, may make our usual assignment unique, up to logical equivalence. In 9.9, I suggest that causal relations which explain reliability play a certain key role in the determinacy of reference.

Quine has supposed that the only physical factors relevant to the determinacy of content are behavioral reactions to perceptual stimuli. But functional facts that go beyond behavior and perception are also relevant; and we have just seen another distinct set of relevant physical factors – correlations between functional states and external states of affairs that transcend immediate observational facts, as well as certain causal relations between functional states and constituents of those states of affairs. On neither the psychological level nor the level of truth conditions do reactions to stimuli exhaust what is relevant to determinacy.

6.2 ARE INDICES ELIMINABLE?

The picture of the role of propositions has so far been this. First, their logical relations *mirror* counterfactual relations among first-order state-types, and the truth conditions of observational and basic action propositions are correlated with causal relations between perceptual circumstances and certain states (observational beliefs) and other states (willings) and certain actions. This mirroring of counterfactual relations enables each proposition (conjoined with some marker of belief or desire) to encode a second-order functional state. Secondly, propositions encapsulate a correlation between functional states and possible states of the world (their truth conditions), this correlation being of interest in part because of the reliability of beliefs as indicators of those states. The interaction between the role of the concept of truth, and the counterfactual relations that constitute the functional theory, determines, among the many possible assignments of propositions to functional states, a certain special one.

Propositions are employed in the functional theory as devices of indirect reference: we refer indirectly to a state as the one whose functional role matches, on a certain projection, such and such logical features of a certain proposition. Compared with the simple black box functional theory of chapter 3, where the terms to be explicated functionally are interpreted directly by quantifiers and variables over the first-order states whose functional roles are being defined, the belief–desire theory must seem odd. On the simpler theory there is no such roundabout indirect reference; why should it be necessary here?

If human beings are functionally organized as required by the belief–desire theory, that is a brute fact from the philosophical point of view, capable of explanation only by a more ambitious psychological, and ultimately neurophysiological, theory. A different sort of understanding of this functional organization might result from an account of its past role in promoting survival.

That this functional system is in that way a brute fact raises the question how we managed to fashion a commonsense theory of it. It could seem I am presupposing that we ingeniously happened to notice that certain exotic entities structurally correspond to certain functional states of which we have an independent grasp. If that were the best we could do, the functional theory would then be too artificial to account for our familiar ascriptions of beliefs and desires; but there is a more likely history.

The semantic properties of the sentences of public language have a derivative status in the theory of propositional attitudes, as I argue in chapter 9. But that is not to say the belief–desire theory could have developed independently of theorizing about language; the natural idea is of an association of functional roles with spoken sentence-types. We may imagine it was noticed that, for a large class of utterances, one could postulate corresponding underlying states whose counterfactual properties differ systematically according to differences in certain *syntactic* structural properties of the utterances. That class of utterances contains those which, in the light of subsequent theory, are taken as sincere, serious, literal and complete. We may imagine our theorist to have noticed that certain syntactic features (the indicative, imperative, or optative moods or the occurrence of 'I want') are associated with general types of functional role, that we call belief, desire and intention. Those underlying states, whose only known properties are their counterfactual roles, are then quite naturally referred to indirectly, by reference to those utterance-types whose structural features systematically correspond to their counterfactual properties. In the original situation, the inventors of the theory were no doubt interested primarily in speakers of their own language, and so the sentences used to index those states could themselves have been uttered by the subjects of the theory to express the states our theorists have used them to index.

It would then have been natural to think of these states as dispositions to assert the sentences that index them, or as realizations of such dispositions – 'the state that is the cause of utterances of that type'. (Cf. Stich, 1978.) Natural, but not inevitable. For on that account the important association of utterance-types with underlying states is not a one-by-one causal relation, but a more systematic correlation of syntactic and counterfactual relations. What we imagine to have been originally noticed, for example, is that when a person is in a situation in which he might utter a sentence of the form 's_1 & s_2', then he might also have uttered s_1; that, when someone would be prepared to utter s_1, and 'if s_1 and I do A then s_2', and 'I want A', then he might do A, an action correlated with 'A' on a certain salient pairing. And so on. Now, part of the initial picture would also be that the underlying state indexed by s is among the normal causes of utterances of s. But that causal relation may itself be then *reconstructed within the theory*; we come to say that x uttered s because x had certain communicative purposes and beliefs, where these are referred to via the more abstract indexing system. This detaches *causal* relations of beliefs to utterances from the defining properties of belief; and the utterance-type acquires the purely abstract indexing function that I have described for propositions.

In consequence of this abstraction, we can suppose that our theorists realized it is irrelevant to the appropriateness of using a sentence to index a certain functional state that it belongs to the subject's language, irrelevant even that he has a language, provided he has a functional organization within the appropriate range. (Of course this is not to deny that linguistic behavior is a crucial part of our evidence for ascribing beliefs and desires, which is discussed in the next two sections.) To introduce propositions would be a further step, and, as I think will now be clear, not one that has any evident point. I shall indicate how to eliminate propositions in favor of sentential indices in section 7.2; invoking them has so far perhaps been useful in keeping questions about language at bay until the theory was somewhat fully presented. But one might see philosophers' invoking propositions as a confused and unnecessary way of marking the non-linguistic nature of both the essential functional roles of beliefs and desires and their truth conditions.

While propositions will be eliminated in favor of less exotic indices, it remains to be considered whether indices as such can be eliminated from the functional system determined by the belief–desire theory. Now there is a way in which the functional role of each belief and desire could be captured more directly – if we were to treat each complex name of the form 'x's belief that p', etc. as replaceable by a variable and then eliminable via the Ramsey–Lewis method. This is not totally preposterous if, as suggested in 4.10, the functional theory of a particular person is to be relativized to a *finite* propositional field, for we may then imagine the following construction. (1) An effective enumeration of the finitely many nominalizations of the form 'the belief that p', 'the desire that q' that arise from a given propositional field. (2) Nominalization of the conditions of the belief–desire theory – e.g. converting '(p) (q) if z believes that p & q then z believes that p' to '(p) (q) if z has the belief that p & q then z has the belief that p'. (3) Instantiation of every such nominalized condition with every nominalization mentioned in (1). (4) For every condition, the (very large) conjunction of its instantiations. (5) The substitution, for every nominalization in each conjunction, of a variable which is subscripted with the number assigned to the nominalization in the enumeration mentioned in (1). (6) The prefixing of quantifiers in the Lewis style of theory interpretation.

The result is a functional theory, or part of one (cf. 4.6), logically equivalent to the functional theory that uses Bel, Des and Int, except for the old theory's quantifying over propositions, not present in the new theory. The equivalence lies in this: necessarily z instantiates the one theory iff z instantiates the other – the functional systems required are identical. This unwieldy theory is a simple black box theory, one that quantifies directly over the relevant first-order states; there is no indirect reference to them via reference to indices.

But, in that unwieldy theory, the general principles whereby we mastered and maintained competence in applying the old theory are quite lost. All *functional analogies* among beliefs, which are essential to our employing the theory, disappear – for example, the functional similarities between the belief that p & q and the belief that s & r.

There is an interesting alternative to the unwieldy theory, and to the ordinary theory interpreted in terms of indices, which is close, but not exactly equivalent to them. Suppose we interpret a conjunctive belief of the form 'x believes that Ft & q' as saying this: x is in a first-order state whose *first-order structure* is as follows. It consists of a first-order structured constituent corresponding to 'Ft' (in a way to be described) conjoined by a relation that corresponds to '&' (to be described) to a constituent that corresponds to 'q'. The constituent corresponding to 'Ft' consists of a constituent corresponding to 'F', conjoined by a relation corresponding to syntactic predication to a constituent corresponding to 't'. The relevant constituents of the first-order states are whatever relations, properties, etc., occur in all first-order states that realize beliefs marked by 'F', 't', '&', etc. So those symbols, as they occur in that-clauses, are defined functionally; similarly for all other expressions and syntactic relations within that-clauses.[3]

How does this differ from my account? Consider the relation between the beliefs 'Ft_1 & q' and 'Gt_2 & p': on my account there is a resemblance in their functional roles, their second-order relations to other beliefs; it is not required that any states which realize those functional roles be similar, in any special way, *in first-order structure*. But on the theory just described they must be; both states must have as constituents a relation corresponding to '&', another corresponding to predication in 'Ft', etc. In other words beliefs would have to be language-like; their structural interrelations would constitute a *syntax*, isomorphic roughly to English, and the belief–desire theory would then imply the "language of thought" hypothesis (cf. 9.1). On my theory the required relations between beliefs are entirely second-order, purely functional. Consider what the units of functional analysis are. On my account, each that-clause marks a distinct functional role, but on the stronger account, each constituent of a that-clause marks one. The latter theory is equivalent to the conjunction of the belief–desire theory on my interpretation, and the further requirement of isomorphism in constituent structure between first-order states and indices.

Which is to be preferred? If the weaker theory generates conservative explications of propositional attitudes, it is the more fundamental. The basic concern is *vindicating* our rational psychology, and the realization of the weaker theory would be strong enough for that.

Can *indices* be eliminated? The answer is yes, *if* we substitute the stronger theory, which then turns out to imply an isomorphism of belief-realizations and that-clauses. But if we want to capture the weaker requirements of functional organization *in the usual structured way*, a theory with indices is unavoidable. The consequences for the analysis of intentionality are interesting. The unwieldy theory, with

---

[3] This is suggested by a theory of Hartry Field's (1978). It differs in several respects. One is this: on this version the functional roles are interpersonally ascribable, while on Field's theory they are not.

indices eliminated, seems to have no claim to expresss intentionality apart from its relation to the theory with indices. But the two theories are logically equivalent (relative to the latter's ontology), and so whether a theory is about "intentional states" then seems a matter not simply of its empirical content but also of how it is expressed; that is, by using indices, of functional roles, with a certain structure. Less paradoxically, we may treat the intentionality of a functional system as its non-trivial *expressibility* by a suitable theory with a language-like indexing system.

How language-like that structure needs to be is an open question. If fine-grained structures are not motivated in the theory of dogs' goal-directed behavior, indices in a canine "belief–desire" theory might be suitably less structured. The possibilities for adjustment here are great, and at what level of fine-grainedness intentionality appears is a somewhat artificial question.

So, in summary, intentionality is a matter of certain functional structures, and physical states can objectively be intentional by being non-trivially describable by a functional theory with suitable indices. This imputes no more arbitrariness to intentional description than the analysis of temperature statements as asserting extrinsic relations to numbers implies arbitrariness for them. Indeed, as I shall be arguing in 8.3, there is far less arbitrariness in the former than in the latter, for, because of the interaction of truth conditions and functional role, there is a set of propositional indices that, given certain *desiderata*, is uniquely adequate to the theory's purposes.

6.3 THE EPISTEMOLOGY OF BELIEF–DESIRE ASCRIPTION

The questions raised and theories proposed so far have been about the metaphysical status of belief–desire ascriptions – their truth conditions, whether they are physically realizable, determinately true or false, etc. Such issues have (all too) often been interwoven with questions about the epistemology of attitude-ascription, so that the principles we rely on in their ascription are counted as constitutive of their truth conditions. An important manifestation of this tendency is the common assumption that an account of belief-ascription must bring in dispositions, or other relations, to overt utterance, or, as in Davidson's theory (1974), that a semantic theory of spoken or written language is not eliminable from the theory of propositional attitudes. The reasoning is clear enough: among the important evidence for beliefs is linguistic behavior; we expect ascriptions of beliefs to fit linguistic dispositions. But while language must have a central place in the full picture of attitudes, it is not necessary to introduce it in the foundation of the theory of attitudes; thus, in my functional theory, connections with overt linguistic behavior are not essential to a belief's functional role.

For this and other reasons the epistemology of belief–desire ascriptions must be kept distinct from their explication; not doing so perpetuates the methodology of the positivists' inevitable, noble, failures, of phenomenalism, behaviorism, and semantic instrumentalism about science. It is difficult to imagine this tendency not to be equally disastrous in the theory of attitudes.[4]

But the distinction between the truth conditions of and contingent principles of evidence for attitude-ascriptions raises the question of the epistemological status of the latter, of how they are better confirmed than principles that lead to different patterns of attitude-ascription.

Somehow, from their behavior, perceptual circumstances, and so on, we are able to ascribe beliefs and desires to others; and it seems this must depend on principles or generalizations of some sort. Let me refer to these putative principles as our *standard scheme* for attitude-ascription. Various preliminary points are in order.

First, the *total* evidence for whether a creature realizes the belief–desire theory, and has certain beliefs and desires, is not exhausted by the behavioral, perceptual and other normally employed evidence which, with the standard scheme, determines our pre-scientific ascriptions. For on the functional interpretation of the belief–desire theory, scientific discoveries in psychology and physiology will be relevant and even telling. So the standard scheme does not contain all the principles via which belief–desire-ascriptions could be confirmed, but rather those we normally rely on in our commonsense use of the theory, those that explain our facility and common agreement in applying the system, and that must be justified if our ascriptions are evidentially sound.

Secondly, the standard scheme is not exhausted by the "belief–desire theory". For while its conditions and constraints are central to our normal evidential situation, we would not get very far in filling out our picture of others' attitudes simply on the basis of those conditions

[4] Gricean explications of semantic concepts, in terms of propositional attitudes, have been seen as implausible *simply because* "reductionist", as if that made them like phenomenalism and behaviorism. But how different the two kinds of reduction are. In the latter, truth conditions are explicated in terms of evidence conditions, and that is the positivist mistake. It is then curious that it is precisely because Gricean theories block *a priori* constitutive connections between attitude-ascriptions and linguistic evidence that such opponents have objected to them.

conjoined with the behavioral–perceptual facts about others. Naturally, the perceptual input condition is important. If Pierre is normal we can infer much of what he believes about his environment from the environment itself. Not only does this generate ascriptions of observational beliefs; given the L-constraints it serves as a check on non-observational beliefs. It is interesting to note that the input conditions cover an important part of the "Principle of Charity", which enjoins us to ascribe to others the beliefs we would have in similar circumstances. (The account of 'similar' determines the sophistication of the version of the Principle of Charity proposed. Cf. Lewis, 1974). The L-constraints of course play an essential adjusting role, although they do not generate new beliefs. Otherwise the belief–desire theory does not on its own enable us to ascribe more of the normal range of ascribable beliefs. The practical problem of radical interpretation is not solved simply by the functional theory.

Thirdly, the belief–desire theory does not provide a direct basis for ascribing *desires*. There are no input conditions for desires; they were not needed in generating a unique functional role for each attitude. Moreover, adding them as constitutive would not improve our evidential situation, as I shall argue shortly about, in general, adding constitutive constraints to the functional theory. Neither the belief–desire–willing condition nor the willing–ability–action condition play a direct role in ascription; but let us take the standard scheme to include the whole belief–desire theory.[5]

Fourthly, the rest of the standard scheme must be simply empirical generalizations, and I shall call them contingent principles of attitude-ascription. They are, as I shall argue, non-nomological generalizations that connect certain behavior, or being in certain environments, with independently specified functional states, or that unconditionally ascribe functional states. (Let us keep in mind that functional organization is partially a matter of contingent non-lawlike anatomical facts.)

The evidential status of the contingent principles needs investigating; to give a theory of the truth conditions of attitude-ascriptions while leaving their epistemology to look after itself would hardly be satisfactory. Certainly it would be nice if on the functional theory we are in no worse position evidentially than we appear intuitively to be; otherwise the functional theory would surely be put in doubt. The

---

[5] This is convenient, since in later assessing our overall evidential situation we must consider the theory which consists of the basic belief–desire theory plus the contingent principles. Instead of having two distinct sets of conditions, it is easiest to identify the standard scheme now with that subsequent overall theory.

threat is an *epistemological indeterminacy* of attitude-ascription: incompatible alternative contingent principles of attitude-ascription that are equally well confirmed. Notice that such an epistemological indeterminacy would not *eo ipso* invalidate the functional explication, at least not on the grounds that the correct assignment of truth conditions to a certain discourse must preclude sceptical alternatives to commonsense ascriptions; that principle leads to positivism.

In the discussion of determinacy in 6.1 such epistemological indeterminacy was not ruled out. There the issue was whether the truth or falsity of attitude-attributions is determined by the totality of physical fact and theory, and not whether normal ascriptions are favored over competitors by a proper part of the possible evidence, our *usual* evidence.

What then are these contingent principles of attitude-ascription? There are at least six major classes that seem worth mentioning.

(1) We may begin with two principles of rationalization[6] – namely, (a) that substantial stretches of a person's waking behavior are intentional – that is, caused by willings; and (b) that most willings are for reasons, are caused by instrumental beliefs and desires.

(2) Nowhere in specifying the functional theory was anything said about inductive procedures for generating beliefs from beliefs. I do not propose to give an account of basic human induction here, but it does seem that we assume a minimal inductive competence in our belief-ascriptions. What generalizations back up our expectations is a well-known question, and much more needs to be said. If there are such generalizations, they cover more of the ground covered by the (umbrella) Principle of Charity.

(3) Next there are "fact–belief" generalizations, of the form: 'if p is a true proposition of kind A and z is a person of kind B, then z believes that p', a further part of the Principle of Charity. They are indispensable in building up our accustomed detailed pictures of the cognitive situations of others. An important subset is about beliefs of the form [if p is the case then my doing A will result in q]; important because, if we can also ascribe the relevant belief that p, we can ascribe the belief [my doing A will result in q], which then can give us a reason (not deductive) for inferring the desire for q from the action A. Fact–belief generalizations are proposed in 8.4 as a principle source of the utility of the concept of truth.

[6] Lewis (1974) suggests a constraint on belief–desire ascription, which he calls the Rationalization Principle, and which in effect combines these two.

(4) Next come the extremely central generalizations that relate utterances to interpretations. For many, one of the more indigestible aspects of my functional theory will be the absence of functional connections between beliefs and overt language. It is worth emphasizing again that such connections are not necessary in establishing unique functional roles for beliefs. The fundamental importance of language and semantic properties in the theory of propositional attitudes does not require locating them at its theoretical core (in terms of which semantic properties are complex constructions). Let me mention three respects in which language is central in the theory of propositional attitudes. First, as was pointed out in 6.2, it is natural to take the theory of propositional attitudes as having arisen from utterance-types being associated with distinct functional roles. Secondly, in anticipation of chapter 9 it may be useful to point out that, on the functional theory, propositional attitudes are non-linguistic only in the sense that functional connections with overt language are not among their defining conditions. It is perfectly compatible that many or most first-order states with the functional roles of beliefs are to be specified in theoretical psychology as linguistic states. The importance of the distinction between non-linguistic functional roles and the linguistic states that have those roles cannot be overestimated in resolving certain problems about language and thought.

Thirdly (to bring us to the main point under (4)), there are interpretative generalizations, which embody a semantic theory of z's language, via which *in part* we infer z's beliefs, desires, and intentions from z's utterances. They evidently must play a central and unique role in the epistemology of attitude-ascription. Evidently, no theory of meaning for z's sentences on its own enables us to infer z's attitudes from z's utterances; we need considerable collateral information about z's other desires and beliefs. In the Gricean form suggested in chapter 10, the interpretative generalizations associate utterance-types with communicative intentions, and only indirectly with beliefs and desires. (This points to further assumptions about z – that z is veracious, etc., included under (5).) Naturally, utterance-meaning principles must have the recursive structure of a semantic theory. A function from sentences to propositions, recursively defined, is not quite right; what is wanted is a function from sentences to certain (complex) entities that take us from non-linguistic parameters of an utterance (e.g. its references, the identity of the speaker, the time of utterance, etc.) to the proposition meant. On the functional theory of propositional attitudes, these generalizations about z, the semantic theory of z's language, are just contingent generalizations relating utterance-types and functional states. (Their form is discussed in 10.4.) How they are evidentially grounded is part of the broader epistemological question, about the contingent principles as a whole.

(5) Here we have conditional and unconditional generalizations about desire – that our fellows normally desire life, food, drink, sleep, not to feel pain, and so on. We take for granted also countless other, less bread-and-butter, ideals, tastes, and social desires, in inferring mediating goals and beliefs. Some play a large role in linguistic interpretation – for example, a certain ideal or recurring objective of communicative cooperativeness: to speak the truth, to be relevant, and so on.[7]

(6) Here are certain beliefs that could be included under (3) but that play a very special role in interpretation, namely the beliefs we have about each other's beliefs, about each other's communicative cooperativeness, and so on. Inferences in communication depend upon assumptions of mutual knowledge between us and our interlocutors and we tend (quite without reflection) to attribute to others the requisite complex background social beliefs. (See Schiffer, 1972, pp. 30–42; and below 10.3.)

Classes (1) through (6) contain some of the generalizations we rely on in ascribing beliefs and desires. They are supposed to explain interpersonal agreement about attitude-ascription; and they justify that agreement only if they are themselves justified. Epistemologically their status is no different from that of far less general assumptions about the attitudes of others that we rely on in making inferences to yet further attitudes. Thus in understanding Pierre I rely not only on (1) to (6), principles we all share, but also on specific things I know about Pierre, e.g. that he believes that Smith is a Russian agent, in my inference to his further beliefs, etc. What makes (1) through (6) *salient* are these two features: first, their *broad scope* – they are applicable in a wide range of attitude-ascriptions; and secondly, their *impersonal origin* – none of us thought them up for himself, they are part of our common cognitive inheritance. In their more positivist moments, philosophers tend to take the broad scope and impersonal provenance of evidentially crucial principles as a sign of some special epistemological status. My contrary view, that they are as contingent and *a posteriori*

---

[7] It is then as wholly contingent generalizations about functional states that I construe Grice's conversational maxims (Grice, 1975b).

as can be, raises the obvious epistemological problem which we must now address.

The standard scheme has two components: the belief–desire theory and the contingent principles. The thought might occur that the epistemological situation would be improved by promoting these principles into constitutive constraints of the functional theory. But this would in fact make no difference to the evidential situation. What initially concerns us is a conjunction: that some particular person or persons are functionally organized in a certain way; and that certain generalizations are true of the functional states, thus defined, of those persons. It we make it a condition of the applicability of the terms 'believes' and 'desires' that an individual satisfy not only the first conjunct but the second, that would affect the truth conditions of 'x believes that p'. But it does not improve the evidential situation; for we still must answer the same questions under another guise: first, does z instantiate that functional *subsystem* (of the new comprehensive functional theory) that is the original belief–desire theory?; and secondly, assuming a positive answer, does z satisfy the rest of the comprehensive functional theory? Any epistemological problems about the original functional theory plus contingent principles also arise about the extended functional theory.

This raises a question about the methodological presuppositions and intentions of much of the literature on indeterminacy. There has been a great emphasis on "constraints" and "principles" that supposedly eliminate the indeterminacy, the Principle of Charity being the most prominent. But generally there has not been much indication of their, as we might say, intended metaphysical status. In chapter 1, I suggested two workable formats for interpreting the belief–desire theory, namely instrumentalist and realist–functionalist. On the former, it is difficult to see how there could be an interesting question about indeterminacy. Perhaps it is an absorbing bit of philosophical anthropology to reconstruct the rules we actually apply; but if there is no fact of the matter about beliefs and desires, it is of no theoretical moment whether certain rules yield determinate attitude-attributions. There is, after all, a single rule that yields a rough determinacy – namely, "observe the normal practice".

Stating constraints that yield determinacy could be intended to avoid instrumentalism – but only if something further is said about how they contribute to objectively determinate attitude-ascriptions. Merely listing them settles very little. If they are supposed to contribute to a functional theory, they ought to have a form that makes that possible. The means they ought to contribute to the eliminative definition of 'x believes that p' in terms of its place in a functional system, and the functional system ought to be reconstructible without the concepts to be defined. Consider the following (somewhat bizarre) rule, one that has not been proposed but that shares relevant features with some that have: 'ascribe to z the belief that p only if you believe p yourself'. How could that satisfy that condition? Nor does 'ascribe to z the belief that p only if p is true' say anything about the functional role of the belief that p.

It may seem obvious that it is only the standard scheme *as a whole* about which the evidential question should be raised; in other words, that it is futile to consider the evidential status of the belief–desire theory independently of the contingent principles. But that does not, upon reflection, seem to me to be obvious; but first two important preliminary points.

First, a functional theory is a theory of an individual, of how its possible state-types are counterfactually related. But that is not to say that our evidence that z has a certain functional organization is confined to facts about only z's behavior and perceptual circumstances. For, that z belongs to a natural kind K other members of which have a functional organization F can be good grounds for taking z to have F. Secondly, solid evidence that members of K have F may not be partitionable into solid evidence e_1 that x_1 has F, evidence e_2 that x_2 has F, etc.; the evidence might be cumulative across K. These two points may be quite important in the epistemology of belief–desire-ascription. We are not, for each new individual, faced with the problem of ascertaining from scratch whether he has beliefs or desires, any more than we start afresh, with each new organism of a well known species, about its internal arrangement of organs.

So, what about the hypothesis that nearly all members of our society, who speak our language, say, have a functional organization that fits the belief–desire theory? Do we also have to bring in the contingent principles? Perhaps the following line is promising. The overwhelming success of our attitude-ascriptions in systematizing human behavior and its connections with perceptual circumstances needs explanation. Given the complexity of the distinct states thus ascribed (not complexity of the belief–desire theory's conditions, but the variety of specific beliefs and desires), and given that our ascriptions obey the constraints of the belief–desire theory, the natural explanation of success includes the hypothesis that human beings are functionally organized in accordance with the belief–desire theory. The inference from instrumental adequacy to truth evidently needs discussion. But as regards the goal of reconstructing the commonsense belief–desire theory in a way that does not conflict with the commonsense epistemology of attitude-ascription, the inference's naturalness is telling. And when we add to the functional theory the possibility that the first-order states that realize the theory's functional roles may be *linguistic* states, the plausibility of the inference is increased. For it is difficult to doubt that normal patterns of dispositions to sincere utterance do correspond to the proposed functional organization; that such dispositions have some systematically corresponding basis in first-order states is a sensible inference.

This line of argument, whatever its merits, is not affected by the usual arguments for indeterminacy. Nothing in the usual contentions that *particular* attitude-ascriptions are indeterminate with respect to physical fact and theory would show that there is some functional system, incompatible with the belief–desire theory, whose satisfaction would equally well explain our usual success in systematizing the perceptual–behavioral evidence. To see this, let us subdivide the belief–desire theory into the perceptual-input law and all other constraints. As regards the latter, the usual contention of indeterminacy is that, *given* those rationality constraints, there are alternative incompatible ascriptions that are equally well supported. Indeterminacy arguments, in other words, would not show that that part of the functional theory is not motivated. As regards the input conditions, let us recall the point made in 6.1 about such allegedly alternative theories. If a different input law, of the form roughly 'if $O(x, p, t)$ etc. then x believes $f(p)$' is substituted, we have, not an alternative functional theory, but rather one that is logically equivalent to the usual theory. So of course we should expect it to be equally well supported by, and explanatory of, the general success of our ascriptions in systematizing the perceptual–behavioral facts, but that is beside the point.

There is then the interesting possibility that the belief–desire theory, independently of the contingent principles of ascription, is more or less highly confirmed by the instrumental success of our overall patterns of ascription. It is important to distinguish two sorts of possible evidential weakness: namely, first, a genuine indeterminacy of the kind that has interested philosophers – i.e. the existence of incompatible and equally supported theories of the propositional attitude-type; secondly, the more general absence of strong confirmation. Nothing of the former sort attends the belief–desire theory, *qua* theory of functional organization; as regards the latter, perhaps all one can and needs to say is that, from a rather casual commonsense point of view, it is natural to take evidence for the functional belief–desire theory as strong.

Now we turn to the question of the evidential status of the contingent principles, or of the standard scheme as a whole. The generalizations in (1)–(6) range over members of our whole society, and assert correlations between having certain features or behaving in certain ways with certain functional states defined independently of the contingent principles. There is no problem then about the empirical content of these principles. Now the foregoing distinction of two types of evidential weakness is relevant here. First, we have to ask whether, *given* the belief–desire theory, there are other sets of contingent principles which, given the perceptual–behavioral evidence, imply patterns of beliefs and desires that (given the L-constraints and the M-constraints) are incompatible with preferred ascriptions and which equally well explain the perceptual–behavioral evidence. I shall argue that the usual arguments for indeterminacy provide no reason for there being such competing principles. As regards the second sort of evidential weakness (general lack of high confirmation), I can say only that, if there is no epistemological indeterminacy of the first sort, the general systematic success of the standard system seems to be a reason to regard it as true. Naturally it may be disconfirmed – e.g. advances in theoretical psychology may make it dubious that we are thus functionally organized. But the only way to protect the belief–desire theory against the *possibility* of such disconfirmation would be to give it an instrumentalist interpretation.

So the question is whether any standard arguments for indeterminacy suggest there are competing principles of ascription that are as well confirmed as the standard scheme. Two somewhat different sorts of argument are relevant. First, a different pattern of ascriptions results from attributing non-standard perceptual beliefs, and then suitably adjusting the usual assignment of desires. But the response should now be clear. The competing principles that would emerge would not be logically incompatible with the standard scheme. For, once again, that amounts simply to changing the input law in the way discussed in 6.1. That does yield a different assignment of propositions to functional states, but the resulting functional theory is logically equivalent to the standard one, and the resulting apparently competing principles of ascription are then logically equivalent to the standard principles; they ascribe the same *functional* states on the same behavioral and other conditions. Quinean constructions that are supposed to generate referential indeterminacy yield ascriptions of functional states that are only notationally distinct.

This point could use some elaboration. It is not that any principles of ascription that explain the perceptual–behavioral evidence as well as the standard system are *eo ipso* logically equivalent to it; I have offered no argument for that. The only way that could be so would be if on the *standard* assignment of propositions to functional roles no set other than the standard one is evidentially equally adequate, and that is still an open question. The point rather was this. Suppose, as in 6.1, f is the function that generates different assignments of propositions to functional roles. If a certain contingent fact–belief principle (say) holds that if (the person) z is (of kind) A and p is (of kind) B then z *believes* that p, the apparently competing fact–"belief" principle is: if z is A and p is B then z "*believes*" that $f(p)$. The two contingent principles are equivalent, since believing that p is logically equivalent to "believing" that $f(p)$.

A second possible argument for epistemological indeterminacy is Quine's claim that the underdetermination of theories by observational data implies that it is indeterminate which of several incompatible theories Pierre believes. In 6.1, I argued that it is determinate which of two incompatible theoretical propositions Pierre really believes; for that is a matter of which of two empirically distinct functional states Pierre is in. But we are still faced with the possibility that Quine's point reveals at least an *epistemological* indeterminacy in the ascription of theoretical beliefs – that is, indeterminacy with regard to the normal perceptual–behavioral evidence.

There is nothing in this worry. It is true that relative solely to our evidence about Pierre's perceptual *non-behavioral* relations to his environment it may be indeterminate which, of a pair of theories that equally well explain the data, Pierre believes. But it does not follow that further *behavioral* facts about Pierre do not make the difference. For consider: if T and $T^\star$ are two such theories they are not logico-syntactically equivalent, for by the general theory of theory interpretation they are then not distinct theories. But if T and $T^\star$ have different logical structures, the belief that T and the belief that $T^\star$ are distinct functional states. But then there can be *behavioral* evidence for Pierre's believing T rather than $T^\star$; for example, certain syntactic facts about what Pierre says may, in the context of our broader theory of

Pierre, point to his being in the functional state which is the belief that *T*. Naturally this would count as evidence only within a well-developed theory of Pierre's beliefs, desires and dispositions thereto.

It has not been my purpose to argue that there is no epistemological indeterminacy, no set of competing principles of ascription that equally well accords with the perceptual–behavioral data. (There are of course no two competing sets equally compatible with the *total* empirical data.) Rather I have argued that certain well-known reasons for thinking there is are not persuasive. In the absence of more telling arguments, the following attitude seems to recommend itself. Here we have the standard scheme, which asserts that all members of a certain group have a certain functional organization and that certain generalizations are true of their functional states. The evidence for that theory is impressive, for it successfully systematizes a vast quantity of perceptual–behavioral facts, including linguistic behavior. So there is no special problem about how the principles in (1)–(6) can be highly contingent, as my theory requires, and still have a firm epistemological status.

That our interpretative task, with a newly encountered individual of our own society, is epistemologically on a par with interpreting a newly encountered Alpha-Centaurian, is a view that has achieved a certain standing. The commonsense dismissive reaction turns out after all to be correct; it took rather sophisticated blinkers to have held it. Evidence that many members of a natural kind instantiate a certain functional system, and certain generalizations about its functional states (the contingent principles), will under certain conditions be evidence that a newly encountered member of that natural kind satisfies them. So we are not faced with the problem of radical interpretation whenever we acquire a new colleague; that would be as though the question of the new colleague's having a heart and kidneys were on a par with some Alpha-Centaurian's having them.

Some remarks, finally, are in order about linguistic evidence for beliefs, which are, I am claiming, non-linguistic functional states. No doubt if linguistic performance were subtracted from our total evidence, the remaining perceptual–behavioral facts would not provide a basis for ascribing anything like the full complement of *abstract*, *fine-grained* beliefs (Davidson's terms) we typically ascribe. It is not easy to imagine non-linguistic or non-communicative behavior, however complicated, that would determinately provide a basis for such ascription. What is the significance of this? There are several points to be made.

(1) It does not follow that the functional states with which beliefs are identified have defining connections with overt language. The standard system may, without adverse epistemological repercussions, be divided into two components; one asserts the existence of functional states whose defining characterization contains nothing about language; the other contains generalizations connecting, in a structured way, linguistic behavior to the functional states. The conjunction of the two is what the linguistic evidence supports.

(2) The *fine-grainedness* of beliefs, which may suggest that they must be linguistic because their fine-grained structure is like that of sentences, has been captured independently of connections with language. For the fine-grainedness of beliefs is a matter of the fine-grainedness of their functional roles. In 4.5 I pointed out that for each logico-structural difference between propositions there is a difference in the functional roles of the indexed beliefs.

(3) It is naturally of considerable importance why linguistic evidence seems so essential to a determinate assignment of fine-grained abstract beliefs; to that I now turn.

6.4 LINGUISTIC EVIDENCE AND FINE-GRAINED BELIEFS

That linguistic evidence has a special status in attitude-ascription has been registered. But since the functional roles of attitudes do not involve connections with overt language, this must appear somewhat puzzling, for that special evidential status could suggest that relations to language are partially *constitutive* of fine-grained belief. First let me make it clear just what the evidential status of language is here, and then show how the functional theory straighforwardly explains that.

Some do not regard language as having in principle a special evidential role. Robert Stalnaker writes: "Imagine that we discovered living creatures – perhaps on some other planet – who did not communicate, but whose behavior was predictable, for the most part, on the hypothesis that they engaged in highly sophisticated theoretical deliberation." (Stalnaker, 1976, p. 82.) (I shall take 'communicate' here to cover all overt linguistic behavior, including working out theories on paper, etc.) I must agree that if we discovered such taciturn creatures building bridges, airplanes, and so on, we would indeed think they engage in 'theoretical deliberation'; we would, as Stalnaker says, be "tempted to attribute to these creatures not just belief and desire analogues but beliefs and desires themselves". That the temptation makes sense *prima facie*, supports a conception of attitudes independent of connections with overt language. (Stalnaker draws a stronger conclusion: "we would not...have any reason to hypothesize that they thought in a mental language or in any language at all". I agree that the language of thought hypothesis does not follow from a fine-grained belief–desire theory (cf. 9.1), but I do not see that this example shows that.)

Stalnaker goes on to speak of "the beliefs that our hypothesis attributed to these creatures". This is quite a further step: it is one thing to say that their non-linguistic behavior, etc., is evidence that they have theoretical beliefs; it is quite another claim that it supports ascriptions of *specific* theoretical beliefs. (The difference is between: (a) we have evidence that they have some beliefs or other and (b) there are certain beliefs $b_1, \ldots, b_n$ such that we have evidence that they have $b_1, \ldots, b_n$.) So the question is: can totally non-linguistic evidence support ascriptions of specific fine-grained beliefs?

Naturally it can, when the creatures belong to groups about whose beliefs we already know a great deal. But we are talking about Alpha-Centaurians. It is doubtful that such technological feats would be explainable only by ascribing a certain specific theory to the Alpha-Centaurians; incompatible theories could dictate the same technological solution to a technical problem. (This differs from Quine's point and my discussion of it in 6.1; lingustic evidence was included there.) Given only the *non-linguistic* behavioral and environmental evidence (without further evidence about the Alpha-Centaurians' internal organization), it is difficult to see how we could ascribe to them specific theoretical beliefs as a better explanation of their feats than any other possible ascription.

But then we have a problem. If the functional roles of beliefs involve no special connections with language, why does the ordinary evidence have to include something about it? This is important, for it might suggest that the earlier conclusion, that the Alpha-Centaurians have theoretical beliefs, was not justified, based on too weak an analogy with our language-using fellows when they display such technological skills.

The problem is not that there is no conceivable non-linguistic evidence for ascribing fine-grained beliefs to new creatures; a theoretical psychology-cum-neurophysiology might uncover a certain fine-grained functional organization. The question is why, in the *ordinary* evidence, language has an ineliminable role – why belief-ascription is radically indeterminate with respect to the non-linguistic behavioral–perceptual evidence.

My answer depends on these facts: (1) linguistic behavior is structured isomorphically to the functional structure of beliefs; (2) no other behavior is similarly structured; (3) nothing else in ordinary non-linguistic behavior warrants such specific hypotheses about functional cognitive structure.

As regards ordinary linguistic dispositions, the syntactic structure of the potential utterances corresponds significantly to the structure of the dispositions; and we explain that dispositional structure in terms of the structure of underlying functional states. Now I take it as evident that no non-linguistic behavior of ours has similar structure, at least not in any way that shows up in our commonsense reasoning.

Why then can we not find evidence about internal functional structure in behavioral–perceptual facts that are not isomorphically structured? Quine has claimed that the general underdetermination of theory by observational evidence implies the indeterminacy of our ascriptions of theoretical beliefs to Pierre. That is correct *provided we throw out our structured, linguistic, evidence.* This will sound odd unless one keeps in mind that we are speaking of ascribing functional states and not truth conditions. The reason we have already seen; given a stretch of Alpha-Centaurian perceptual–behavioral data, however impressive their technological products, a sufficiently ingenious theory-constructor among us might suggest several incompatible theories whose application by the Alpha-Centaurians would lead to the same non-linguistic behavior. The general underdetermination of theory by observational evidence thus explains the indeterminacy of ascriptions of certain fine-grained beliefs with respect to ordinary non-linguistic evidence.

There is nothing constitutive of belief-ascription in this; it is an empirical fact about the evidence normally available to us. That brain scientists could discover on the basis of non-ordinary evidence that the correct explanation of Alpha-Centaurians' abilities to build airplanes and bridges is certain theoretical deliberations – internal events involving certain functional states – shows that *our ordinary non-linguistic evidence is simply deficient,* crucially more rudimentary than the scientists' evidence (and than the linguistic evidence). This no more needs philosophical explanation than our inability to deduce the nervous system of a newt from its observable behavior.

7

Intentionality without intensions

To understand the role of propositions is to be able to dispense with them; that is a guiding idea of this chapter. Beliefs so far are, in one sense, relations to propositions; but that must be treated cautiously. The relation is abstract, and the proposition serves as an extrinsic indicator of functional role; that beliefs are relational does not imply that their *relata* are in the believer's natural environment.

'Beliefs are...' admits of rather different completions; the following are each appropriate: (a) beliefs are relations to propositions; (b) beliefs are functional states; (c) beliefs, for a given person and time, are physical states with certain functional roles. On the last two, that beliefs are relations to propositions rather drops out of the picture. This is not unlike the case of temperatures, which are in one sense extrinsic relations to numbers, and in another intrinsic states of molecule collections. 'Temperature' could denote the complex states of affairs expressed by 'the temperature in degrees Celsius of $x = n$', or it could denote properties of x by virtue of which (given our indexing system) such relational states of affairs obtain.

Another feature of temperature is relevant: we do not expect the underlying states of molecule collections themselves to be relational in a way that parallels the relation to numbers. No underlying entity corresponds to the number, and no underlying relation corresponds to 'x has temperature n'. Similarly, while my explication of belief does not preclude the underlying state from being, in some interesting sense, relational, it does not imply it either.

One might discern the following structure in the development of the analytical theory of belief. From a platonist conception of belief, based on the notion of grasping a proposition, there emerged the more naturalistic idea of beliefs as relations to sentences, belief-*ascriptions* being taken to describe the underlying relation indirectly, via the underlying sentence's meaning. So $\ulcorner x$ believes that $s \urcorner$ would mean:

$$(\exists s')\ B^\star(x, s')\ \&\ R(s', \text{that-}s).$$

Here B★ is more basic than the relation expressed by the ascription – call it *accepting* the sentence s' of one's own language; R is some relation like 'means' or 'means the same as' to a proposition, sentence, or utterance. Then it became apparent that R, while not as overtly drawn from an antiquated psychology as "grasping" a proposition, nevertheless is still difficult to account for naturalistically.[1] The next move was to eliminate meaning and to concentrate on B★ as the only real belief-relation. This preserves the intuition that belief is relational while avoiding propositions and meaning. But the cost is high, for it eliminates full classical intentionality, on which the ordinary structure of rationalizing action appears to depend. (cf. 2.4).

Now the first-order states that realize the functional roles of beliefs and desires might be language-relative internal linguistic states, and perhaps that would interpret B★ after all. But the relation *x's being in state y* does not vindicate the underlying-relation theory. For on this theory there is not just one relation; there are believing★, desiring★, intending★. No doubt they can be reintroduced by definition, given my theory, but their philosophical point, as primitive terms of a basic sentential attitude theory, is then lost.

B★ is not drawn upon by the functional theory of chapter 4. The proposition does not give the meaning of a sentence which the speaker accepts (that is, in some independent sense of 'meaning'); it rather indicates a functional state, and that state's truth conditions. The sentential replacements of propositions, to be introduced in 7.2, are the ascriber's sentences; again, their function is not to *translate* the believer's sentences but to index functional roles, and to provide a peg on which to hang truth conditions.

The ontological issue, of meanings as abstract entities, has not been the main point in scepticism about intentionality; the usual substitution of sentences or utterances merely exchanges propositions for the equally problematic concept of equivalence in meaning. But not only is eliminating propositions not *sufficient* for a naturalistic account, in a certain notable way it is, oddly enough, not *necessary* either. For the functional theory yields *necessary and sufficient physical conditions* for z's believing that p. Even though propositions are not in the domain of natural science, this relation to a proposition is determined entirely by

---

[1] There is the possibility of explicating that relation in terms of equivalence in functional role. But that does not lend support to the B★ pattern of explication. As I pointed out in 2.3, "equivalence in functional role" is too short; some functional system has to be specified to generate a useful equivalence relation. But to specify that (as I claim to have done in chapter 4) is to explicate belief-ascriptions without bringing in B★.

the physical facts. How can that be? Consider again the unwieldy functional theory of 6.2, on which all instances of 'the belief that...' are treated as semantically simple. To each sentence 'x believes that p', there corresponds a preposterously unmanageable sentence that does not quantify over propositions and is equivalent to 'x believes that p' *apart from* the latter's reference to a proposition. They agree *exactly* on x's functional state; relative to the ontology, each entails the other. When a naturalistic account of *truth conditions* is also provided, the contribution of propositions is fully naturalized, in a way that permits their elimination. Ontological scruples can then be humored.

In 6.2 I argued that, given certain *desiderata*, indices cannot be eliminated. But if there were no alternative to propositions, the index theory of intentionality would (as I see it) be only partially illuminating, leaving an annoying opacity in an otherwise limpid physicalism. It is that, and not the absence of a naturalistic account of the relation to the proposition, which motivates finding surrogates for propositions. The motivation is ontological, but depends upon a certain further concern. If the concern were just to find necessary and sufficient conditions for ⌜z believes that...⌝, the unwieldy theory of 6.3 would do, and propositions could be viewed simply as convenient *fictions*. But we are after a theory of intentional structure – that is, those general interrelations among beliefs and desires that depend upon logical form, the mastery of which in large part constitutes our mastery of attitudes. The importance of purifying attitude-ascriptions of reference to propositions lies in this: only then is it clear that intensionality is irrelevant to intentionality.

Propositions have two overlapping functions: to index functional roles, and to encapsulate truth and fulfillment conditions. I say "overlapping" because the truth and fulfillment conditions of some attitudes figure in their functional roles. In the next section I discuss how to replace propositions in the functional theory, and defer the general question of truth conditions to the subsequent section.

7.2 PROPOSITIONS ELIMINATED FROM THE FUNCTIONAL THEORY

Two features of propositions are exploited in their employment as indices, namely their interrelations of logical structure and, for some propositions, their truth conditions. The former are deployed in the *internal* constraints, those that generate functional connections between beliefs and beliefs, and among beliefs, desires and willings. On the other hand, truth conditions are invoked on the *periphery* of the functional theory, in the input and output conditions. That exhausts the contribution of propositions to the functional theory. If non-intensional entities like sentences, and their non-intensional properties, can suitably imitate propositions and their intensional properties, then, as regards functional role, intensionality will have been eliminated, while the full classical criteria of individuating beliefs interpersonally will have been preserved.

The adequacy conditions of this elimination are as follows. First, the new deintensionalized theory should be satisfied by z at t if and only if the propositional theory is satisfied; furthermore, for each p, 'x believes that p at t' ought to be satisfied by z at t just in case its replacement is thus satisfied. Let us call this conjunction the condition of *functional equivalence*. Secondly we want something more, since the unwieldy theory of 6.2 satisfies that condition. That theory fails to treat 'x believes that p' as semantically complex, and therefore to preserve the generalizable structure in interactions among attitudes, and between them and perception and action. The new theory must parallel the old theory's ascriptions of intentionality. Call this the condition of *equivalence in intentional structure*.

The new theory substitutes sentences for propositions, but, unlike the semantic relation theories of 2.3, no pragmatic semantic concepts are here invoked – that is, nothing about what the sentence means in the ascriber's language or mouth. That is how the reconstruction escapes a circular interaction of theory of meaning and rational psychology.

No doubt the claim that this can be done is surprising. How can belief-ascriptions assert relations to the ascriber's sentences except insofar as the latter have meaning? It is necessary to take a somewhat abstract view, to escape from the grip of the semantic-relation model (which is quite intuitive). In place of something equally intuitive, let one's guide be the adequacy of the two stages of explication: first to reconstruct the functional theory non-intensionally, substituting sentences for propositions subject to the requirements of functional equivalence and equivalence in intentional structure, and secondly, to reconstruct truth conditions using only a non-intensional apparatus.

I am supposing all propositions to be first-order expressible; for those who demur, this may be viewed as a simplifying strategy that leaves open the possibility of supplementing the L-constraints. Let L be quantificational English, adequate for expressing all relevant propositions and propositional functions. A one–one mapping from propositions to the sentences of L that express them will be useful; so let us take L to be rid of synonymy and ambiguity, through suitable contraction and supplementation. Our propositions are fine-grained, so their structure imitates the syntactic structure of the regimented L. (Henceforth I shall simply say 'propositions' and 'sentences' when it is clear that propositional functions and open sentences are to be included.)

Although 'expresses' is a semantic term, to be avoided if unexplained, think of it as defined abstractly for L as in a formal semantics. But its converse is more to the point: let 'p's expression in $L = s$' capture that converse function from propositions to sentences, similarly abstractly defined. The sentence to be substituted for a proposition, in the new theory, is then its expression in L. (This notion is not part of the new theory; I use it to avoid tedious description of the new theory.)

In the propositional theory, some indices contain singular propositions, for example, in beliefs about perceived particulars, tensed beliefs and self ascriptive beliefs (cf. chapter 5). In replacements for such indices in the new theory, it will help to have initally taken singular propositions to be pairs of n-ary propositional functions and n-tuples of particulars; the former can then simply be replaced by open sentences. Let us call the new indices, with sentences or open sentences in place of propositions or propositional functions, the sentential analogues of the latter. Now the sentential analogue of p is just its expression in L. In what follows there is no harm in thinking of all old and new indices as simply propositions and sentences; nothing turns on the more complex structures of indices.

The intended effect of the replacement is that the new belief–desire theory defines new functions Bel′, Des′, Int′ which map sentential indices, persons and times onto (sets of) underlying states, according to their functional roles. Naturally the new theory and the old theory should conjointly entail, whenever s is p's expression in L, that Bel′$[s, z, t]$ = Bel$[p, z, t]$; similarly for Des′ and Int′. If that is so, and the new theory restricts itself to the ground covered by the old theory, the conditions of functional equivalence and equivalence in intentional structure will be met.[2] Let us see that there is no problem for the new theory's appropriately defining Bel′, Des′, and Int′.

[2] The two theories are to be logically equivalent relative to their ontologies. That is, if Q captures the ontological commitment to sentences and propositions and T is the old theory and T' the new theory, then what ought to be true is: $\Box(Q \rightarrow (T$ is true of z at t iff T' is true of z at $t))$.

First, consider the internal constraints, say the L-constraints and the belief–desire–willing condition. The new theory must contain a suitable syntax for the sentences of L, to permit generalizing syntactic forms: $\ulcorner s \ \& \ s' \urcorner$, $\ulcorner (\exists x) \ldots x \ldots \urcorner$, etc. We replace internal constraints using the expressing function; '$B[p \ \& \ q] \Rightarrow \text{not } B[\sim p]$' is replaced by '$B'\ulcorner s \ \& \ r \urcorner \Rightarrow \text{not } B'\ulcorner \sim s \urcorner$'. (That is: 'if z is at t in Bel'$[\ulcorner s \ \& \ r \urcorner, z, t]$ then z is not at t in Bel'$[\ulcorner \sim s \urcorner, z, t]$'.) And so throughout. Where formerly the constraints were expressed in terms of relations of logical structure among propositions, they are now in terms of syntactic relations among sentences.

The L-constraints impose conditions on what underlying states are candidates for being z's beliefs at t: they must be counterfactually related as the L-constraints say such and such beliefs are related. Now consider some instantiations of the old and new L-constraints:

Bel[[roses are red and violets are blue], Jones, t],

Bel[[not: roses are red], Jones, t],

Bel'[['roses are red and violets are blue', Jones, t], and

Bel'[['not: roses are red', Jones, t].

If α and β are first-order states that are candidates for being denoted by the first and the second, respectively, and the third and the fourth, respectively, then the old and new L-constraints impose exactly the same condition: if Jones were in α at t then Jones would not be in β at t.

Of course it is the complex counterfactual position of α and β in a vast network of states that determines whether they can be those beliefs. But every counterfactual condition imposed on the belief that p and the belief that q by the old theory, is imposed by the new theory on the belief' that s and the belief' that r, when s and r are the expressions of p and q in L. In general, the internal constraints of the two theories do not distinguish the belief that p from the belief' that s, if s is the expression of p in L – do not, that is, distinguish Bel[p, z, t] from Bel'[s, z, t].

That purely syntactic relations serve just as well in indexing internal functional connections among beliefs and desires as relations of logical structure among propositions is not surprising. For what matters in capturing functional connections is their *structure*; if certain relations among propositions mirror those connections, so do isomorphic relations among sentences, on a certain one–one correspondence with propositions. This is the first step in deintensionalizing the belief–desire theory. As soon as belief-contents are seen as, in part, functional roles, intensions become irrelevant to that extent. But to vindicate that fully, we need to reconstruct the input and output conditions.

An important point needs emphasis. L is not the language of the believer, nor are the syntactic relations involved supposed to hold among underlying states. L is our artifact; with it we index functional states via the ordinary syntax of L. To what extent the first-order structure of the underlying states resembles that syntactic structure is a further question. If those states are in some sense linguistic, then to speak of syntax at that level is also appropriate (cf. 9.1).

The perceptual input conditions of chapter 4 rely on the concept of truth, for they say that if p is a *true* observational proposition and z is related at t to p by O, etc., z at t believes that p. What role does truth play here? There is a correlation between certain perceptible states of affairs and certain functional states whereby one of the defining conditions of the latter is that, if a certain of the former obtains, etc., z moves into that functional state. A proposition is an economical index for an observational belief; via its truth conditions, it looks outward to the perceptible state of affairs that is functionally tied to the belief, and, via its logical structure it looks inward to the other beliefs and desires whose functional relations to the belief are definitive.

How can we duplicate the proposition's contribution to the input law? What counts as success is quite simple. If the new theory is logically equivalent to the old (relative to their ontologies), there must be a (non-intensional) predicate T of sentences such that, if s is p's expression in L, then necessarily p is true if and only if Ts. Suppose that, if s is p's expression, there is a condition '...' such that (1) the definition of T logically implies 'Ts iff...', and (2) 'p is true iff...' is a necessary truth. Then 'Ts' and 'p is true' are strongly equivalent. (For we then always have both '$\Box$(Ts iff...)' and '$\Box$(p is true *iff*...)'.)

But there is such a predicate – namely, the homophonic Tarski-type truth predicate on L (Tarski, 1956; Quine, 1970). Since L is quantificational English, not only does it serve as our set of indices of functional roles, but it can be part of our theoretical metalanguage (in which the new functional belief–desire theory is expressed, not the meta-metalanguage in which this book is written). So for each sentence s of L let the definition of T logically imply $\ulcorner$T$\bar{s}$ iff $s\urcorner$, where $\bar{s}$ is a structural–descriptive name of s. There is no problem in constructing such a predicate without using intensional or pragmatic semantic concepts; the techniques are the standard Tarskian ones.

That the truth predicate is homophonic plays no essential role in the

148

construction. All we need is a Tarski-type predicate T' such that '$T's$' and 'p is true' are strongly equivalent whenever s is p's expression in L. Because L may be part of the metalanguage, the homophonic T suffices; but we could always construct a non-homophonic predicate T' with the same result. This point will become clearer when the role of T is revealed more fully.

For observational beliefs with singular propositions in their indices, it is not exactly 'true' that needs replication, but 'true of' or 'satisfies'. We need a relation Sat such that, necessarily, the propositional function p is true of n-tuple x if and only if, where s is p's expression in L, $\mathrm{Sat}(s, x)$. Again a suitable Tarski-type Sat relation on L is easily forthcoming.

Let us now look at the new input conditions. Assuming there was no problem originally in defining the class of observation propositions in terms of their constituents (without using the concept of belief), there will be no problem in syntactically defining the class of observational sentential indices. In the original theory we have the relation '$O(z, p, t)$', a necessary condition of which is that p be observational. So similarly for observationality in the new '$O'(z, s, t)$'.[3]

The new conditions are as follows; where formerly we had

'If p is true and $O(z, p, t)$ etc., z is in $\mathrm{Bel}[p, z, t]$',

where 'p' ranges over general propositions, we now have

'If Ts and $O'(z, s, t)$ etc., z is in $\mathrm{Bel}'[s, z, t]$'.

When, in the former condition, 'p' ranges over singular propositions, which have the form $\langle q, \langle \alpha_1, \ldots, \alpha_n \rangle \rangle$, we now instead have:

'If $\mathrm{Sat}(s', \langle \alpha_1, \ldots, \alpha_n \rangle)$ and $O'(z, \langle s' \langle \alpha_1, \ldots, \alpha_n \rangle \rangle, t)$ etc., z is in $\mathrm{Bel}'[\langle s', \langle \alpha_1, \ldots, \alpha_n \rangle \rangle, z, t]$'.

Suppose α is a candidate for being denoted by '$\mathrm{Bel}[p, z, t]$' and '$\mathrm{Bel}'[s, z, t]$' where s is p's expression in L. The old and new input conditions impose logically equivalent constraints on α: the former

---

[3] The idea of observational relations to sentences may appear odd. But the general idea is in terms of spatial and sensory relations to objects and spatial regions that stand in our Sat relation to the appropriate sentences of L. Think of the observation sentences as syntactically subclassified in form and constituent predicates. For example, let K contain sentences of the form 'there before me is an F', where the relevant F's are Sat only by objects of types we expect normal people to recognize as such in normal circumstances – 'cat', 'house', 'hill', through a finite list of simple predicates and their conjunctions ('black cat') up to some limit of recognitional abilities. Then $\ulcorner O'(z, s, t) \urcorner$ for the K sentences means 'if $s = \ulcorner$there's an $F \urcorner$ then $O'(z, s, t)$ iff, for some object x such that Sat $(\ulcorner Fy \urcorner, x,)$, z is spatially and sensorily related to x thus and so.' That other observation sentences can be treated roughly in that manner seems safe enough. As '$O'(z, s, t)$' has been defined, it entails that s is true, or rather T. I have chosen to treat the truth of s as a separate clause of the input law to make its point and presence as clear as possible.

requires that if p were true and $O(z, p, t)$, z would be in α at t, and the latter that if Ts and $O'(z, s, t)$, z would be in α at t. But $\ulcorner p$ is true$\urcorner$ and $\ulcorner Ts \urcorner$ are logically equivalent, as are $\ulcorner O(z, p, t) \urcorner$ and $\ulcorner O'(z, s, t) \urcorner$. Hence the old and new conditions are logically equivalent (relative to their ontologies).

Consider a family of first-order states that are candidates for being z's possible beliefs at t (under a certain assignment). The old input conditions plus internal constraints and the new input conditions plus internal constraints impose logically equivalent requirements on that family of first-order states — the same counterfactual connections of beliefs with perceptual input and with each other.

Finally, the output condition in the old theory has the form 'if z is at t in Wills[[y does A], z, t] and in Able[[y does A], z, t] then [y does A] is true of z at t'. On the definition of Sat envisaged, '[y does A] is true of y at t' is always logically equivalent to 'Sat('y does A', z, t)', where 'y does A' is the expression in L of [y does A]. Substituting open sentences for propositional functions and 'Sat' for 'true of' produces a strongly equivalent output condition.

How can non-intensional Tarski-type predicates replace propositional truth and satisfaction? Think of a Tarski-type truth predicate as abstractly correlating sentences, syntactically described, with independent states of affairs. That correlation is in its way arbitrary; infinitely many non-equivalent truth predicates are definable on a given language. Now I hasten to add that states of affairs, as entities, are not introduced by T; for 'Ts iff...' does not assert a relation between s and something named by '...'; it says that s satisfies T just in case .... But speaking of states of affairs may clarify two important points. (1) The association established by T between syntactic objects and certain conditions is as formal and abstract as the functions from sentences to propositions that count as languages in formal semantics. (2) Even when T is homophonic, its point here is not to be a disquotation device; those equivalences associate sentences with non-linguistic conditions. That abstract correlation signifies nothing, of course, except within an appropriate pragmatic framework. In the belief–desire theory, it sums up a correlation between certain functional states and perceptible states of affairs. Since what is needed is something that is given pragmatic significance by being embedded in the functional theory, the non-intensional, non-pragmatic, Tarski-type truth and satisfaction predicates are completely adequate. In the old theory, the intensionality of the construction is superfluous.

The argument for the logical equivalence of the old and new functional theories shows that entities other than sentences will do equally well. Gödel numbers and arithmetical relations on them can isomorphically index internal functional connections, and as regards truth, we merely need a predicate T′ of Gödel numbers such that necessarily s is T iff the Gödel number of s is T′, which results from appropriately imitating the definition of T. So that theory would by my criteria capture everything functional that our commonsense theory captures; but it would look wildly different, so much so that it seems preposterous to count it as an explication. Is this not a *reductio ad absurdum* of my account?

Let us keep in mind what a conservative explication is supposed to do. It is only slightly artificial to explicate our that-clauses as employing structural descriptions of quantificational English; but it is more than a little artificial to take them to employ the Gödelian arithmetical concepts. (Explication is a matter of conceptual replacement; hence, the "inscrutability of reference" is not relevant here.[4]) But once the theorist has become convinced that a successful explication of attitude-ascriptions must merely capture the appropriate interpersonally ascribable functional organization and truth conditions, Gödel numbers could then seem acceptable. The conservativeness of an explication is theorist-relative.

So, while the reconstruction involving Gödel numbers is *logically* equivalent to my reconstruction, we are not forced to accept it as *explicatively* equivalent. There is a nice parallel in the relation of English attitude-sentences to their translations in other languages. Suppose we had a one–one correlation C between Italian and regimented English that intuitively, isomorphically, preserved fine-grained meaning. Let '$s′$' range over Italian. Then we could define 'Bel$_1$' so that whenever $C(s) = s′$, $\mathrm{Bel}[s, z, t] = \mathrm{Bel}_1[s′, z, t]$; and this would be *a priori*. Moreover, there would exist a Tarski-type predicate T′ on Italian such that $\ulcorner T′s′ \urcorner$ is strongly equivalent to $\ulcorner Ts \urcorner$.[5] If the Italian 'credere' is then construed via Bel$_1$, the Italian sentence '*Maria crede che la neve è bianca*' is *strongly* equivalent to 'Maria believes that snow is white', a surprising but satisfying result.[6]

---

[4] Naturally I am assuming that the difference between syntactic and arithmetical *concepts* can be accounted for within my theory of content.

[5] For each pair s and $s′$ there would be some condition $\ulcorner \ldots \urcorner$ such that, if T′ is appropriately defined, $\ulcorner s$ is T iff...$\urcorner$ and $\ulcorner s′$ is T′ iff...$\urcorner$ would follow from the definition of T and T′; hence it would be true that $\square(s$ is T iff...$)$ and $\square(s′$ is T′ iff...$)$.

[6] This assumes that interlinguistic modal equivalence makes sense; but whoever had found a difficulty for sentential theories of attitudes in facts about translation will assume that it makes sense.

There is no problem in the result that a sentence which refers to an Italian sentence (and not to an English sentence) is strongly equivalent to a sentence which refers to an English sentence (and not to an Italian sentence). For it is not by virtue of any *contingent* properties that those sentences figure in the truth conditions of attitude-sentences on my explication; syntactic properties of sentence-types are among their *essential* properties. Evidently, the predication of truth predicates T and T′ on s and s' can be strongly equivalent even though s and s' belong to different languages.

Thus Church's arguments against sentential analyses do not apply here. Suppose a theory implies that $\ulcorner x$ believes that $s\urcorner$ depends on s's *contingent* semantic properties. There are possible worlds in which Columbus believes that the earth is round, but in which 'Columbus believed that the earth is round' would be false, because 'the earth is round' means there: 'smoking causes cancer'. For an analogous reason, '*Colombo credeva che il mondo è rotondo*' would not be strongly equivalent to the English sentence. It is not that these are incontrovertible arguments against semantic-relation theories; but to my theory neither point constitutes even a *prima facie* objection.

Two other points worth clearing up concern synonymy and ambiguity in that-clauses. Suppose some pairs of English sentences, e.g. 'Hume was a bachelor' and 'Hume never married', yield synonymous results in 'x believes that...'. Nothing so far in my theory accounts for that equivalence; but the lack would be easily remedied by adding to the functional theory an M-constraint to the effect that Bel['...bachelor...', z, t] and Bel['...never previously married adult male...', z, t] are always identical.

Suppose that when s is ambiguous so is $\ulcorner x$ believes that $s\urcorner$. No sentential analysis that did not introduce ambiguity into the belief-relation itself can capture that. But if successful explications must match ambiguities with ambiguities, then make 'Bel' suitably ambiguous: first define 'Bel' as if s had only its first reading; then define it again as if s had only its second reading, etc. Then interpret $\ulcorner z$ believes that s at $t\urcorner$ as ambiguous between the two or more readings of $\ulcorner z$ is at t in Bel[s, z, t]$\urcorner$ on those two or more definitions of 'Bel'. Alternatively, the explication might simply eliminate the ambiguity; nothing in the purposes of conservative explication seems to me to rule out such marginal adjustments.

The replacement of propositions by sentences allows capturing fully the functional roles of beliefs and desires. But nothing in the functional theory explains ascribing *truth conditions* to beliefs in general; for non-observational beliefs, functional role is a matter of lateral connections with other attitudes and not of vertical connections with the world. Any adequate theory of belief *content* should, however, account for truth conditions (or at least account for their appearance of relevance).

The explication of attitude-ascriptions so far has relied on nothing about speaker's meaning, or the meaning of a sentence in a certain population; if a theory of truth conditions for beliefs could be carried through on a similarly non-pragmatic–semantic basis, the concept of truth for beliefs would then serve as the foundational concept of truth, with the concepts of the truth of sentences, statements and utterances derivative from it. In recent decades it has been assumed that if the concept of truth for beliefs were basic that would be by virtue of an intensional sort of truth conditions or of some irreducible form of intentionality. Russell and Ramsey (1912, 1927) had sketched a theory that avoided those alternatives, while nevertheless taking the truth of beliefs as basic, but serious logical problems scotched it. (For a reconstruction of Ramsey's theory that meets his basic *desiderata*, along the lines of the theory of this book, see Loar, 1980.)

Tarski's techniques (Tarski, 1956; Quine, 1970b) for assigning truth conditions to sentences elegantly avoid intensionality. It is essential to those techniques, however, that the bearers of truth conditions should have a *structure* that suitably parallels the recursive assignment of truth conditions, and the natural candidates are sentences. But as soon as sentences are seen as the bearers of truth, the idea that interlinguistically ascribed beliefs (not described as sentential attitudes) are the fundamental bearers of truth is quite naturally overshadowed.

On the sentential-index theory of beliefs, however, the situation is radically altered. For to each belief a certain sentence is assigned, but that sentential index is not thereby in the language of the believer. Consequently, the Tarskian apparatus can now be employed in ascribing truth conditions to beliefs, not under their descriptions as sentential attitudes, but as interlinguistically ascribable "propositional" attitudes. Now if T is the appropriate Tarski-type truth predicate for the content language L (i.e. if it captures the preanalytically correct truth conditions), the belief that s is true just in case Ts. The inductive characterization of T thereby gives us an inductive characterization of truth for beliefs. The upshot is that neither ontological nor formal reasons now preclude taking truth for beliefs as the basic truth concept. But there is still a philosophical problem which is not how to represent the truth conditions of beliefs but rather what makes it appropriate to assign them truth conditions; but much more needs to be said about defining 'true' before we can turn to that, in chapter 8.

To get a Tarskian characterization of truth for L there are two strategies. First we may take 'true' as undefined, and lay down axioms which determine under what circumstances each sentence of L is true. For philosophical purposes, this would not count as an explication of 'true'; it is not eliminative. The second strategy is an explicit definition of a predicate T on L, from which, for each sentence s of L, something appropriate of the form $\ulcorner$T$\bar{s}$ iff $p\urcorner$ follows. Tarski showed how to construct such a predicate for any first-order language which is in a certain respect weaker than the metalanguage (so the definition of T is not inconsistent in the manner of the liar paradox). Now in the subsequent treatment, the truth predicate is to be regarded as having a Tarski-type explicit definition; otherwise the reconstruction pre-supposes an unexplicated 'true'. That means some restriction of the beliefs for which truth is explicated, i.e. those beliefs for which the concept is independently unproblematic with regard to the semantic paradoxes. Let us suppose that L, the set of indices of beliefs, has been appropriately restricted. It will be simpler if L belongs to our metalanguage, as well as serving as the set of indices; so let T be the homophonic Tarski-type predicate on L, from whose definition, for each s, something of the form $\ulcorner$T$\bar{s}$ iff $s\urcorner$ follows, where $\bar{s}$ denotes s itself.

A technical point needs to be dealt with. The indices of some beliefs have the form $\langle \ulcorner Fx_1,\ldots,x_n\urcorner, \langle a_1,\ldots,a_n\rangle\rangle$, i.e. are sentential analogues of singular propositions. Let 'Sat' be the homophonic Tarskian satisfaction-relation on L – that is, each instance of the following schema follows from its definition:

$$\text{Sat}(\ulcorner Fx_1,\ldots,x_n\urcorner, \langle a_1,\ldots,a_n\rangle) \text{ iff } Fa_1,\ldots,a_n.$$

Now we can allow T to be also a predicate of those ordered pairs, and extend its definition:

$$\text{T}\langle \ulcorner Fx_1,\ldots,x_n\urcorner, \langle a_1,\ldots,a_n\rangle\rangle = \text{def. } \text{Sat}(\ulcorner Fx_1,\ldots,x_n\urcorner, \langle a_1,\ldots,a_n\rangle)$$

Then we have the following convention about the metalinguistic '$\bar{s}$' and 's': their instances may be either names of sentences and sentences, respectively, or names of ordered pairs of the form '$\langle \ulcorner Fx_1,\ldots,x_n \urcorner, \langle a_1,\ldots,a_n \rangle \rangle$' and sentences of the form $\ulcorner Fa_1,\ldots,a_n \urcorner$, respectively. We can then count the schema '$T\bar{s}$ iff s' as covering not only the expected cases but also all instances of

$$T\langle \ulcorner Fx_1,\ldots,x_n \urcorner, \langle a_1,\ldots,a_n \rangle \rangle \text{ iff } Fa_1,\ldots,a_n.$$

The theory of truth for beliefs may begin with this observation: $\ulcorner$*the belief that $\bar{s}$ is true* $\urcorner$ (where 'true' is the preanalytic term) *is strongly equivalent to* $\ulcorner T\bar{s} \urcorner$ (where T is the explicitly defined truth predicate). This can be shown as follows. For every $\bar{s}$, $\ulcorner$the belief that $\bar{s}$ is true iff $s \urcorner$ holds necessarily; this seems uncontroversial. But $\ulcorner T\bar{s}$ iff $s \urcorner$ also holds necessarily for every $\bar{s}$, since it follows from the definition of T. Given that 'true' and T have nothing in their extensions apart from beliefs and sentences of L respectively, it follows from the universal necessary truth of each schema that the equivalence above holds. It can hardly be over-emphasized how important this simple fact is in the general theory of truth: it means that in a very strong sense Tarski's construction solves the definitional problem of truth. (Later I discuss the question of redundancy and correspondence; here we may simply observe that the equivalence just noted constitutes a sort of redundancy theory; but that is compatible with a strong sort of correspondence theory.) So we have, it would seem, a full explication of attitude-ascriptions and of truth-ascriptions: 'z's belief that $\bar{s}$ is true' is explicated as 'z is in $Bel[\bar{s}, z, t]$, and $T\bar{s}$'.

But nothing in this explication answers our initial question: if truth conditions are irrelevant to specifications of functional role, what makes it *appropriate* to ascribe them? Indeed that this question is not thereby answered might make one sceptical of the claim that the Tarski construction in that way strongly captures the basic concept of truth.

Suppose our problem were different. We are presented, let us say, with speakers whose sentences are syntactically English, and we want to know how to understand them. We have at our command the Tarski predicate T, and we know that their sentence 'snow is white' is T iff snow is white, etc. Does this help us to interpret their sentences? No, indeed. For all we know, that sentence, *qua* sentence of theirs, is *false* iff snow is white; or perhaps the T-condition of that sentence corresponds to no interesting semantic properties of it as they use it. Our only information about them, we are supposing, is syntactic; what 'snow is white' means in their mouths depends upon substantial further facts about their individual behavior and psychology, social interactions, causal connections with natural kinds, etc. The Tarski predicate contains no such information; it says nothing specifically about those speakers.

If one has this sort of thing in mind, the strong equivalence of the Tarski predicate T on $\bar{s}$ and the truth of the belief that $\bar{s}$ could be surprising, for nothing in the specification of the functional roles of (non-observational) beliefs requires truth conditions. It could then seem that whatever explicates 'true' for beliefs must contain pragmatic information about a belief other than its functional role – e.g. its other causal connections with the world, etc.; the Tarski predicate contains no such information.

The resolution of this problem has to be, I think, as follows. While specifying functional roles requires no general assignment of truth conditions, the functional role of a belief strongly determines its truth conditions in this sense: for reasons to be investigated, we associate certain conditions with beliefs which we *dub* 'truth' conditions. Perhaps this will help. There are infinitely many functions from sentences to sets of possible worlds. For whatever reason, we pick out one such function and dub it '$\mathcal{T}$'. We then define a new predicate 'true' on beliefs thus: 'the belief that $\bar{s}$, that functional state, is true' = def. '$\mathcal{T}(\bar{s}) = p$ and the actual world belongs to p'. Even though $\mathcal{T}$ and 'true' play no role in specifying it, the functional role of a given belief strongly determines its 'truth' conditions, but that is due simply to how we defined 'true'. The interesting philosophical problem is then to explain the apotheosis of $\mathcal{T}$ or the Tarskian predicate T. But as regards the *explication* of 'the belief that $\bar{s}$ is true', nothing further needs to be said; the theory of that-clauses as denoting indices of functional roles, coupled with the Tarskian construction, gives us an eliminative theory of 'true'.

The argument has two premises: first, that $\ulcorner z$ is at t in $\text{Bel}[\bar{s}, z, t]\urcorner$ is an adequate explication of $\ulcorner z$ believes at t that $\bar{s}\urcorner$, and secondly that $\ulcorner z$'s belief that $\bar{s}$ is true$\urcorner$ is strongly equivalent to $\ulcorner T\bar{s}\urcorner$. What gives us the second premiss is that we always have both $\ulcorner \Box$ the belief that $\bar{s}$ is true iff $s\urcorner$ and $\ulcorner \Box$ T$\bar{s}$ iff $s\urcorner$, and that 'true' has in its extension nothing but such beliefs. (The reason why, while T is adequate in explicating the truth of beliefs, T is inadequate in explicating truth for the sentences of those speakers of syntactic English, is then simply that we do not have: $\ulcorner \Box$ the sentence $\bar{s}$ as they use it is true iff $s\urcorner$.)

There are two points about how functional role "determines" truth conditions that need explanation. First consider indexical beliefs, e.g. beliefs that are self-ascriptive. Suppose Jones and Smith each believes that he himself is clever; their beliefs are equivalent functionally but not in truth conditions. Consequently, for such beliefs, it is better to say that functional roles "determine" (in the relevant sense) *satisfaction* conditions. That indeed is how the definition works out, for when you consider how T was introduced earlier for beliefs in "singular propositions", truth for self-ascriptive beliefs comes to this:

a's belief that a-self is F is true = def. Sat(F, a).

Secondly, are truth conditions, on this account, attached to the functional role of a belief, or rather to the belief's *index*? This would be unattractive, for the assignment of indices is arbitrary. It is important in the next chapter that truth conditions correspond to objective properties of functional states, regardless of how they are described. Consider the following alternative indexing scheme. Let f be a one–one function from sentences of L to sentences of L, and let f-Bel be a function from triples $\langle s', z', t' \rangle$ to first-order states such that, for all s, z, t, Bel$[s, z, t] = f$-Bel$[f(s), z, t]$. Given that truth conditions are assigned to beliefs according to their functional roles, z's belief that s is true iff z's f-belief that $f(s)$ is true, which is captured by a truth predicate T' such that $\square$ T'$f(\check{s})$ iff T$\check{s}$. Given that f is not identity, T' is not homophonic, but it is nonetheless adequate, for we have: $\square$ z's f-belief that $\check{s}'$ is true iff T'$\check{s}'$ iff T$\check{s}$ iff z's belief that $\check{s}$ is true.

So our favorite truth predicate T captures the truth conditions of beliefs only relative to our favorite system of indices. But that does not mean that a belief's truth conditions are relative to a conventionally chosen system of indexing; the belief that $\check{s}$ and the f-belief that $f(\check{s})$ have the same truth conditions – they are the same belief. What depends on the system of indexing is which truth predicate succeeds in associating with a belief, *via* its index, the truth conditions that it can be taken to have *invariably* under all systems of indexing. The question of the next chapter is what makes the usual truth conditions special, but I shall put it in terms of what makes T special, which naturally presupposes our favorite system of indices. It will be convenient to use T as a predicate, both of sentences of L and of beliefs: a belief b is T iff b = the belief that $\check{s}$ and T$\check{s}$.

T is defined without independent semantic terms. In the basis of a Tarski truth definition, where simple predicates are assigned satisfaction conditions, the procedure is purely enumerative: the individual y satisfies 'F' just in case either 'F' = 'x is a dog' and y is a dog, or 'F' = 'x is a bat' and y is a bat, and so throughout the finite list of basic predicates; this partially defines 'satisfies'. Hartry Field has argued

(Field, 1972) that a Tarski construction with such an enumerative basis does not adequately explicate 'true', and he proposes a new construction on which an independent semantic concept, "primitive denotation", is used (but not explicated): 'dog' primitively denotes y iff y is a dog, etc. It is true that a pure Tarski predicate does not adequately explicate 'true' for *sentences* if it is not embedded in something pragmatic, as with those speakers of syntactic English. Now as I have used T, it is embedded in something pragmatic in a sense: '$\text{Bel}[s, z, t]$' is defined so that s is associated with a certain functional role. But T itself correlates belief indices and "truth conditions" in a purely abstract and even arbitrary way; it does not capture any causal, etc., basis for the association. But my argument has been that it does not have to in order to capture strongly the concept of truth for beliefs; the argument is solid for the pure Tarski predicate. (It may help to keep in mind that, *qua* systems of indices, we treat L as having a special status; it is not just one among many languages.) So finally the point is that we must distinguish the adequacy of an explication of 'true' for beliefs from that of an explanation of the point of 'true'.

There is an intuitive conception of the truth of beliefs that goes back to Russell and Ramsey; it can be expressed in terms of three conditions. The first is complex: something objective about a belief, independent of the believer's language, determines its truth conditions and its details are captured by the that-clause. Second, beliefs are not relations to Meinongian objectives, Fregean senses, etc. Third, belief can serve as the foundation of the theory of meaning; their ascriptions are then not to be explicated in terms of (pragmatic) semantic relations to the sentences or utterances of the ascriber. One difficulty in vindicating that conception has been how to capture, in a finite way, truth conditions for beliefs of all logical forms (cf. Loar, 1980). The difficulty is overcome on this way of applying Tarski to beliefs; that is, I suggest, a further argument for interpreting that-clauses as denoting *indices* of functional roles – indices that are sentences or complexes involving sentences. As indices they are interlinguistically ascribable but, being linguistic, they serve as the basis for applying the unproblematic apparatus of Tarskian semantics to beliefs. By virtue of their syntactic structure, they have enabled us to capture functional generalizations, and now truth conditions. Both functional roles and truth conditions are independent of the indexing system; but for their structured *expression and systematization* a particular assignment of sentences needs to be invoked, and that is what 'believes that s' achieves.

Hilary Putnam has argued against the classical view that meaning, or (what is relevant here) truth conditions, are determined by psychological (or functional) states (Putnam, 1973). One sense of that I have already emphasized: functional roles in general do not explain truth conditions. But Putnam's point goes further, and apparently conflicts with something implied in the previous section – namely that whatever the motivation for assigning truth conditions to functional roles, there is just one way of doing it (regardless of differences in environment, etc.).

Suppose on Twin Earth there are people like us, who speak "English" and have similar beliefs; but the stuff they call 'water', that they bathe in, that fills their lakes and oceans, is not H_2O "but a different liquid whose chemical formula is very long and complicated" which we may abbreviate as 'XYZ'. From the non-expert point of view XYZ is indistinguishable from water, and whatever in general we non-expert Earthlings believe when we think 'water', non-expert Twin Earthlings also believe. In short, they are in many of the same relevant functional states as us. Now to apply Putnam's point to the current context, it seems the truth conditions of their beliefs are different from those of ours. For their beliefs that 'water is...' are true iff XYZ is such and such, while ours are true iff H_2O is such and such. Consequently, functional role seems not to "determine" truth conditions, even in the sense of the previous section. For the Twin Earth example appears to show that truth conditions are not assignable to functional roles in one standard way, but depend on facts (perhaps about reliability, and causal relations to natural kinds) that may *vary* while functional role remains constant.

Now despite the intuitiveness of this, it is not so clear what Twin Earth considerations in fact show about the relation between functional role and truth conditions. Much depends on how we construe beliefs about natural kinds; Putnam's point rests on assuming that a certain natural theory – a description theory in fact – is false. Let me first present that theory, and then discuss what is to be said if we reject it. What makes 'gold' true of x is not those observable features of x that allow us to recognize x as gold, but rather x's belonging to a certain natural kind. There are several possible views about how 'gold' is related to the natural kind it denotes. One is that some causal relation constitutes reference; another is that 'gold's' reference depends on what the experts hold. A usual concomitant view is that 'gold', as we use it, is a *rigid designator*, that it picks out the same stuff in every possible world (in which it refers). This means it is not equivalent to any description that is only contingently true of gold.

The point is that reference to the natural kind, rather than the observable properties, is compatible with a *description* theory, e.g., one on which 'gold' means 'the natural kind our experts call 'gold''. What about the rigid designator claim? Consider a statement like: 'If English had not been our language this thing would not have been made of gold.' This is, on normal assumptions, false, and so the rigid designator theory counts it; but doesn't the description theory count it true? Not if the description theory takes such terms normally to have *wider scope* than the counterfactual modality, for then it says: 'the natural kind K which our experts call 'gold' is such that if English had not been our language this thing would not have belonged to K', which is false. But consider 'Gold is called 'gold' by our experts.' The description theory marks it as *analytic*, and therefore as *necessary* – true in all possible worlds in which the description is satisfied. The proper reaction is, I suggest: so what? It does not follow that gold is called 'gold' by our experts in all possible worlds; for that amounts to 'the stuff called gold by our experts is in all possible worlds called gold by our experts', which we all agree is false. That is, (A) 'Gold is called 'gold' by our experts' is true in all possible worlds, does not imply, on the description theory, (B) Gold, in all possible worlds, is called 'gold' by our experts. For in (B) (the theory goes) the definite description equivalent to 'gold' has wider scope than the quantifier 'in all possible worlds', whereas in (A) 'gold' is confined within quotes. Thus the metalinguistic description theory has no untoward metaphysical consequences; (A) is harmless and there seem to be no considerations that have *independent* standing and imply its falsity.

Back then to Twin Earth. This description theory implies that, say, 'water is plentiful on Twin Earth' contains an indexical: it means 'the stuff *our* experts call 'water' is plentiful on Twin Earth'. Now on *classical* theories of meaning, that, as said by Twin Earthlings, is true, and as said by us, false; 'water' in their mouths refers to XYZ, and in our mouths to H_2O. Naturally functional role does not then determine exactly *truth* conditions; it determines (as in all indexical cases) the *satisfaction* conditions of the predicates of the fully spelled out beliefs.

But, for all that, is the metalinguistic theory plausible? I daresay it will seem unattractive to many contemporary ears, despite the absence of a metaphysical refutation. What are the consequences then of the rigid designator theory for the connection between functional role and truth conditions, given the Twin Earth case? In 8.3, I suggest that the real-world reliability of our beliefs under the truth predicate T explains our promoting T to a special status. The idea is not that you consider the reliability of each person's beliefs, but rather the reliability of the society's beliefs (given certain procedures in stable environmental conditions). If 'water' is a rigid designator, the Twin Earth case shows that the reliability facts about a given society's beliefs that determine our assignment of truth conditions must be relative to their environment, a rather natural constraint. (This would carry over to subsentential reference, given the theory of reference in 9.9.) Then functional role does not "determine" truth conditions *simpliciter*.

This is all in the spirit of my account, but there is a problem. I claimed that the pure Tarskian predicate T can be used to explicate 'the belief that $\bar{s}$ is true' – i.e. that the latter is strongly equivalent to T $\bar{s}$. But 'the belief that $\bar{s}$' denotes a second-order state, and that would seem to mean that, necessarily, the second-order state Twin Earthlings are in when they assent to 'water is plentiful on this planet' is true iff H_2O is plentiful on Twin Earth, which gives the wrong truth conditions.

But consider. Are we obliged to treat those conditions which, given the rigid designator theory, we are inclined to assign to Twin Earthlings' beliefs, as the conditions under which they are *true*, in the sense in which we call Earthlings' beliefs true? Suppose we say that, while of course we would use the word 'true' to abbreviate those conditions, in each case it demands a distinct explication. Both predicates may, in relation to their respective populations and worlds, correspond to associations of functional states and possible states of affairs that share a common feature: the former are reliable indicators (within certain parameters to be specified in 8.3) of the latter. (I assume that Twin Earthlings are supposed to be like us in this respect.) So it is not *arbitrary* which conditions we choose to express via 'x is true iff...' in the two cases. But what the predicates have in common, relative to Earth and Twin Earth, is registered at the metalevel. Thus we may distinguish the theory of 'true', on a given use, from the theory of what makes a predicate a 'truth predicate' for a population-world pair. And we may want to use the term *truth conditions* so that it is defined univocally at the metalevel.

Before considering two somewhat obvious objections, I would like to clarify two points. First, this proposal in no way reneges on the goal of explicating a univocal *interlinguistic* truth predicate – a foundation for a univocal 'true in *P*', for variable '*P*'. If the theory of communication provides for the meaning of some sentences of *P* to be a function of a certain relation between them and the beliefs of members of *P*, then a univocal 'true' for all Earthling beliefs gives us a univocal 'true in *P*' when '*P*' ranges over populations of Earthling speakers. So the proposal does not proliferate senses of 'true' as applied to real world beliefs, utterances or sentences.

Second, I am not sure that it is possible to state fully general conditions for a given T*'s being 'the correct truth predicate' for *every* arbitrary population-world pair, regardless of that population's conceptual organization, and degree of reliability as indicators of a broad range of facts about their world. Our doppelgangers on Twin Earth are meant to be like us in all relevant respects, except for the interchange of natural kinds, and thus it is not surprising that our intuitions about the truth conditions of their beliefs are relatively unproblematic. But, if conceptual organization and degree of reliability (relative to the most favorable assignment of truth conditions that roughly satisfies the parameters of 8.3) were quite different for the former, and unimpressive for the latter, it is not obvious that applying any truth predicate would be motivated either intuitively or theoretically, at least without a far greater degree of arbitrariness than seems to be present in our case (cf. 8.3).

Two objections to the proposal that 'true' is equivocal for Earth and Twin Earth have perhaps occurred to the reader. (A) Is this not *ad hoc* – simply a way of slipping past a good objection? (B) Shouldn't what those truth-predicates have in common in relation to those population-world pairs be part of a univocal conception of truth? These may be answered together. I suggest that there are just three possible approaches to explicating truth conditions against the background of the functional theory and the reliability factors that are explained in 8.3. (1) 'True' is a theoretical-explanatory concept, whose meaning is determined by its role in some theory that incorporates or predicts the reliability facts. (2) The notion of reliability is built into the meaning of '*x*'s belief that such and such is true iff *p*', e.g. something like: 'For some truth predicate T* under which the beliefs of *x*'s society are in *x*'s world reliable, *x*'s belief that such and such is T* iff *p*'. (3) We take the Tarski predicate to capture 'true', and therefore take 'true' to be equivocal as predicated of beliefs on Earth and on Twin Earth, given the rigid designator assumption.

As for (1), it seems just false that 'true' is an *explanatory* concept in some theory about the reliability of beliefs. Quite disparate facts about belief-forming processes and about the independent worldly facts will conjointly be involved in explaining reliability under T. As regards (2), building reliability into the definition of 'true' implies that we cannot imagine a way in which it might have turned out that our beliefs were not true to anything like the extent they are. Any reasons for rejecting an *a priori* status for tendencies among our beliefs to be true, in the sense in which we apply that predicate to them, are reasons for rejecting this approach. So that leaves (3), which is then, against this background, hardly *ad hoc*.

Does functional role then 'determine' truth conditions? In a way it does, but not because there is some intrinsic connection. Moreover, we had better say that functional role determines $truth_1$ conditions and $truth_2$ conditions and so on. There is no inconsistency here, for the belief that s can be $true_1$ iff H_2O is such and such *and* $true_2$ iff XYZ is such and such.

If we were to visit Twin Earth as anthropologists (who hold the rigid designator theory, know about XYZ, etc.), we probably would want to index Twin Earthlings' beliefs, those functional states, differently from ours. Suppose we called XYZ twin-water. Then, perhaps, it would be natural to call a certain belief of theirs the belief that one bathes in twin-water, the functional state, that is, which among us we call the belief that one bathes in water. The upshot would be that we could then use our homophonic Tarski predicate T to capture the 'truth' conditions of their beliefs. But it would capture an assignment of truth conditions to functional roles that is different from ours, and so generate a distinct truth predicate on those functional roles, given the shifting of indices.

What impact does this have on the explication of 'believes'? If we shift indices to preserve the redundancy of 'true', then we have, not only '$true_1$' and '$true_2$', but also 'Bel_1' and 'Bel_2', so that, for example, Bel_1 ['one bathes in water', z, t] = Bel_2 ['one bathes in twin-water', z, t]. Thus 'believes' stands systematically for different such functions (captures different ways of indexing the relevant functional roles) in a way that matches the use of 'true' for different truth predicates. Outside science fiction, on Earth, this matters not at all, for we do very well with '$true_1$' and 'Bel_1'.

On the sentential index theory, only the *syntactic* properties of indices come into the definition of Bel. Without the foregoing account of truth it might have appeared that 'z is in Bel$[s, z, t]$' cannot capture 'z has the belief that s', for the latter holds only if z has a belief with certain truth conditions, while the former does not depend on the ascribed state's having any particular "truth conditions". But as we may well say, it is part of the meaning of '*true*' that certain functional states have certain truth conditions, even though the latter need not be mentioned in specifying the former. Consequently, from 'z is at t in Bel$[s, z, t]$' it *does* follow that z is in a state that is true iff such and such.

But the explication still appears not to satisfy a natural constraint – that the *meaning* of $\ulcorner x$ believes that $s\urcorner$ must somehow be a function of the meaning of s; or perhaps that understanding the former requires understanding the latter. Frege's theory satisfies this condition preeminently; but what about my functional theory? It seems one could understand what functional state is ascribed by $\ulcorner x$ believes that $s\urcorner$ without understanding s, for all that is relevant to the definition of Bel are the syntactic properties of s; hence the theory fails that intuitive requirement. But suppose the assignment of truth conditions is an important ingredient of our *use* of the functional theory (cf. chapter 8). Then we could say one has not really "*understood*" 'z believes that s' *unless one has mastered that assignment of truth conditions to functional roles*. In other words, the sense of "understanding 'z believes that s'" appropriate to the intuitive constraint simply incorporates "knowing the truth conditions" of the belief thereby ascribed. Given that the content language is also part of the metalanguage, truth conditions are captured by the homophonic truth predicate T; but that means that to "understand" 'x believes that s' one must understand 'Ts iff s', and, since s is used and not mentioned on the right hand side, that means that one must understand s.

7.6 POSSIBLE-WORLD TRUTH CONDITIONS

On classical intuitions a belief's content involves its conditions of truth in any possible state of affairs. This has sometimes been captured by taking a belief's object to be the set of possible worlds in which it is true, or something more fine-grained that determines that set. There is something intuitive in the idea that a belief's content determines its possible-world truth conditions; the question arises whether, on the nonintensional theory of content, that intuition is accommodated.

My answer is unreservedly yes; a Tarski predicate on beliefs does a lot more than determine their truth *values*. So if Ts iff snow is white, and Ts' iff grass is green, T determines one truth value for s and s', but those equivalences evidently do not say the same thing. Indeed while nothing intensional is involved in T, the belief that s and the belief that s' are assigned different possible-world truth conditions *by* T; for (if one invokes possible worlds) there are worlds in which the belief that s and the belief that s' differ in respect of being T. Introducing possible worlds into the *objects* of beliefs cannot improve upon *that* difference between those beliefs.

The point is not that some modal or intensional notion is explicated on my theory of belief. Rather the situation is this. Suppose a philosopher is assessing the explication in an intensional metalanguage, and wants to require that the explication provide the means for generating predicates of beliefs such that any two beliefs differ in possible-world truth conditions (as judged by intensional intuitions) *iff* they satisfy intensionally distinct such predicates. Now my explication of truth conditions satisfies that intensional adequacy condition even though *it* employs no intensional concepts, the relevant predicates being those of the form ⌐is true iff s⌐.

Why then has it seemed plausible that intensionality is to be built into the objects of belief? The explanation lies in a certain preconception about belief *individuation*. Suppose one thought that to understand what a belief-ascription ascribes to a belief is *just* to understand its possible-world truth conditions, and, say for Church's reasons, one rejected semantic-relation analyses. Then one would have to take the that-clause to capture the belief's truth conditions by somehow *denoting* them. Now of course the purely extensional Tarski-type truth construction does not yield an entity with which then to identify truth conditions; what occurs on the right hand side of 's is true iff...' is a sentence and not a name. Thus, taking the content of a belief to be nothing more than its truth conditions leads to making them into an abstract entity.

But beliefs are individuated not by truth conditions but by functional roles. To take that-clauses to denote indices of suitably individuated functional roles eliminates the need for taking truth conditions to do the individuating. Then the Tarski predicate perfectly captures, in the only form there is any preanalytic reason for wanting, possible-world truth conditions. The inadequacy of extensional truth-condition semantics as a complete theory of meaning is due, not to any failure in capturing intensional refinements in truth conditions, but rather to its not yielding *individuation* conditions for content and meaning. Because they are a matter of functional role, to which intensions are irrelevant, that inadequacy is not to be remedied by introducing possible worlds.

7.7 REDUNDANCY AND CORRESPONDENCE

The foregoing account of truth is a kind of redundancy theory, of which it will be useful to have an explicit characterization. Let "$\Phi\ldots$" stand for expressions that refer to bearers of truth conditions, e.g. 'z's belief that$\ldots$', or 'z's statement that$\ldots$', or the sentence '$\ldots$' itself. On a redundancy theory (within restrictions required by the Liar), there is a strong equivalence between '$\Phi\ldots$ is true' and '$\ldots$', or better, we have all instances of '$\square$ if $\Phi\ldots$ exists, then $\Phi\ldots$ is true iff $\ldots$'. This is *case by case* redundancy, and my account evidently yields it; for the bearers of truth conditions are denoted by 'z's belief that s', and ⌜necessarily if z believes that $\bar{s}$ then z's belief that $\bar{s}$ is true iff s⌝ holds for all cases. The *homophonic* aspect of the criterion is not the main point; what really matters is that the predication of truth is *strongly equivalent* to something that contains no mention of truth and its bearers (except when the bearer of truth has semantic subject matter). So if for some peculiar reason we wished to adopt a non-standard indexing scheme, we could have '$\square$ z's f-belief that $f(\bar{s})$ is true iff s' ($f(\bar{s}) \neq \bar{s}$) and yet still have case by case redundancy in the sense that matters.

While for some philosophical purposes case by case redundancy is enough, one can hardly say 'true' is redundant unless it is eliminable from all contexts, including those in which '$\ldots$' is not explicitly given, as in 'his theory of quasars has turned out to be true'. A redundancy theory explicates 'true' eliminatively in all contexts and implies case by case redundancy. My theory is a redundancy theory, thanks to the Tarski predicate T, for 'z's belief b is true' is explicated by '$b = \text{Bel}[\bar{s}, z, t]$' and T$\bar{s}$. This is genuinely eliminative; nothing in the definition of T or Bel is from among the problematic concepts that include 'true'.

It is perhaps worth remarking that Tarski-type constructions may well be essential to any unproblematic redundancy theory. The alternative seems to be to use higher-order variables in Ramsey's style, thus: the belief that p is true iff p, or, the belief that aRb is true iff aRb. Such higher-order quantification appears (to me) to require a first-order gloss, so 'p' and 'R' occur in name positions, thus requiring supplementation: '...iff p is true' '...iff R is true of $\langle a, b \rangle$'. Of course, to intuitions on which second-order quantification is primitively given, the Ramsey formulation is genuinely eliminative, and the Tarski construction would not be the only means to a redundancy theory.

That the Tarski truth definition is the key to a redundancy theory will to many be no surprise, but it may be surprising that it and redundancy are ingredients of a theory of *interlinguistically* ascribable truth. For a common view of the use of Tarskian constructions is as follows. On the one hand we have 'true in L', or better 'true in population P'; on the other, there is the Quinean 'true', a predicate of sentences of our language, an *intralinguistic* disquotation device. As regards the former, one doesn't expect redundancy, that is, a *strong* equivalence between 's is true in P' and some '...'; for that equivalence is always contingent, depending on contingent facts about P, even when $P = $ us. In the latter case, we have genuine redundancy, but nothing interlinguistically ascribable. If 'true in P' is basic, truth conditions depend on social and psychological facts about P. But on the disquotation view, the explication of 'true' is independent of any such facts: 'true' is used to generalize over object-language truths, "...' is true' being a variant of '...'; nothing psychological or social is relevant.

The last point is worth elaborating. That 'true' can be an intralinguistic disquotation device, implying nothing about the use of language or psychology, is demonstrated by the Tarskian definition of T. For consider. The hypothesis is that the function of 'is true' is to be a predicate whose application to a sentence is equivalent to that sentence; this can be put thus: all instances of "'...' is true iff...' are analytic. But all instances of "'...' is T iff...' are analytic as well; they follow from the definition of T. Assuming that 'true' and T have only English sentences in their possible extensions, it follows that 'true' and T are strongly equivalent.

It could then appear that a redundancy theory of 'true' is incompatible with an account that takes pragmatic conditions to be part of the concept. This may be reinforced by a certain view of the relation between redundancy and *correspondence* theories of truth. The concept of truth as correspondence is neither clear nor univocal. For some, mere case-by-case redundancy captures it; the equivalence "'...' is true iff...' mentions words on the left and objects on the right. But on other intuitions something more substantial is required – a *representation*, by language or thought, of the world. There doubtless is more than one such conception of correspondence, but a key ingredient is this. Maps and graphs are representations by virtue of contingent facts of individual or social psychology, and so with the bearers of truth conditions. Truth depends not just on the non-linguistic facts but also on non-trivial pragmatic properties of the bearers of truth, which put them in potential correspondence with the facts. Call this a strong correspondence theory.[7]

The impression could arise that strong correspondence theories and redundancy theories must be incompatible. If it is a contingent fact about x, whether x be sentence, utterance or mental state, that x is true iff..., then the truth of x, it might seem, cannot be *strongly* equivalent to '...'. But there is of course a mistake here; strong correspondence and redundancy are in fact compatible.

The bearers of truth so far are the referents of 'z's belief that...', that is, first-order state-types (sets thereof) which may for these purposes be thought of as mental sentence types. A plausible alternative is to take bearers of truth to be tokens, mental utterances. Either way, the bearers of truth have truth conditions contingently; truth conditions are assigned to functional roles, and it is contingent about first-order states that they have certain functional roles.

But it also happens that 'z's belief that...is true' and '...' are (relative to the belief's existence) strongly equivalent. Thus, we have both:

(1) about z's belief that...it is a contingent fact that it is true iff...;

(2) necessarily, if z believes that...then z's belief that...is true iff....

The former shows that the account is a strong correspondence theory and the latter that it is a redundancy theory. There is no mystery about the compatibility; the contingency in (1) is *de re* and the necessity in (2) is *de dicto*. It is contingent that x is the belief that...; it is necessary that anything satisfying that description is true iff....

I shall call this a *de dicto* redundancy theory. *De re* redundancy theories are not hard to find, that is, where the bearer of a truth condition has it in every world. Propositional theories are pre-eminent

---

[7] An ingredient of classical correspondence theories of truth has been *realism*, the position that the truth of a proposition is not strongly equivalent to any *epistemic* property, that is, about whether it is verifiable, etc. Call that "metaphysical realism" (following Putnam). In the text I am more concerned with another ingredient of the classic correspondence theory, namely semantic realism – the position that truth conditions are properties of their bearers by virtue of certain determinate and contingent facts about them (or about things that stand to them in certain pragmatic relations). Metaphysical and semantic realism are independent; but they conjointly define the strongest classical correspondence theory.

examples; and on a disquotation theory, a sentence-type's truth conditions are the same in every possible world, because T-conditions depend only on syntactic properties, which are essential properties of sentence types.

The most famous redundancy theory is Ramsey's, but what he says in some places makes it a *de re* and in others a *de dicto* theory (Ramsey, 1927). Thus he writes: 'truth...[is] primarily ascribed to propositions'. But this must be a manner of speaking, since propositions are not real entities for Ramsey. But he also says that it is "the mental factor" in a judgment that is true or false, that is, the words towards which one has a "feeling of belief"; it is a contingent fact about them that they are a judgment that such and such, by virtue of their "causal properties". On this second interpretation, Ramsey's redundancy theory is *de dicto*, and counts as a strong correspondence theory.

A possibly oversimplified view of Austin's and Strawson's opposing theories of truth is this. For Austin (1950) truth is predicated of statements, that is, utterances; and in the analysis of a statement's truth, its contingent conventional properties are crucial. For Strawson (1950), truth is predicated of a statement in the sense of what is said – the proposition. Strawson proposes a Ramsey-type redundancy account which is then a *de re* theory, for propositions have their truth conditions non-contingently; he holds contingent conventional properties to come into the picture in the account not of truth but of what statement is made.

It would be a mistake to interpret the issue as turning on redundancy; for it is not difficult to fashion a Ramsey-type *de dicto* redundancy theory from Austin's account. For Austin, (certain) utterances are true just in case the state of affairs correlated with the statement by the "demonstrative conventions" is of a type correlated with the sentence uttered by the "descriptive conventions". Identify states of affairs with place–time pairs $\langle s, t \rangle$, and say an utterance is a statement that Pst provided that P is the relevant type and $\langle s, t \rangle$ the relevant state of affairs. 'True' is then defined in Ramsey's style: a statement that Pst is true iff Pst. This is equivalent to Austin's theory.

The real issue in that dispute was not redundancy, but whether the bearer of truth has truth conditions essentially or contingently – whether the redundancy is *de re* or *de dicto*. Can the apparently important matter of truth as correspondence depend on that? Let us see that there is a much more fundamental conflict between theories of truth. Consider those two theories again. On both we have a redundancy theory. On both a person makes a statement with such and such truth conditions just in case certain conventions, etc., obtain. Regardless of whether truth conditions are contingent or essential properties of their bearers, they are interlinguistically ascribable by virtue of certain contingent social facts. This suggests a more basic divergence between theories of truth – namely between theories of this sort and Quine's disquotation theory. For on Quine's theory truth conditions are not essentially a matter of psychological or social facts at all, and that affects the picture of truth as correspondence. The two theories' fundamental concordance ought to make us regard the *de re* version as *virtually* a correspondence theory, in the sense that certain contingent psychological – social facts are, according to it, necessary for there being something (an utterance that makes a certain statement) that has truth conditions. The disquotation theory, despite having in common with the latter theory that they are both *de re*, differs from it substantially: on it, truth conditions are not a matter of potential correspondence between the linguistic and the extralinguistic by virtue of contingent representational properties of the former.

So, in summary, my account of truth as a property of beliefs – the first-order states – is both a redundancy theory and a strong correspondence theory. The fact that it is a *de dicto* redundancy theory is interesting, but ultimately not crucial to its correspondence status. Even if truth conditions were an *essential* property of, say, the relevant second-order functional states, the theory would still deserve classification as a strong correspondence theory. What matters to truth conditions, as we shall see in 8.5, is a certain striking correlation between contingencies of functional organization and independent features of the world.

8

Why truth?

8.1 TWO UNHELPFUL ANSWERS

'True' as a disquotation device

There is a clear sense in which functional roles "determine" truth conditions, but it rests, trivially perhaps, on the dubbing of T as 'true'. Nothing about the functional roles suggests why we isolate that correlation between beliefs and possible states of affairs as special, still less as justifying the pre-eminence of the concept of truth. That T is *homophonic* is striking, but helpful only given a more basic reason for having such a predicate of functionally described states. The thought occurs that making functional states the primary bearers creates an unreal problem; perhaps characterizing others' beliefs as true is derivative from our intralinguistic use of 'true', that is, as a predicate of our own sentences which is then, rather naturally, transferred to states indexed with them.

What might explain the intralinguistic utility of 'true'? Quine suggests that its role in certain generalizations supplies its *raison d'être*.

> When we want to generalize on 'Tom is mortal or Tom is not mortal', 'Snow is white or snow is not white', and so on, we ascend to talk of truth and of sentences, saying 'Every sentence of the form 'p or not p' is true'...' What prompts this semantic ascent is not that 'Tom is mortal or Tom is not mortal' is somehow about sentences while 'Tom is mortal' and 'Tom is Tom' are about Tom. All these are about Tom. We ascend only because of the oblique way in which the instances over which we are generalizing are related to one another. (Quine, 1970b.)

As an explanation of the *point* of 'true', this leaves me puzzled. Evidently 'when we want to *generalize*...' does not bear its meaning on its face. One way of generalizing with regard to sentences of the form '*p* or not *p*' is to say we would *accept* all instances; but that does not require 'true'. No, 'we want to generalize' must mean "with regard to their *truth*". But how does that tell us what is important about truth? Why do we *want* to generalize in terms of T and not some other T'? Why *any* truth predicate?

Quine goes on to say:

> By calling the sentence ['snow is white'] true we call snow white. The truth predicate is a device of disquotation. We may affirm the single sentence just by uttering it, unaided by quotation or by the truth predicate; but if we want to affirm some infinite lot of sentences that we can demarcate only by talking about the sentences, then the truth predicate has its use. We need it to restore the effect of objective reference when for the sake of some generalization we have resorted to semantic ascent.

The idea is to descend from semantic ascent. Consider this reply. If we want to affirm some infinite lot of sentences, why not simply say that we would affirm any sentence of such and such form? Again, no need for 'true'. But again, 'to affirm some infinite lot of sentences' is really supposed to mean 'to say they are all true'. But how does that explain what is special about 'true' nor T? What about the need "to restore the effect of objective reference"? This does not get us very far. Either we "restore the effect of reference" to non-linguistic objects by saying something in the object language; or, if we want to "generalize" in a way that can't be done in the object language – i.e. with respect to the *truth* of an infinite lot of sentences, we use 'true'. But, to reiterate, that does not explain what is of interest about truth.

It is clear that I accept a kind of redundancy theory. So, what I am resisting about Quine's account is not the emphasis on equivalences of the form "'...' is true iff...', which are indeed central to the meaning of 'true', but rather the idea that we have in them a *motivation* for having a truth predicate. I do not wish to deny that there is something intuitive in looking to the first-person case for an explanation of the interest of 'true' or T. But we must ask why generalizations about our own sentences are not theoretically on a par with those about the sentences of others; short of an answer, foundational questions about truth should be about the third-person case.

The principle of charity

Davidson (1974) has suggested that in ascribing truth conditions we should thereby maximize truth. But why should *charity* be constitutive of truth conditions? Perhaps this is the intended picture. Ascribing truth conditions is essential to achieving a certain understanding of others, of a different sort from our understanding non-mental aspects of the world. It is essential that we see others' thoughts and desires as reasonably like our own, and that means their beliefs should largely be true by our lights.

This is radically different from the functional theory, and I shall not undertake a comparative evaluation here. My point is not to assess the merits of the principle of charity in the setting of Davidson's account, but to consider whether it illuminates the problem of truth conditions on the functional theory. What gets said on Davidson's theory and on mine are commensurable only if sentential attitudes are suitably related to propositional attitudes, and the obvious idea is that what x believes is determined by the functional role of what x accepts. But then my theory could force us to be *uncharitable* in how we assess truth conditions to an individual x's sentences; there may be no room for charity. For it is determinate what functional role x's accepting $s^\star$ has, and so it is determinate, for some s, that x's acceptance of $s^\star$ is a belief that s. But there is no further question of how to assign truth conditions; a theory that implied that the most reasonable way of understanding x requires *denying* that x's belief that s is true iff s, would be an odd theory indeed. Naturally this is no objection to Davidson, who would say that whether x believes that s depends on a prior choice of truth predicate for x's sentences. But on my account the *choice* of truth predicate (for members of our society) is not separate from the ascription of functional states.

If the principle of charity is to help, then it must explain why we ascribe truth conditions to functional roles, and, in particular, why T? Suppose it is said that the motivation for selecting T is that it maximizes truth. But that does not explain why maximizing *truth* is of interest. Presumably we must look to that special kind of understanding. Now, if the motivation is to make others enough like us to be comprehensible, why aren't functional states enough? They, after all, capture others' *reasons* for their beliefs and decisions and enable us to translate their sentences into ours. Suppose it is said that knowing reasons implies knowing truth conditions, that we would not *understand* them unless we knew what their beliefs were *about*. This merely raises the problem under another guise: what is so special about truth conditions that makes us interested in the "reasons" of others? In some form the question must be faced; the principle of charity (and the concept of *verstehen*) sheds no independent light.

The problem is not how to explicate truth. Within restrictions that isolate the destructive impact of the liar, the Tarski predicate T (or some ascending sequence of suitably related predicates) is all we need. The question is rather why we are interested in truth. Put that way it could mislead – could suggest this: our interest in truth is our interest in how the world is, our reasons being as various as our reasons for wanting to know how cold it is outside, when dinner will be ready, and so on. But my question is about the beliefs of others. There we have certain organisms with certain functional states; here is a predicate T of these states that plays a central role in how we think about those organisms. What makes T *salient*?

A Tarskian truth definition sums up an infinite correlation of sentences and possible states of affairs. It does this in a structured way, but that is not what makes T special, since other truth predicates sum up different correlations in equally structured ways. With this *correlative* function of Tarskian constructions in mind, let me suggest that we should not think of truth as a *theoretical* predicate whose meaning is elucidated by its explanatory role. Truth is simply T-hood; its meaning is independent of any explanatory role. Let us see the correlation it embodies as an abstraction from a certain *empirically interesting* fact, which requires explanation; then T is not part of any *explanans* but part of an *explanandum*.

The salience of T could be accounted for if we identified such an empirically interesting fact. Now it is too narrow to ask simply what makes the concept of truth *useful*. We have mentioned reliability in connection with truth; beliefs formed in certain ways tend to be T, are reliable *under* T. That is a very useful fact, enabling us to infer how the world is from what others believe, i.e. from their functional states. But being useful is not the only way of being interesting. Suppose a certain machine's states are highly *projectibly* reliable under a truth predicate T' where T' is defined on sentences somehow associated with those states; and suppose this reliability turns out to be *informative*. This may not be *useful*, since we may independently be aware of these external facts, which are inferrable via T' from its states. Nevertheless, reliability under T' may be extremely *interesting – because it requires systematic explanation*. So if we put the question about the salience of T as 'what is the *point* of the concept of truth?', we ought not to interpret that too pragmatically.

It has been supposed that truth is specifically connected with communication. No doubt much of our interest in it stems from its essential role there, the Tarski predicate on our interlocutors' utterances playing a substantial role in our inferences from them. Communication, however, is too narrow a setting for the general concept of truth; the *inferential application* of T or 'true' is to be distinguished from those facts about T that are its basis. Now those facts may be seen as facts about functional states, independent of connections with utterances.

Given the irrelevance of the truth predicate to belief–desire functional explanation, truth conditions must somehow depend on other relations to our environment. This is not to say they are not intimately bound up with the application of the functional theory; in addition to reliability, I shall be suggesting, as salience factors for T, its indispensability in inferences to others' beliefs, in calculations about what beliefs to induce in others, in certain ways of thinking about successful action. These considerations show how closely we rely on the truth predicate in applying the belief–desire theory; but they go beyond the constraints that define that functional theory, and are external to it in that sense.

We apply the same truth predicate T to all believers; so the question is not: in what empirically interesting facts about each believer x is T embedded? Individuals who satisfy the belief–desire theory, to whose states we ascribe truth conditions, may deviate, even radically, from those generalizations about our fellows that explain the salience of T. So let us look for T's role in the whole interpersonal class of beliefs.

Naturally a completely satisfactory account would reveal salience properties of T that are possessed by it *uniquely*; and, indeed, key questions about *determinacy* are in effect about such a uniqueness. As we shall see, while T's empirically interesting features do not determine any truth predicate uniquely, even up to logical equivalence, other striking properties of simplicity, etc., are naturally invoked to resolve the problem.

8.3 RELIABILITY AND THE DETERMINACY OF TRUTH CONDITIONS

Informative reliability

It is striking that our beliefs tend to be true in far greater quantity than could be expected simply from their functional roles. This is quite contingent; truth is T-hood and no *a priori* principle of charity implies that those functional states are highly reliable under T. Here we have a promising start to an account of T's empirical salience.

The reliability of beliefs is not merely statistical, not just that so many belief-tokens have been T. Reliability under T is *projectible*: if competent humans form their beliefs according to certain procedures in certain circumstances, those beliefs would significantly tend to be T. What are those circumstances? They have to do with the continued stability of those background conditions which permit our usual dealings with our environment. Of these *stability conditions* I cannot give a detailed picture, but a certain vagueness in background stability conditions normally attends assessments of the capabilities of physical systems. That is, in assessing the properties of some complicated machine, counterfactuals would abound without our being able to say precisely what factors must remain constant for the conditions not to be falsified.

Mere reliability is in itself of no interest. So if $T^\star$ assigns to all beliefs the "truth" condition that ice is cold, beliefs will not get any credit for being reliable under $T^\star$. The deficiency is not only a lack of *variety* in $T^\star$-conditions, but also the one-sided distribution of truth *values*, among belief-*types*. A minimal condition for reliability under $T^\star$ to be noteworthy is that, relative to $T^\star$'s distribution of truth values among belief-types, there is an *antecedent improbability* of the totality of belief-*tokens* being more than moderately reliable. If they turn out to be immoderately reliable, $T^\star$ becomes of interest; something is afoot.

That is a basic ingredient of the *informative* reliability of beliefs under T; here is another. Consider the following pairs of propositions: (1) [a is scarlet], (1') [a is not scarlet]; (2) [there are exactly three cats on the fence], (2') [there are not exactly three cats on the fence]. Of each pair the first contains more information, is bolder, than the second. Suppose most belief-tokens that are true under $T^\star$ have $T^\star$-conditions that are not very bold. It may still be an impressive fact that beliefs tend to be highly reliable under $T^\star$. But if an impressive proportion of those beliefs are T' (where $T^\star \neq T'$) and have *bold* T'-conditions, naturally T' will overshadow $T^\star$; beliefs are more informative under T'. Now a truly impressive fact about our beliefs, especially perceptual and other ordinary beliefs, is not only how many are T, but how many of those that are T have bold T-conditions.

Another striking aspect of informativeness is the diversity and quasi-universal range of the truth conditions of true belief–tokens. Any $T^\star$ that diminishes that diversity and range will, *ceteris paribus*, thereby not be as worthy as T of special status.

Back to reliability. There are two other equally important concepts: our beliefs' being *reliably approximately* T, and their increasingly *approximating to being T*. It is not only that so many beliefs *are* T that makes T salient, but also that many beliefs are *nearly* T. After counting the people at a party, I believe there are nineteen when there are twenty. That our beliefs often come so close to being T is part of a broader pattern in our interactions with the world that makes T salient. This concept of *approximation* is of course difficult; but it is of considerable importance in any naturalistic theory of truth.

There is also the idea that our theoretical and investigatory procedures in the physical sciences continually lead us closer to the truth, which is different from our already being close. I am afraid my point here must seem a gratuitous assertion to the anti-scientific realist; but let me register two points. First, it does not seem that "truth" is equivalent to anything epistemic, not even 'what our scientific procedures tend towards', *pace* Peirce, and Putnam (1978). Consequently, *if* our theories do continue to get closer to being T, that would be a wholly contingent fact and relevant to T's empirical salience. Secondly, some of us *do believe* that physical theory is (in some sense that needs explication) getting closer to being T; the current point can have appeal only given that non-sceptical attitude. There are several ways of not accepting realism. One may be instrumentalist about *interpretation*, holding physical theory not to be true-or-false, and thus not to require an account of the salience of T. But for the sceptic for whom, while theories do have realist interpretations, i.e. under T, we can never have grounds to believe them true (cf. van Fraassen, 1980), there is a problem: what makes T *salient* if not what I have said? The functional or conceptual roles of our theories do not explain our equating truth-conditions and T-conditions. What then *interprets* them? Is semantic instrumentalism forced on the anti-scientific realist?

In the following I shall speak simply of reliability; but the considerations extend equally to being reliably approximate to T, and continually getting closer to being T. In other words, when I argue that such and such would make beliefs not as reliable under T* as under T, one should read that as also covering: 'beliefs will not then tend to be as approximately T* as T, and not tend as quickly to approach being T* as they do being T'.

Perhaps the most serious impediment to a realist theory of truth has been a failure (engendered in part by certain disquotational intuitions), to appreciate how *remarkable* it is that beliefs are reliable under T—that a certain wide range of our states, under an enormous variety of T-conditions, tend projectibly to be highly informatively reliable. If this reliability was limited to our immediate environment, that would be remarkable enough. But the T-conditions of many true beliefs are independent of their functional and local settings; the T-conditions of the belief that at the poles there are large areas of ice and snow has nothing to do *a priori* with its functional role.

The uniqueness of T

Perhaps other truth predicates, not logically equivalent to T, make beliefs equally informatively reliable; there is certainly no obvious *a priori* reason why not. But if that is so, it seems our choice is a matter of convention. Then the question arises why we should have singled out T. Why have such a convention? Perhaps it is practically important to have agreed on one truth predicate under which beliefs are informatively reliable, because of its predictive value, say; and an obvious explanation of the choice of T in particular is that it is homophonic. Then Quinean indeterminacy would be vindicated; truth conditions, while based upon natural facts about T, would be not uniquely determined by them, and therefore underdetermined by "physical fact and theory". Truth conditions would then in part be a matter of convention.

My question at this point is the uniqueness of T up to logical equivalence, and not the uniqueness of our assignment of references to words, etc. In giving truth theories T_1 and T_2 for another language we might assign under T_1 the set of bats to the expression 'flick' and on T_2 the set of undetached bat parts, so that '*est flick*' is true on T_1 iff bats exist and is true on T_2 iff undetached bat parts exist. If the rest of T_1 and T_2 were in step, then, for present purposes, T_1 and T_2 would count as the same. If no other truth theory for that language were relevantly adequate, we would have determinacy of truth conditions, but not perhaps of reference (but see 9.9).

Something important that is easily lost about indeterminacy is this: even if truth conditions were indeterminate relative to the natural facts T is embedded in, beliefs are still informatively reliable under T. That there are other such truth predicates does not make this correspondence less notable. One might see only two alternatives: (1) there is a naturalistically determinate assignment of truth conditions, and with it a vindication of a strong correspondence theory; or (2) the only intelligible role for 'true' is to be an intralinguistic disquotation device.

It is obvious from the discussion of informative reliability that they are not the only two possibilities. We should detach the question of a correspondence between thoughts and facts from the issue of determinacy, that is, the uniqueness of T. Even if classical determinate propositional content had to be scrapped, a substantial part of the picture remains: intersubjective intentional sameness of belief in terms of functional role, and a certain non-trivial correspondence between beliefs and facts, via beliefs' informative reliability under T.

Given this, one could then underestimate the interest of the question of uniqueness, pointing to the strong equivalence of ⌜Ts⌝ and ⌜the belief that s is true⌝ as showing that it does not matter whether natural features make T unique. It is not as though we can't naturalistically explicate 'true'; the Tarski predicate does the job. Granted that our account of the *point* of truth doesn't make T unique, we have still adequately defined 'true'. What is being left out? Now as a fall-back position, that might be a reasonable compromise between Quinean anti-intentionalism and the full Brentanian picture, one that manages to retain crucial ingredients of the classical conception of objective content. But reasonable only if necessary; for something is left out, as we can see if we look once more at the propositional theory.

The normal assignment of propositions to beliefs is radically underdetermined by their functional roles; suppose it is also underdetermined by facts about informative reliability. We could *say* that the normal assignment is built into the definition of 'believes'. (This corresponds to the strong equivalence of 'true' and T.) But suppose someone replied to Quine's claim about the indeterminacy of *translation* thus: "What we mean by 'correct translation' is what gets produced by the conventional procedures, and they do not underdetermine the translation, except marginally." But, to shift Quine's emphasis slightly, his argument is: translation is correct if it preserves something called meaning; all that is plausibly relevant to sameness of meaning is such and such; it determines no unique translation scheme; hence there is no determinate fact of correct translation. The ordinary language reply is hardly impressive. Something similar can be argued about belief: ascriptions of content are correct only if they assign the right propositions; the only facts plausibly relevant to assigning propositions are such and such; they do not uniquely determine an assignment; hence there are no determinate facts about content.

The meaning of 'believes' does not prevent the assignment of content from being arbitrary; if nothing prevents it, we have a conflict with something fairly entrenched in the classical conception of intentionality. If that is so for the propositional theory, it must also be so on the sentential theory as regards the choice of truth predicate. Invoking the meaning of 'true' no more forestalls arbitrariness than does invoking the meaning of 'believes'.

But, as I shall argue, our choice of T is not arbitrary; given informative reliability and two other conditions, simplicity and a certain epistemic accessibility, it seems no other truth predicate is a serious competitor. Whether this shows that truth conditions are determinate in a *physicalist* sense is not completely clear. A similar question arises about the determinacy of reference, at the end of 9.9. The point is that the notion of determinacy is, while tolerably clear, not totally clear; nor is it likely to become so except by fiat.

The question is whether informative reliability together with some other factors make T unique *up to logical equivalence*. Let me explain the role of such intensional notions as logical equivalence in my account; it does, after all, purport to eliminate intensionality. We can distinguish the occurrence of an intensional concept in an explication from the concern that an explication should satisfy an intensional criterion of adequacy. In 2.5 we discussed a naturalistic sort of explication; a certain psychological feature of a conceptual replacement can make it conservative for a given person. Now if an explication appears to satisfy an unreconstructed intensional standard of adequacy, that psychological feature presumably will be present. I shall talk as though truth conditions were propositions that a truth predicate assigns to a sentence, rather than move up a linguistic level to speak of equivalences that deductively follow from the definition of the truth predicate. That is harmless enough. But I shall also consider whether the conditions a truth predicate $T^\star$ assigns to L are logically stronger or weaker than what T assigns; one should read 'logically stronger', etc., as the full modal notion. But no such notion occurs in the explication of propositional attitudes and truth; 'true' is *not* being explicated as 'satisfies the truth predicate that uniquely satisfies such and such conditions'. ⌜The belief that s is true⌝ is strongly equivalent to ⌜s is T⌝; nothing intensional is used in defining that Tarski predicate. When questions of determinacy arise intensional notions crop up; but they are about the explication, and not part of it.

The argument has this form. First, I argue that any truth predicate $T^\star$ under which *observational* beliefs are as informatively reliable as they are under T, and which satisfies a further condition, is logically equivalent to T with respect to the truth conditions of observational beliefs. Secondly, we have the inductive part; any T* under which beliefs are as informatively reliable as they are under T, and which satisfies a certain simplicity condition, resembles T in the inductive clauses of its definition, that is, in how it assigns truth or satisfaction conditions to complexes on the basis of their constituents. Throughout I speak ambiguously both of beliefs and of sentences of L as being T.

The uniqueness of T for observational beliefs

The functional roles of observational beliefs depend in part on their input conditions, which are about independent features of the environment. In explaining the sentential index theory in 7.2, I pointed out that 'if p is true etc.' in the input condition can be replaced using the truth predicate T: 'if s is T etc.'. So it may seem we have a ready made answer to the first part of our problem: what is unique about T with respect to observational beliefs is that it captures their input conditions, which in part define those second order states. This is not trivial; a logically distinct T* in the input clause yields a distinct functional theory. In 6.1 I pointed out that we might take some non-identity function f, and write the input clause thus: 'if p is true etc. then z f-believes that $f(p)$'. The point now is that, regardless of how we *index* that belief (that f-belief, that second-order state) one and the same input condition is associated with it by our theory. So it is tempting to take T's uniqueness for observational beliefs to be determined by the functional theory itself; the truth conditions of observational beliefs are determined by their functional roles. (This is not supposed to yield determinacy of *subsentential reference*.) Then what remains to be shown is that, among truth predicates that resemble T for observational beliefs, any T* under which all other beliefs are as informatively reliable, etc., as they are under T, is logically equivalent to T. That is, I think, sufficient for determinacy of truth conditions. But would it not be odd if considerations about informative reliability did not also pick out T as uniquely capturing something about observational beliefs? The emphasis on informative reliability would be more persuasive if it were relevant to determinacy at all levels of truth conditions.

Informative reliability alone does not yield uniqueness for T. Some T' which is not logically equivalent to T could be *counterfactually* equivalent to T in this sense: any observational s would be T', *given* the stability conditions, iff s were T. Beliefs under T' would then be as informatively reliable as they are under T. So the procedure will be to argue that if beliefs are as informatively reliable under T′ as under T, they are at least "counterfactually" equivalent, and then to point out an interesting respect in which, in that equivalence class, T is unique up to logical equivalence.

If $T^\star$ is not counterfactually equivalent to T there is at least one sentence s of L to which $T^\star$ assigns truth conditions that are counterfactually weaker or stronger than, or independent of those assigned by T to s. Now it is not obvious that if $T^\star$ differs from T in one of those ways that *eo ipso* means that beliefs are less informatively reliable under $T^\star$ than under T. Suppose $T^\star$ assigns to Bs a condition counterfactually *weaker* than that assigned by T; so, Ts iff the thing there is blue, and $T^\star s$ iff the thing there is blue or blueish green. Tokens of the belief that s are less informative under $T^\star$ than under T. But they are potentially more reliable under $T^\star$ than under T; for among the situations compatible with the stability conditions are those in which one carelessly believes something blueish green to be blue. Given how informative reliability was introduced, the mere fact that Ts is *more informative* than $T^\star s$ is not enough to explain our predilection for T. It may be that, somewhere else in L, $T^\star$ makes up for this decrease in informativeness by making another belief more informative, even if less reliable, than under T.

Parallel remarks are in order if $T^{\star\star}s$ is counterfactually stronger than or independent of Ts. Suppose $T^{\star\star}s$ is independent of Ts – e.g. $T^{\star\star}s$ iff the thing there is hexagonal. Given even the vague characterization of stability conditions and favorable epistemic procedures, it is clear that our belief that s, the one that is functionally the belief that the thing there is blue, would in general be more reliable under T than under $T^{\star\star}$. Similarly if $T^{\star\star}s$ is stronger than Ts. But why shouldn't the decrease in the reliability of Bs under $T^{\star\star}$ be *compensated for* by the increase in informativeness, especially since other beliefs might be more reliable (if less informative) under $T^{\star\star}$ than under T? That is, after all, the relation between T and the weaker $T^\star$.

The apparent problem is that if $T^\star$ deviates from T somewhere in respect of reliability or informativeness, that could be compensated for by an increase in the opposite factor on that belief or in the same factor on other beliefs. In showing what is special about T, then, I must make it plausible that, within certain motivated parameters, such compensations are not forthcoming.

It is useful to have a standard representation of observational beliefs of the form 'that object there is F' or 'this object here is R to that object there'; let us use 'the belief that Θ is *F*' or 'the belief that Θ is *R* to Θ'', with 'Θ' representing the demonstrative. What a truth predicate really assigns to such beliefs are satisfaction conditions for open sentences; so let us represent their truth conditions using individual variables: '*x* is *F*', or '*x* is *R* to *y*'. I shall first present the account in an unhedged and general way, then explain an apparently question-begging notion (astuteness), and finally turn to refinements.

Suppose T* assigns weaker conditions to the observational belief B*s* than does T, thereby making it less informative under T* than under T. This decrease in informativeness is not *guaranteed* to be compensated for by an increase in reliability. For suppose B*s* is *completely* reliable under T; it cannot be more reliable under T*. There would then be a strong reason to prefer T, *ceteris paribus*, to T*. It is a more interesting indicator of the empirical properties of B*s*; it represents more fully the discriminative capacity of B*s*. But our observational beliefs are not in general fully reliable in all the circumstances compatible with the stability conditions. Suppose that T* assigns to the belief that Θ is blue (the functional state we express as 'that is blue') the truth conditions: *x* is blue or blueish green; and that tokens of that belief tend to be more reliable under T* than under T. Now if we increase the *astuteness* with which we form that belief, the difference between the reliability of that belief under T* and under T will generally diminish; we would increasingly tend not to believe of merely blueish-green things that they are blue. Now consider T**, which assigns to that belief stronger truth conditions than T – say, *x* is cobalt blue. Normally tokens of the belief that Θ is blue are more reliable under T than under T**, because of the non-cobalt-blue blue things that we believe to be blue. But unlike the case of T* and T, it is *not* generally true that an increase in astuteness would diminish the difference in reliability of that belief under T and under T** – it does not tend to make us restrict *that* belief to cobalt blue objects. The idea then is this. Consider the class of truth predicates T' such that increased astuteness in forming an observational belief B*s* tends to diminish the difference between the reliability of that belief under T' and under truth predicates which assign *weaker* truth conditions to B*s*: T is in that class, and no truth predicate is in that class which assigns to B*s* truth conditions counterfactually *stronger* than or independent of what T assigns. This is a contingent fact about T and each observational belief B*s*: *T captures the strongest discriminative capacities of B*s. Each functional state that I am calling an observational belief has such optimal discriminative capacities (given the stability conditions) and T captures them.

Perhaps the most glaring difficulty here is this notion 'astuteness'. To form beliefs astutely is to form them using sound epistemic procedures, and in defining 'sound', a philosopher will most naturally invoke truth – 'tending to promote true beliefs and to generate true beliefs from true beliefs'. But truth is T-hood, and if we insert that in the above account, the resultant characterization of T also holds of non-equivalent predicates T′: astuteness relative to T′ tends to produce observational beliefs that are T′. It does not help to explain "sound" epistemic procedures by reference to their promoting the *satisfaction* of our *desires*; for the satisfaction conditions of desires are as problematic as the truth conditions of beliefs.

There is a general strategy for characterizing sound epistemic procedures that does not rely on truth. Certain properties of organisms – behavioral tendencies, anatomical features, *and* belief-forming proce- dures – make positive contributions to the probability of their survival (or their genes' survival). The biologist does not even implicitly have to attribute wants or want-satisfaction conditions to organisms, in order to describe complicated interlocking sets of properties as having survival value. Sometimes a feature's contribution to survival is discoverable only with great ingenuity, but that it does make a contribution can be clear without the details. So it seems likely that certain human epistemic tendencies (the ones that happen to be truth- and information-promoting), such as careful attention, general alertness, curiosity, certain simple patterns of reasoning, would naturally form a unified class in an evolutionary–ecological approach to explaining our nature. All we need now is for them to have something in common that can be described independently of truth; it may then be introduced non-circularly into the account of what makes T special.

The idea has been that the more astutely an observational belief is formed the smaller the difference between its reliability under T and under any weaker truth predicate. This seems to imply that optimal astuteness guarantees truth, which seems rather strong. Now it is not implied that observational beliefs are infallible in any strong sense; not that optimal astuteness could not lead to error, but at most that it would not lead to error in most real-world situations. Nor is it implied that background theoretical and factual beliefs are not operative in forming observational beliefs, that all one needs is astutely governed perception. It is a highly contingent property of T that I wish to characterize; our background beliefs ordinarily are such that they and our perceptual experiences, given astuteness, tend to result in observational beliefs as reliable under T as under weaker predicates, while this is not so under predicates stronger than T.

Still, perfect reliability, even in real-world situations, is not guaranteed by astuteness, and if only approximate reliability obtains, can T be unique? Consider again the belief that Θ is blue, and the predicates T* (which assigns to it 'x is blue or blueish-green') and T** (which assigns to it 'x is cobalt blue'). In nearly all real-world situations, for nearly all members of our society, increased astuteness tends to diminish the difference between observational reliability under T* and under T, whereas this is *not* true of T and T**. So although reliability is imperfect, the difference in the relation between T and the weaker T*, and between T** and the weaker T, is marked. The suggestion then is that for every belief *b*, for every pair of predicates one weaker and the other stronger than or independent of T, the same asymmetrical tendency will be found with respect to *b*. T captures the optimal discriminative potential of each observational belief relative to normally prevailing circumstances.

Are we to count as observational those beliefs involving *natural-kind* terms – e.g. lion, or gold? If so, there is a problem for my account of T's uniqueness for observational beliefs, at least given the usual view of natural-kind terms. The properties by virtue of which we normally *recognize* an object as of a certain kind may not be co-extensive with those that *constitute* it as being of that kind. Some things that look and behave like lions might not be lions, and some lions might not appear to be so, if being a lion consists in being of the genetic kind of certain lion paradigms. Suppose there were a substantial discrepancy between being a lion and being normally perceptually identifiable as one; then my account of T's uniqueness, for the belief that Θ is a lion, is not correct. Suppose some things that are lionlike aren't lions. The difference between reliability under the weaker predicate T* which assigns 'x is lion-like or a lion' to that belief, and reliability under T, will not then tend to diminish with increased astuteness; mere observational astuteness (which does not cover applying molecular biology) will not prevent classifying lion-like non-lions as lions. Or suppose that, while everything lion-like is a lion, some lions are not lion-like. Then if T** assigns the stronger condition 'x is a lion-like lion', then, given ordinary astuteness, that belief will be as reliable under T** as under T. The upshot is that, if we count beliefs with such *hidden* truth conditions as observational, my account of what makes T special is not correct.

Suppose we count no beliefs about natural kinds as observational? Contrary to one's instinctive reaction here, the class of observational beliefs would *not* thereby be significantly impoverished, given their intended role in the functional theory. They generate distinctiveness of content for all beliefs because enough of them have unique input conditions to induce uniqueness of systematic role for all beliefs, given the L-constraints and a realistic set of M-constraints. The last condition is important: if observational beliefs contain only minimal concepts – about colors, shapes, relative spatial position and changes in those factors over time – the M-constraints required to relate B-type beliefs uniquely to observational beliefs would count as unrealistically complicated. To eliminate natural-kind concepts from observational beliefs however, does not leave merely physical versions of empiricist simple ideas. We can recognize an array of *gestalt* observational concepts; it is required merely that they not have hidden satisfaction conditions. Which concepts are they? 'Lion-like' is a good candidate. If you will permit, they are the meanings that words like 'water' have or would have independently of meaning-reform directives issued by scientific essentialists in the form: 'that clear, thirst-quenching, stuff in the river wouldn't be water if it weren't H_2O'. After the reform, they are the *gestalt* concepts under which we perceptually identify certain natural kinds; it seems we are fitted out with a huge, varied array of them. Which words and phrases express them? Natural-kind words themselves might be regarded as having two functions: to express the *gestalt* observationally identifying concepts that scientifically unaided observation ascribes, and to denote the corresponding natural kinds. Beliefs that invoke natural kinds are then B-type. Eliminating them from observational beliefs leaves a large and varied class, whose optimal discriminative capacities T captures.

However well T captures the discriminative capacities of observational beliefs, if $T^\star$ assigns them conditions that are *counterfactually* but not logically equivalent to T's conditions, then $T^\star$ is equally adequate. (This counterfactual equivalence is relative to the stability conditions.) The question now is what further properties make T special within that equivalence class. First I consider certain artificially constructed equivalent truth predicates, and then a certain other class, with the idea that what accounts for one or the other class accounts for all cases.

Suppose p is counterfactually but not logically sufficient for q, and that Ts iff p. If T$^\star s$ iff p and q, then Ts and T$^\star s$ are counterfactually equivalent but not logically equivalent. Observational beliefs are as reliably informative under T* as under T. Or suppose p is counterfactually but not logically necessary for q. Then if T$^{\star\star}s$ iff $p \lor q$, again T$^\star s$ is counterfactually but not logically equivalent to Ts. But these equivalences reveal an asymmetry between T and T*: under T* there is a constituent of the truth condition that is not represented by a constituent of the belief – namely q.

Lest this talk of constituents seems arbitrary, let us keep in mind that beliefs do have constituent structure, given fine-grained functional individuation. So, the belief Bs is less complex than the beliefs B$s \& s'$ or B$s \lor s'$; its functional role is determined by fewer functional connections with other beliefs. As for T*, which assigns to Bs the truth condition $p \& q$, since Bs is not truth functionally complex, it has no constituent s' such that T$^\star s'$ iff q. T satisfies a certain *isomorphism* condition that T* fails to satisfy; this is a kind of *simplicity*.

The isomorphism condition eliminates many truth predicates that are counterfactually but not logically equivalent to T on observational beliefs, but probably not all. However, the ones it does not eliminate perhaps all have the following feature: they depend on scientific investigation for their discovery. There are no doubt such counterfactual equivalences between some *gestalt* recognitional conditions and natural kinds; but none is available to scientifically untutored common sense. So if T* assigns such a condition to an observational belief, while T assigns the observational condition, there is another interesting asymmetry between T* and T; the T-conditions have historically been *epistemically accessible*,[1] whereas the T*-conditions have not.

So to sum up: I have suggested that only T, and truth predicates counterfactually equivalent to T, capture the optimal discriminative capacities of observational beliefs. Within that class, I then suggested, truth predicates that satisfy certain conditions of isomorphism and epistemic accessibility are logically equivalent to T for observational beliefs.

The uniqueness of T: molecular, quantified, and non-observational beliefs

Philosophers have been sanguine about the determinacy of the truth conditions of truth-functional connectives. Thus Quine says, "The

---

[1] Bringing in epistemic accessibility does not introduce a vicious circle. We are not now *defining* 'true': truth is T-hood, and insofar as truth and belief come into what 'epistemically accessible' means, we have them independently of the current discussion of uniqueness.

semantic criterion of negation is that it turns any short sentence to which one will assent into a sentence from which one will dissent, and vice-versa. That of conjunction is that it produces compounds to which one is prepared to assent always and only when one is prepared to assent to each component." (Quine, 1960, pp. 57–8.) What this identifies is, in my terms, functional role; but Quine also proposes a maxim of charity, and that together with the foregoing criteria of course has implications about truth conditions. Nothing there, however, apparently implies the *unique* appropriateness of T's assignments to the connectives; I have found that a plausible motivation for that must be somewhat more complex, but not enormously so.

As a preliminary, a reminder about 'reliability under T': this is a matter of counterfactuals, relativized to the stability conditions; it is, moreover, not meant to hold of all beliefs, but of those guided by "good" epistemic procedures. One may suspect a vicious circle: what makes epistemic procedures good if not their truth-promoting tendencies? Merely to *list* them, under their functional descriptions, would raise the question why the reliability, under T, of beliefs formed in accordance with *those* procedures is especially notable. Now the foregoing discussion of acuteness gives the clue to how that class may be unified. What matters is the effect of the epistemic procedures on our needs and survival; and it seems likely that ecological evolutionary considerations will be adequate for marking off what is special about our "good" inferential tendencies.

Again we must be careful not to smuggle in the concept of the fulfillment of wants *unless* independently motivated. This last proviso suggests a more subtle structure of the justification of T's uniqueness – namely, to think of it as established in stages, the first being for a certain subset of beliefs, those formed in accordance with relatively simple epistemic procedures whose immediate usefulness for survival is unproblematic. On that level of truth conditions, assigning satisfaction conditions to certain wants (cf. the remarks in the following section about want termination) would then be motivated and, on that basis, a class of more sophisticated epistemic procedures would be marked off non-circularly as those which tend to promote the fulfillment such wants, which enables us to proceed to the next stage.

Suppose then that the class of good inferential procedures has been marked off as salient without begging any questions about truth or want fulfillment. In what follows, an important step in the argument is that certain *deductive* procedures ought to be exceptionlessly truth-preserving under any suitable competitor of T; but that means we cannot usefully characterize the class of deductive procedures in terms of their truth-preserving – i.e. T-preserving – properties. One strategy would be this: to try to distinguish among the good epistemic procedures those that are non-risky and conservative from those that are risky and information-productive and that therefore expand one's set of behavioral strategies, not in terms of truth conditions, but in terms of their ecological environmental properties, of what contributions the procedures make to an organism's achieving its "goals". The idea would then be to argue for a salience connection between being "deductive" in this non-truth-oriented sense and being T-preserving; and from that to argue that the deductive procedures should be $T^\star$-preserving for any suitable truth predicate $T^\star$. But in fact it seems unlikely (to me) that the risky/non-risky distinction can be made (except enumeratively) without 'true'.

A much more productive idea is this. It is difficult to doubt that the enormously striking, substantive, empirical fact of the reliability of beliefs under T (those produced in accordance with good epistemic procedures) is to be *explained* in part by the fact that those procedures include certain ones (those we call deductive) that are *exceptionlessly T-preserving*. I am suggesting that this is essential to any empirical explanation of reliability. The point is now this: it would be a sort of miracle if there were another truth predicate $T^\star$, under which those beliefs (formed according to the good epistemic procedures) are as projectibly reliable (relative to the stability conditions) but such that the deductive procedures are *not* also exceptionlessly $T^\star$-preserving. I cannot prove this, but it seems clear that if it turned out to be so it would be an amazing fact. On this basis we would be entitled to expect any interesting competitor of T to make the deductive procedures exceptionlessly truth-preserving.

In what follows the only procedures that come into play are simple "introduction" and "elimination" rules for connectives. Now the considerations advanced so far would clearly entitle us to assume only that those rules are exceptionlessly truth-preserving relative to the stability conditions – in the possible worlds that satisfy those conditions. So let us say that $T^\star$ must be such that the deductive procedures are "counterfactually" truth-preserving under $T^\star$. That is evidently not enough to secure T's uniqueness for the connectives up to *logical* equivalence. The idea will be to show that this counterfactual truth-preserving property of the deductive procedures under $T^\star$

implies that $T^\star$ is logically equivalent to T *given* two rather different further conditions: a pair of assumptions about negation and universal quantification, and a certain simplicity requirement. Let us consider some properties of deductive rules for the connectives.

Conjunction is easiest; neither its introduction nor its elimination rules involve negation. They are '$Bs_1, Bs_2 \Rightarrow Bs_1 \& s_2$' and '$Bs_1 \& s_2 \Rightarrow Bs_1, Bs_2$'; *ex hypothesi*, they are counterfactually truth-preserving under any adequate $T^\star$. Consider the following assignments to instances of those forms, by a truth predicate $T^\star$ that is not logically equivalent to T: $T^\star r_1$ iff α has a heart, $T^\star r_2$ iff α has a human brain, and $T^\star r_1 \& r_2$ iff α is human. We may suppose that this assignment to the beliefs Br_1, Br_2 and $Br_1 \& r_2$ keeps the two conjunction rules counterfactually truth-preserving. But evidently there is no *principle* in what $T^\star$ assigns which is extrapolable to other instances of $Bs_1 \& s_2$, and which keeps the rules counterfactually truth-preserving *in general*. This is evident when s_1 and s_2 are simple, and even more so given that '&' is iteratively bedded in complex beliefs. There is nothing *arbitrary* about eliminating such a $T^\star$ from among the serious competitors of T. To count our standard assignment of truth conditions as *indeterminate* because of $T^\star$ would rob the issue of determinacy of philosophical interest. (Not that Quine denies this.)

Now there is a *unified* condition for '&' which yields a $T^\star$ that is not logically equivalent to T but makes the rules counterfactually truth-preserving. Let q be some proposition that follows from the stability conditions; then '$T^\star s_1 \& s_2$ iff $T^\star s_1$ and $T^\star s_2$ and q' makes the introduction rule for conjunction counterfactually truth-preserving, and evidently makes the elimination rule so. I considered a similar sort of thing about observational beliefs and suggested an "isomorphism condition" to rule it out. How does this sort of constraint (or, say, a judgment of *adhocness*) relate to the issue of determinacy? This is a hazy area; if 'determinate with respect to physical fact and theory' excludes all *formal* considerations, then indeed our assignment of truth conditions to beliefs is not determinate, not even up to logical equivalence. But would that conflict with our vague pre-Quinean intuitions about the *objectivity* of truth conditions? Here the best we can do is to register the vagueness. Given the theorist-relativity of conservative explication, we may observe that one person's 'objective' is another's 'arbitrary', one's 'determined by the physical facts' is another's 'merely partially determined by the physical facts'. An appropriate reaction might be: if that is what is meant by 'indeterminacy' how interesting is it?

It is clear, I think, that there is no T^*, which is not *ad hoc* in one of those ways, which makes the conjunction rules counterfactually truth-preserving, without being logically equivalent to T, for Bs_1 & s_2. Certainly no other truth function does it, nor any binary sentential operator like 'because'.

Here let us observe that a strict demonstration of T's uniqueness would cover not only its assignments to occurrences of connectives with widest scope (as in the deductive rules) but also to all their embedded occurrences. But I think it should be clear that any T^* that does not generate interpretations *uniformly* through all levels of embedding (as T does) must deviate from T in respect of simplicity and *non-adhocness* in something like the manner we have seen.

Now T's assignments to negation and universal quantification are not fully determined by any "deductive procedures". Let us first see how far we can get with *negation* along the lines suggested; there are various methods, and one of them requires first establishing something about disjunction. We have '$Bs_1 (Bs_2) \Rightarrow Bs_1 \lor s_2$' among the deductive procedures. No unified and non-*ad hoc* T^* that makes this counter-factually truth-preserving also makes '$T^*s_1 \lor s_2$' logically stronger than or independent of '$Ts_1 \lor s_2$'. Now consider the rule *modus tollendo ponens*, which uses negation: '$Bs_1 \lor s_2$, $B \sim s_1 \Rightarrow Bs_2$'. Given that '$T^*s_1 \lor s_2$' cannot be logically (or counterfactually) stronger than '$Ts_1 \lor s_2$', $T^* \sim s_1$ must be counterfactually as strong as $T \sim s_1$. (Here we assume inductively that T^*s_1 iff Ts_1.) Once again the simplicity considerations enable us to strengthen that: $T^* \sim s_1$ must be logically as strong as $T \sim s_1$.

Now the question is: can $T^* \sim s$ be logically stronger than $T \sim s$? The relevant deductive procedure would appear to be excluded middle: 'believe any instance of $s \lor \sim s$'. Now there are complications here, introduced by the possibility of T^*'s being defined via supervaluations, but we may ignore them at this point, for we cannot in any case rely on the assumption that $T^* s \lor \sim s$ holds for every s to show that $T^* \sim s$ can't be stronger than $T \sim s$. The reason is that we haven't yet shown that $T^*s_1 \lor s_2$ is equivalent to $Ts_1 \lor s_2$; for we haven't shown that the former can't be counterfactually weaker than the latter, and to do that by reference to *modus tollendo ponens* would presuppose we had already established that $T^* \sim s$ is not stronger than $T \sim s$.

A frontal attack is needed. It seems that if $T^* \sim s$ were *counterfactually stronger* than $T \sim s$ (whatever the latter amounts to – i.e. whether s is vague, has presuppositions, etc.), then our beliefs would as a matter of fact be less reliable under $T^\star$ than under T. For it seems quite likely that there is no single unified way to strengthen $T^\star \sim s$ which does not employ *ad hoc* clauses, and which would not make the reliability of beliefs under $T^\star$ so much lower than it is under T that we would judge T the more empirically significant property by far.[2]

Notice finally that this approach is compatible with intuitionism, which may accept T as the optimal truth predicate; that acceptance does not imply excluded middle, for T itself may be defined in an intuitionistic metalanguage.

Given that $T^\star \sim s$ must be logically equivalent to $T \sim s$, it is now simple to establish the same for the other truth-functional connectives. What about the quantifiers? Consider the deductive procedure: '$B(\forall x)(\ldots x \ldots) \Rightarrow B(\ldots t \ldots)$'. Can we show that '$T^\star(\forall x)(\ldots x \ldots)$' must not be counterfactually weaker than '$T(\forall x)(\ldots x \ldots)$' on that basis? Suppose that, while beliefs of the form $(\ldots t \ldots)$ are highly reliable, that is so only because they all, given the stability conditions, fall within a *restricted range* of denotations for 't' and hence of values for 'x' in '$(\forall x)(\ldots x \ldots)$'. If $T^\star$ restricts the quantifier correspondingly, the elimination rule would be exceptionlessly truth-preserving under $T^\star$, and there would then be no empirical motivation to prefer T to $T^\star$. Two things can be said. First, it seems unlikely that there is a unified and non-*ad hoc* restriction with that effect. Second, it is hard to see how such a restriction could become *accessible* to us – how we could know that our potential reliability extends only to a certain range of entities.

If we are then justified in supposing that if $T^\star$ is a competitor it must be no weaker than T with respect to '$\forall$', the question finally is whether it can be stronger. There is nothing among the deductive procedures that would rule this out – nothing that corresponds to conjunction introduction. But as with the question how strong $T^\star$ can make negation, it is difficult to see how any non-*ad hoc*, unified, strengthening of '$\forall$' could fail to make our universally quantified beliefs significantly less reliable under $T^\star$ than they are under T.

[2] Suppose $T^\star$ treats s as vague, so that to have $T^\star s \vee \sim s$ requires a supervaluation definition of $T^\star$. We have, *ex inductive hypothesi* that $T^\star s$ is strongly equivalent to Ts, and so the two must match vagueness for vagueness. It is difficult to see any motivation there for making $T^\star \sim s$ stronger than $T \sim s$. But suppose $T^\star$ is *presuppositional* and T is not; might that ever be a reason for preferring $T^\star$? We are here speaking of truth conditions for *beliefs* and not *sentences*; consequently there is going to be no reason not to take (e.g.) the belief that 'not the F is G', to be *functionally equivalent* to the belief that 'not there is a unique F which is G', and hence identical with it. $T^\star$ had better not be presuppositional, then, if beliefs are as reliable under $T^\star$ as under T.

No new issues are raised by the existential quantifier or by identity. Thus, I am claiming, the empirical properties of beliefs, when conjoined with certain fairly dramatic differences in *simplicity* between T and its empirically adequate competitors, make T's assignment to the logical connectives unique, up to logical equivalence.

The considerations so far have been about observational predicates and logical operations. What about B-type beliefs? I shall try to make it plausible that the uniqueness of T may be extended in that direction as well.

First, a distinction among B-type beliefs. In 4.7 beliefs whose only non-logical and non-observational constituents are quantification over properties and relations, some mathematics, and (say) the concept 'x causes y', were noted in connection with uniqueness of systematic role. They include the Ramseyfied forms of all theories whose O-terms consist in that special vocabulary plus observational predicates – call them Ramsey beliefs. T's uniqueness for Ramsey beliefs would imply that they are as reliable under no other equally simple $T^\star$, which assigns to 'x is a property', 'x is a relation', 'x causes y', and the mathematical predicates, satisfaction conditions logically distinct from what T assigns. Now the idea is that any suitable $T^\star$ would have to maximize the truth-preservingness of certain inferential patterns involving those predicates. Hence the strategy would involve specifying those patterns and showing that any assignment to, say, 'x causes y' which deviates from T's assignment would not maximize reliability or the tendency of beliefs continually to approach truth. That this is on the cards is quite plausible if one keeps in mind the simplicity condition: how likely is it that there is some non-standard interpretation of 'x causes y' that is not *ad hoc*, under which our most entrenched reasoning procedures involving 'causes' (essentially) remain truth-preserving?

The uniqueness of T for Ramsey beliefs has directly broader implications, given their intimate connection with large-scale scientific views – conjunctions of non-Ramseyfied theories and theoretical–observational connections. It is safe to assume that any suitable $T^\star$ will make the latter equivalent to some Ramsey "belief" under T. But what about ordinary B-type beliefs, those simple enough to have one by one? Apart from the obvious resort to hard work, that is, in discussing alternatives to T predicate by predicate, let me make the following general reflection on this final question about the uniqueness of T. Every B-type predicate is, at any given time, so closely associated in our overall framework with a certain Ramsey-type predicate, that if we assigned to the non-Ramsey predicates a truth predicate T★ different from T, while assigning T to the Ramsey beliefs, so many conditionals and biconditionals would thereby be falsified (because of the non-equivalence of T★ and T) that the overall reliability of beliefs under that mixed assignment would be less than under T. This is especially important if those equivalences and conditionals have a large part in scientific theorizing.

8.4 TRUTH AND THE APPLICATION OF THE FUNCTIONAL THEORY

The informative reliability of our beliefs under T is the foundation of T's salience. But there remains a curious gap between the two components of content: functional role and truth conditions. The former does determine the latter, in the sense that follows from the dubbing of T as 'true'; furthermore, functional states are reliable indicators under T. But our *application* of the functional theory in explaining and predicting behavior is not thereby shown to rely on truth conditions, except for observational beliefs. Might the truth conditions of beliefs be so detached from our ascription of them? In this section I mention ways in which truth conditions are invoked in our use of the functional theory.

Fact–belief inferences

Ascribing beliefs and desires on the basis of z's behavior is backed by substantial assumptions about the rest of z's beliefs and desires, and evidently those presuppositions are for the most part not based one by one on bits of z's past behavior. We have no difficulty in reconstructing, with varying degrees of probability, a cognitive framework from the few remarks of a stranger – a framework that includes both general and quite specific factual beliefs. How do we make such inferences? On a plane a stranger tells me she studies singing at a certain institute. I am then able to make many unqualified and probabilistic assumptions about her beliefs, that is, her knowledge. The likelihood of her believing that Haydn composed a work called *Missa in Tempore Belli* is not low. What is my basis for that assumption? It is not that I have sampled students of classical music and found they tend to believe *that* proposition; although I believe they do, that is not because of an induction by enumeration. The natural answer is more general: *such people* tend, with varying probability, to know *such facts*. It is a belief of a certain sort; it is *true*; she is a person of a certain sort; hence (probably) she has that belief. What I am suggesting, then, is that a large and important part of our basis for ascribing beliefs consists in generalizations, whose epistemological status has been discussed in 6.3, to which the truth predicate T is essential, of the form: if z is a person of such and such kind and b is a belief of so and so kind *and* b is true, then z has b. These generalizations are not part of the functional theory; but it is likely that without them our belief-ascription would be considerably impoverished, that the vast cognitive prerequisites of ordinary social interactions would be seriously diminished.

In the discussion of reliability I emphasized the *obtaining* of generalizations that certain beliefs tend to be true more than inferential *applications* of them. Regardless of their usefulness in inferring how things are, the mere fact that they obtain makes T of great empirical interest. That I am now emphasizing the inferential usefulness of the converse sorts of generalizations, from facts to beliefs rather than from beliefs to facts, should not obscure the more basic fact that such generalizations obtain, which itself contributes further to the salience of T. Not only are we reliable under T; we are *well informed* relative to T. Reliability also plays an important role in belief-ascription, but negatively; that s is not T is often a reason for taking z to lack the belief that s. So, belief–fact and fact–belief generalizations have essential roles to play, each in two sorts of inference – from how the world is to how z is functionally organized, and from how z is functionally organized to how the world is.

Is it possible that, in cases in which we appear to make such fact–belief inferences, there exists a reconstruction of them which does not employ the concept of truth? Consider a particular case. It is safe to assume that the French President believes, indeed knows, that in 1979 Cyrus Vance is U.S. Secretary of State, even though we may have no direct evidence of his belief. By my reckoning, my basis for this ascription is that such persons tend to know such facts. But perhaps there are other ways we could have arrived at the conclusion, not using the concept of truth. We may suppose that at a certain time, the French President was informed that Vance was the new Secretary of State, that nothing in the meantime changed his belief, etc. The fact is, however, that that does not capture my inferential situation; for my confidence that he has that belief outweighs any particular conjecture about *how* he acquired it. He was bound to come to know the fact, somehow.

But then perhaps we assume a certain disjunction of causal processes that would lead from the fact to the belief, without having to bring in T. Now I do not doubt we have such a disjunction in hand in this case. But how do we arrive at it? Our evidence consists in the many cases that have constituted direct evidence that humans tend to know salient facts about their areas of concern and activity and about the world at large. For in our assumption of such a disjunction of processes leading from a fact to a belief, our reasons for thinking that one or other of those processes *occurred*, and that the person has the belief, depends on our assumption that such people tend to come to know such facts *in some way or other*. Unless that has independent credibility, our confidence that one of *those* processes obtained, actually produced that belief, would be considerably diminished.

So I propose that 'true' is essential to certain generalizations which we rely on in ascribing beliefs. The examples I gave, of a Haydn mass and a well-known fact of public affairs, are not special cases. Think of anyone you meet and how, after discovering a few facts about that person, your potential ascriptions of beliefs and therefore your potential presuppositions in conversation, etc., expand enormously; then consider how much of that is based upon fact–belief inferences. In every case, I believe, you will find that the proportion appears to be great *prima facie*, and that that appearance stands up to further examination.

The fulfillment of wants

An important role for truth is in a certain explanation of the success of action, to which I shall turn shortly. Success consists in the fulfillment of the want or wants that motivate an action. As with truth the concept of fulfillment is not generated by any role in the functional theory. Nevertheless, for the reasons that make T adequate for explicating truth for beliefs, T is adequate for explicating the fulfillment of wants: $\ulcorner z$'s desire that s is fulfilled$\urcorner$ is strongly equivalent to $\ulcorner Ts \urcorner$, i.e. given the desire. So the question is not how to define 'fulfillment', but what makes it of interest.

One may be tempted to mistrust the question: for how could anything be more crucial to x's want that p than what would fulfill it? This is evidently to be granted. The point is that the concept has two components, functional role and fulfillment conditions; the question is why the two should go together. What about human beings gives a point to such a correlation of functional roles and (in general) extra-mental conditions?

When we ascribe attitudes it is important to be able to determine when wants *cease*. Here is a type of generalization we constantly apply: when such and such wants are fulfilled they tend to cease. Desires for food, sleep and sex let up in varying degrees when satisfied. Desires for means to ends, e.g. to take steps to board a plane, cease when fulfilled. Desires for certain amusements, to read a certain book, to see a certain view, to converse with a certain person, to play a certain game, often cease when fulfilled. While some desires persist through fulfillment, the others are numerous enough to provide a sufficient reason for our interest in whether wants (not our own, but those of others) are fulfilled. There is an empirical fact about the relation of wants and T here, as much in need of explanation as the parallel fact about beliefs and T.

There is an over-simplification in this suggestion. Often when we infer want cessation from fulfillment there is a premise involving belief. For even if a want is fulfilled it will often not cease unless *believed* fulfilled. It is not that beliefs about wants are involved, but that, in these cases, unless one believes that *s* one will not cease to desire that *s*. Moreover, in those cases the belief is sufficient for the termination of the desire. Naturally not all desires are under cognitive control; the more basic desires normally cease when satisfied.

This is a conclusive objection to the claim that the concept of *fulfillment* is essential to the range of cases I described, many of which may be redescribed in terms of inferences from facts to beliefs to want cessations, and thus the concept of the truth of beliefs at most is essential. However, in explaining the empirical interest of the concept of fulfillment it is perhaps not necessary that it be *ineliminable* from the reasoning involved. Given that we can so often infer cessation from fulfillment (when we are in a position to infer the corresponding beliefs), the concept of fulfillment is bound to take on a life of its own, even if by the grace of the more essential concept of truth.

Considerations about want cessation may not be enough to explain the extremely fundamental status of the concept of want fulfillment; but they may explain more than they seem to *prima facie*. Thus, our altruistic interest in the fulfillment of others' desires could be explained in terms of the beneficial effects of cessation on frustration and anxiety, given an independent explanation of our desire that others should not feel frustration, etc. Naturally our interest in the fulfillment of others' desires may to some extent be incapable of explanation at any level of rationality; it is perhaps a fundamental aspect of socialization.

What about our interest in the fulfillment of our own desires; does that not make the concept of fulfillment essential? Isn't desiring s and desiring that one's desire that s should be T virtually the same thing? Now, the project is to explain the salience of T as a predicate T of the beliefs and desires of *others*; otherwise there is no naturalistic basis for interlinguistic truth and fulfillment conditions. So the question becomes: does the fact that, for persons in general, desiring that s is often virtually the same as desiring that one's desire that s be T explain the interest of T as a predicate of wants? I think not. That is a fact about functional states which, from our theoretical perspective on others, may be expressed without using T *predicatively*. 'T' occurs in the sentential indices of certain reflexive desires; it is still an open question what the point is of an *observer*'s noting that another's desire *is* T, or using T at any level of *extensional* embedding.

This point is worth extending to certain other accounts of how truth conditions come into the theory of meaning, e.g. those on which language mastery is said to consist in mastery of truth conditions. It is true that one has not mastered a public language as a means of communication unless one has mastered the truth conditions of its sentences. But the role of our T as a predicate of others' beliefs, of their functional states, is not explained via its conceptual role for them, in their mastery of their language, for that is just a fact about their functional organization. T's interest as a *predicate of* their beliefs would still require explanation.

Truth and the success of action

We are generally successful in getting what we want, appearances to the contrary resting on a small proportion of cases. Now a certain way of systematizing and in a sense explaining this fact involves the concept of truth. Given our evident interest in success, that is, the fulfillment of desire, that would constitute a further important role for truth. But the matter is not exactly simple. I shall first give a rough sense in which truth explains success, then consider a counter-argument that the concept has no essential role there, and finally distinguish two *explananda* covered by 'the success of action', with two concomitant roles for truth.

The intuitive point is that our actions tend to be successful because our beliefs tend to be true. The point lies in the pattern of beliefs and desires that motivate intentional actions, namely:

> x wants s
> x believes ⌜if s', then doing A leads to s⌝
> x believes s'.

The truth of that pair of beliefs *entails* success for *A*; thus any tendency of such pairs to be jointly true implies a tendency of actions thus motivated to be successful; and, given that the truth of those beliefs is not counterfactually dependent on the success of the actions and is sufficient for success, it is *prima facie* plausible to speak of truth as explaining success.

Now let us turn to a line of reasoning on which truth is not essential in explaining success. Take this example: Jones reaches Smith by telephone; his dialling stems from the desire to speak with Smith, his beliefs about Smith's location and the line's condition, and his belief that if those things are such and such his dialling will result in contact. Need we mention truth in explaining Jones's success? To explain that is to explain his contacting Smith; but that is explained by certain electronic facts, by Smith's location, etc. While those facts imply the truth of his beliefs, that concept is not essential to the explanation of his achieving contact. Those beliefs caused his action, but their *truth* was not relevant; and once the action was done the beliefs have no further explanatory role and, *a fortiori*, their truth has no such role. So the concept of truth has no essential function in explaining success in particular cases.

But, the argument proceeds, truth does not then figure in the explanation of the *general* success of action; for, given the foregoing, there is no general explanation of success, in the sense in which there is a general explanation, say, of iron rusting. The causal chain that leads from one action to the state of affairs that constitutes success may have virtually nothing in common with the one operative in another case. Those actions are produced by similar patterns of beliefs and desires, but *that* neither involves truth nor explains success.

This line is essentially correct, if one takes the *explanandum*, 'the success of action', to consist in the fact that all those actions tend to result in certain states of affairs (the ones that happen to fulfill the motivating wants). Let this be the first sense of 'the success of action'; before distinguishing another sense, another *explanandum*, let us note a generalization which in a way systematizes all particular explanations of success (first sense), which employs the concept of truth, and which may not improperly be called an "explanation" of the tendency of actions to be successful (first sense).

Consider this analogy. Suppose Brown died from eating food containing arsenic, which he got from Pierre's kitchen. Suppose also that Pierre's kitchen contained other foods, each of which was contaminated with a different poison, and suppose a number of others have died from eating different bits of that other food. First question: is it correct to say that the explanation of Brown's death is that he ate food from Pierre's kitchen? Certainly, in a sense; it extensionally captures something that explains Brown's death. Naturally, the more intrinsic explanation instantiates a less accidental generalization. Second question: can it be said that the explanation of all those deaths was the victims' having eaten food from Pierre's kitchen? Again that is correct in a sense. But it is doubly removed from a more basic explanation, for it generalizes over particular explanations only via extrinsic descriptions of them; moreover, those particular explanations are heterogeneous, the poisons' working chemically, neurally, etc., in different ways.

There is a parallel between this "explanation" of the multiple deaths, and the sense in which the success of actions is explained by the relevant beliefs being true. In a particular case, to say that z's action was successful because z's beliefs were true captures *extensionally* the more essential explanation — namely the facts that make the beliefs true. And the generalization is doubly removed from a proper unified explanation, for the particular explanations it extensionally covers are quite heterogeneous, the facts that explain success in one case being quite different from those in others.

Naturally in the poison case there are reasons to be interested in the generalization, and similarly in the truth case; they give a further point to the concept of truth. Let us notice that the concept of truth does not thereby become a "theoretical" concept; truth is T-hood, and T sums up a correlation between beliefs and states of affairs which enables us to generalize extrinsically over heterogeneous explanations in a useful way.

Earlier I promised a second sense of 'the success of action'. Consider this. In situations consisting of beliefs-and-wants-leading-to-actions-according-to-the-practical-syllogism-pattern, the relevant wants tend to be fulfilled. Now that projectible correlation gives us a new *explanandum*. Previously, the *explanandum* was actions' leading to certain results. Now, how the actions come about is built into the *explanandum*. Does 'true' occur essentially in an explanation of that projectible correlation? Given that the practical syllogism is built into the *explanandum*, that the relevant pairs of beliefs tend to be jointly true *entails* the *explanandum*. So it yields only a somewhat attenuated sense of explaining success. But the important thing is that 'true' does not occur here merely to sum up heterogeneous explanations. For the tendency of those beliefs leading to action to be true generates a *projectible* feature of our actions. What explains success in the second sense is then whatever explains that projectible tendency. We have, on the one hand, the world's stability in certain respects, and, on the other, those facts about our belief-forming mechanisms which it is the business of cognitive psychology to discover. 'True' plays an essential intermediary role in formulating how cognitive psychology would explain the success of action in the second sense. Once again, truth is not thereby a "theoretical" concept in the sense that it gets its meaning from this role; truth is T-hood.

Getting one's way by telling the truth

The connection between true belief and successful action is one we must exploit constantly. For example, getting what we want is often achieved by z's getting what z wants, thus providing us with a motive to get z to fulfill z's wants. This happens not only when our desire is altruistic, but also when what z wants coincides with what we independently want, and this covers a wide variety of cases. One way to get z to advance z's goals effectively is to get z to have true beliefs, given the connection between true belief and success. In certain cases z knows more than we do of the background facts but lacks specific information needed for effective action. Suppose z is a medical specialist to whom I go for relief from pain. To get z to advance z's goal of relieving my pain, the most effective thing may be to produce in z true beliefs about my symptoms, past ailments, etc. Sometimes getting z to do something I want merely requires causing z to have a certain belief, *regardless of its truth*: if I want z to go to Chattanooga, it may be enough to tell him his long lost brother is there. But in the medical case, since I do not know what specific actions of z's would satisfy my wants, and since I think that z's technical background beliefs are likely to be true, or approximately so, my best strategy is to get z to have true beliefs about the specifics, thereby contributing to the successful satisfaction of z's wants, which I suppose to coincide with mine.

It may seem that another maxim for such cases would be equally effective, one that does not involve truth – namely, say what you believe. But it seems that one's concern is *still* with truth, but of z's beliefs about one's beliefs. Moreover, 'a maxim for such cases' raises precisely this question: what cases are they? Their very conception would seem to be: cases in which it is important that z have certain *true* beliefs if z is to bring about the desired result.

If one reconstructs the reasoning behind such cases, I think it is impossible to eliminate the concept of truth. I mean, of course, that the medical example is not special, and that much practical communicative activity has that sort of reasoning behind it.

9

Language and meaning

Let us turn to the relation between meaning and propositional attitudes now that we have a theory in hand. Theories that take attitudes as the foundation of semantic description have been greeted by many with something like amazed incredulity. One reason has been a strong intuition, central in modern empiricist philosophy, that thoughts, beliefs, intentions, are in large part linguistic states and that, consequently, concepts of the content of such states cannot be invoked non-circularly in explicating linguistic meaning. That intuition has stemmed largely from laudably naturalistic tendencies – a rejection of the Platonic–Cartesian–Brentanian conception of thought. Now my theory of beliefs, their functional semantic properties and truth conditions, would show that those concepts *can* be explicated without bringing in language and within a naturalistic framework. But while the functional organization required for beliefs involves no essential connections with natural language, the spirit of the enterprise has not been to show that beliefs are non-linguistic. It is even perfectly consistent with the theory that, in a sense to be explained, beliefs are linguistic states. But that is by no means obviously true, depending upon the truth of a non-trivial psychological hypothesis. A non-linguistic account of content provides an attractively flexible basis for sketching the manifold possible dependencies of thought upon language; the key point is that the ascription of content to propositional attitudes is at a more abstract level than ascriptions of meaning to natural language.

A second source of resistance to regarding beliefs as basic has been their apparent dependence on intensional properties, relations and entities. Naturalistic theories of meaning have tended to substitute dispositions to utterance or sentential attitudes for propositional attitudes. For it seemed that something intensional is required to capture appropriate *individuation conditions* for beliefs, while counting sentences as the primary bearers of content permits an entirely extensional semantics. The point is, if my functional account of belief-individuation is correct, intensions are not required in the theory of propositional attitudes and their intentional properties.

203

A third source of resistance has been epistemological. Fine-grained attitude-ascription inevitably depends on linguistic evidence, and a not unnatural conclusion to have reached is that the attitudes themselves must be linguistic, their content being equated with linguistic meaning. But in this sort of reasoning there is the risk of a positivist assimilation of theory to evidence. The foundational status of propositional attitudes, within our content- and meaning-ascribing theory of linguistic and non-linguistic behavior, does not imply that we normally can have non-linguistic access to fine-grained content. Moreover, the special role of linguistic evidence can be explained within the theory itself (cf. 6.4).

Recently there has been a tendency to argue that beliefs have to be linguistic because they are both representational, and structured like sentences. Harman (1973) has argued that beliefs, and more generally thoughts, are in one's natural language, and Fodor (1975), for related reasons, that they are in an innate language, this being necessary to explain natural language learning. Both hold that a system of beliefs must exhibit linguistic structure – that the existence of a *language* of thought follows more or less directly from the existence of thought.

While it is possible that beliefs are in one's natural language, it by no means follows from the relevant structure of the set of our possible beliefs that they are, nor that beliefs are in an underlying "language". In this difficult area, precipitate obliteration of distinctions may introduce unnecessarily strong empirical requirements. As I shall argue in the next section, 'people have beliefs' makes a lesser claim than 'there is a language of thought', and is more likely to be true. If the distinction is eliminated, it becomes that much less likely that our rational psychology has objective application.

Why try to explicate concepts of the semantic properties of natural language in terms of propositional attitudes? One rather evident motivation is simply that that would reduce the question of the objective determinacy of semantic concepts to that of the objective determinacy of the content of beliefs, given that certain theories along those lines have seemed promising (independently of the objections just discussed). The idea that semantic concepts are *coordinate* with, and not reducible to, propositional attitude concepts must be treated seriously, but my intuitions have been strongly in the direction of a subordinate status for the latter, for reasons that will emerge in chapter 10. Given that worries about mentalism and circularity have been stilled, we can again take seriously the intuitive idea that linguistic meaning, at least its public language aspect, consists in sentences being conventional devices for expressing thoughts.

In this chapter I shall sketch possible connections between propositional attitudes and language that could account for meaning, by no means exhausted by the Gricean framework (although it is bound to be prominent in the semantics of public language). I shall also consider the concepts of subsentential *reference*, and of *grammar* (also treated in 10.4), which of all central semantic concepts are perhaps the most refractory to naturalistic vindication.

9.1 THE LANGUAGE OF THOUGHT

Suppose our functional organization meets the constraints of the belief–desire theory. The question arises whether the underlying first-order states having the relevant functional roles collectively make up a *language*. Now, unlike recent proponents of the language of thought hypothesis, I do not think the answer is trivially yes. For there is a structural property, present in all uncontroversial cases of language, natural and artificial, which is not guaranteed simply by the *functional* structure required for having beliefs and desires. But while it is a further question whether there is a language of thought, the further conditions may well be satisfied.

Ordinary linguistic structure is a matter of two structural levels, syntactic and semantic, being in a certain way parallel. So, for 'rats eat cheese' and 'cats eat cheese', the syntactic description 'consists of a noun phrase followed by 'eats cheese'' applies to both, and it is a further fact that they have in common something semantic that matches the syntactic similarity. That two symbols share semantic properties is, conversely, not sufficient for their having that sort of linguistic structure, for two unstructured signals could be used (in a code, say) to mean what those sentences mean. Now, by 'semantic' I mean not only the referential – truth condition level of description but also the functional; if linguistic structure is to be discerned in a functional system, it would seem there must be *two parallel structures*, syntactic and functional. For example, consider a rule like 'from $\ulcorner s \& s'\urcorner$ infer s'. For sentences with a certain syntactic property, this determines a common functional role; a system of inferential rules not founded on independently describable syntactic structure would not yield what would look like linguistic structure. So we might say linguistic structure depends on syntactic–semantic (referential or functional) structural parallels.

What is the analogue of syntactic structure in beliefs and desires? Being in a functional state is being in an underlying "first-order" state with certain counterfactual properties. In the inference rule example, the syntactic description intrinsically characterizes sentence-types that are then given certain inferential roles. So it is natural to look for the "syntax" of beliefs in whatever intrinsically characterizes those "first-order" state types that have the relevant functional roles; if people had blackboards inside their heads, then the first-order state with the functional role of the belief that rats eat cheese might be, among French people, the occurrence of '*les rats mangent le fromage*' on their internal *tableaux noirs*, and there would be no problem about what to count as syntax. Linguistic structure would be present here precisely because of further parallel syntactic and functional structures: the state with the functional role of the belief that cats eat cheese would be the inscription of '*les chats mangent le fromage*'. If there is then linguistic structure in our beliefs, the first-order states must have a suitable structure, constituted *independently of their being beliefs*; otherwise there would be no interesting parallel with the internal blackboard story, and thus no point in speaking of a language of thought.

Would the syntactic structure have to be physiological? What else could the relevant first-order states be? But I have been using 'first-order' loosely; for the relevant distinction is not, strictly speaking, first-order/second-order, but nth-order/$n + 1$th order. The state types that contingently have the functional roles of beliefs and desires might themselves be intrinsically characterized at some other level of functional description. Even neurophysiology itself might be functionally defined if, say, a creature made out of wire, etc., could nevertheless have neurons, axons, synapses. But apart from that, there could be, in an information-processing model that abstracts from neurophysiological structure, a systematic characterization of states which (like the syntactic description of marks on blackboards) does not imply the further functional roles which make those states beliefs. So, for beliefs to have a syntax, it is not required that some states be suitably isomorphic in physiological structure to English. But if the functional states defined by the belief–desire theory are $n + 1$th order states, then an appropriate syntactic structure should be found among nth order states if beliefs constitute a language.

It evidently does not follow trivially from z's being functionally organized in accordance with the belief–desire theory that some of z's states (beliefs and desires) have syntactic structure. Suppose $x = z$'s belief at t that rats eat cheese (i.e. the type), and $y = z$'s belief at t that cats eat cheese. Must there be an underlying structure in x and y which they have in common with all and only beliefs that A's eat cheese? Clearly not, however fruitful and interesting an empirical hypothesis that may be. But then it is not a trivial consequence of the functional belief–desire theory that there is a language of thought.

Not everyone has seen matters thus. Gilbert Harman holds that that structure of beliefs by virtue of which we generalize over their contents using variables, as in 'the belief that p & q', is enough to warrant speaking of the language of thought. He writes: "we can take these states to be instances of sentences because they have structure and representational characteristics that depend on their structure" (Harman, 1973, p. 58). But, since 'structure' here means 'functional structure', this remark conflates functional and syntactic structure; without an independent status for the latter, the interesting analogy with language vanishes. In 7.2 I maintained that the syntactic structure of sentential *indices* is sufficient to capture functional interconnections of beliefs. But that involves the syntax of the content language; the underlying states that have the indexed functional roles need not be syntactically isomorphic to the indices. To generalize systematically over the functional roles of conjunctive beliefs, as in 'the belief that p & q', we require syntactic structure only in the indices; the variables do not refer to underlying constituents.

This is not meant to deny that the language of thought hypothesis is extremely interesting, or that it stands a good chance of being approximately correct. On the contrary, it is a natural hypothesis that beliefs of the same form, such as 'A's eat cheese', have something structural in common which accounts for their similarity in functional role. Suppose it is true. The functional theory of beliefs and desires could then count as the semantic theory of sentences in the language of thought: if x is such a sentence, x's meaning (indicatively) p is simply x's being the belief that p (for person z at time t). It may not be useful to call this property 'meaning', but a strong analogy with the semantic description of overt language is clearly established: the conditions that map underlying states onto belief-types would have the generative structure we expect of the semantic theory of a language.

Suppose a language of thought hypothesis were true of z. What would be the connection between z's language of thought and z's spoken language? Could they automatically be identified? Harman has proposed identifying the language of thought with the language we speak: "My present claim is that the relation between some of these 'sentences' and sentences in the language we speak is more like the relation between written and spoken English than like that between English and Russian" (1973, p. 89). This would be secured by virtue of a word–word/structure–structure isomorphism between the languages in which we think and speak, the isomorphism that obtains between written and spoken English but not between English and Russian. Would that imply that we think in English, as we write in English? The identification is made in a further part of Harman's account: in an ordinary linguistic communication "the speaker's thought [is] a token of the sentence under analysis, and the hearer's perception is another token of *the same sentence* [my italics] under the same analysis". Whether this is a further hypothesis than (or is intended to be implied by) the isomorphism is not clear from Harman's text. My position is this: that we think in English is a non-trivial, interesting, hypothesis, not secured by an isomorphism of our language of thought and natural language. After all, two distinct natural languages could be relevantly isomorphic. One may think of further *causal* constraints on identifying inner and outer languages, but even that may not be sufficient to capture the most interesting sense in which we may "think in English". I shall make a suggestion about this shortly (pp. 214–15).

The issue is not terminological (although one ought not to insist too much on one's own ways of speaking). The real question is how to conceptualize the possibilities, rather than when to say "we think in English". It makes a difference to the overall picture of what properties of natural language are its semantic properties if it is true that we think in English in some substantial sense.

In summary, then, the fact that z's internal states are functionally organized in according with the belief–desire theory does not entail that z's beliefs exhibit linguistic structure; and the fact that our beliefs exhibit linguistic structure, even isomorphic to that of our spoken language, does not entail that we think in the language we speak. Both are further empirical hypotheses that would make a substantial difference to a psychological theory.

9.2 NATURAL LANGUAGE MEANING

The rest of this chapter is concerned with the semantic properties of natural language. This is not altogether easy to demarcate firmly, but let me say what it is *not* meant to cover. Suppose there is a language of thought which does not meet appropriate requirements for being identified with a natural language. While we could speak of sentences in the language of thought as having *meaning*, that would not be part of my topic here. (My theory of belief is a theory of meaning for such a language.) But if z's language of thought is appropriately identified with z's natural language, then those properties of z's sentences which constitute their *content* − as being a belief that p − are part of the current topic.

I wish to construe 'natural language meaning', then, as broadly as possible. A theorist can always then say: I am interested merely in this part of your broadly defined topic. There has been some misunderstanding among philosophers of language about just what it is about meaning and reference that concerns them, especially as regards whether the concern is communication and linguistic behavior, or something broader, or something more fundamental. (Gilbert Harman has been admirably clear on these matters, but that has not altogether prevented misunderstanding.) Now I do not mean to preclude without further discussion the claim that, say, the theory of communication completely exhausts the topic of natural language meaning; but given the following characterization, that would take an argument.

Regardless of what else it includes, I take natural language meaning to cover the use of language in communication, and whatever truth-conditional, referential, locutionary and illocutionary properties sentences and utterances thereby possess, as well as non-conventional utterance meaning, if it exists.

Here is a further condition on what is to count as natural language meaning, and an important empirical assumption. That a child learns, comes to understand, something linguistic, s, is sufficient for s's having meaning. This is trivial, but it has important consequences. For, if a theory says that meaning consists in XYZ, and a child at early to middle stages of language learning has not mastered XYZ, then the theory does not state a necessary condition of meaning in the broadest relevant sense. Whether this is crucial depends on whether what the child masters is something *weaker* than XYZ or *independent* of it. Thus consider the theory that meaning consists solely in certain complex social–psychological properties which are a function of communicative use; if the child, because of not possessing a sophisticated enough set of concepts, has not mastered such properties of language, that might be either because the child's learning consisted in mastery of something weaker than those properties (cf. 9.6), in which case that theory of meaning would need merely a minor adjustment to cover the developmental stage, or because the learning consists in something independent, e.g. in sentences coming to have certain roles in thought, in which case the theory would need more than minor revision.

For some, speculation about first language learning and conceptual development may seem irrelevant to what interests them most – namely, those properties of fully developed language which constitute meaning. Theorists of chess, of modern warfare, of the economics of modern societies, of mathematics, all might with some plausibility claim that those early developmental processes which led to the full blown forms of their subjects are beside the point in understanding their synchronically interesting properties. But the difference with meaning is this. It is a plausible empirical assumption that what the child learns, what his understanding consists in, is retained in its general form by the adult. Consequently, if that consists partly in something independent of XYZ, it must be counted as a further component of full blown linguistic understanding, and consequently a distinct and ineliminable part of my topic.

9.3 PROPOSITIONAL ATTITUDES AS THE BASIS OF MEANING

An important and illuminating model in the theory of meaning has been the Gricean one (Grice, 1957, 1969; Schiffer, 1972). The basic idea is that semantic properties of utterances and sentences are a function of the communicative intentions of their utterers, or of conventions that associate sentence-types with such intentions. A related model is David Lewis's (1975), in which semantic properties are explicated in terms of conventions that associate sentence-types with beliefs. Both types of explication depend for their interest on the viability of a foundational framework of propositional attitudes which does not in its turn depend upon the semantic properties to be explicated; and that has by now, I think, been amply demonstrated.

There is a quite different way in which propositional attitudes may serve as the basis of meaning. Consider how Russell and Ramsey conceived the matter, especially Ramsey in 'Facts and propositions' (1927). (Cf. Loar, 1980.)

The idea is that you give the meaning of a sentence of z's by saying what z would be *believing* if z accepted that sentence. On Ramsey's theory the content of a belief (which Ramsey called the belief's objective factors) is a matter of its causal role. But the important thing is that the primary ascription of content or meaning has the form 'z believes that p', and it is only via such an ascription that meaning is ascribed to a sentence s, depending on the causal role of z's "attitude" in accepting s (which Ramsey calls the belief's mental factor).

Thus Gricean and Ramseyan explications of meaning via propositional attitudes depend on rather different relations between beliefs and sentences: on the former, utterances of sentences *express* beliefs; on the latter, acceptances of sentences *are* beliefs. But on both the *primary ascription of content* has the form: 'z believes that p'. Thus the thesis that propositional attitudes are the basis of meaning is quite general. Let the full topic of "content and meaning" include all ascriptions of propositional attitudes, locutionary acts of saying, etc., illocutionary acts, speaker's meaning, sentence meaning, the concept of what makes a language the language of a certain population, word meaning, truth conditions, reference, and so on. The thesis then is this: first, propositional attitude-ascriptions can be explicated without relying on any other ascriptions of content or meaning; and, secondly, all other ascriptions of content and meaning can be explicated on the basis of propositional attitudes. I hope the interest of the thesis is clear. Any motivation for wanting a physicalist explication of propositional attitudes applies to meaning also; and we have an explication of propositional attitude content compatible with physicalism. Moreover, reconstructing semantics on the basis of propositional attitudes (rather than sentential attitudes and their extensional semantics) accounts for classical intuitions about *individuating meanings*, and, as we have seen, we can achieve the relevant fineness of individuation without intensions.

Consider accounts on which sentential attitudes are taken as explicatively primary. Sentential attitudes may be invoked either as radically eliminative replacements of propositional attitudes or as a basis for their explication. In the latter case we would have something like this: 'z believes that p' means '$(\exists s)$ z accepts s and s means p'. Now, on my view, the likelihood of accounting independently for 's means p' is negligible, for reasons discussed in 2.3. The advantage of taking 'z believes p' and not 's means p' as basic is that the former can be explicated in a functional belief–desire theory of the sort I sketched.

This is not to say that the idea of sentential attitudes and their meaning is to be eliminated. Suppose "thinking in English" were vindicated – that inner states which are somehow in English have the functional roles of beliefs. It would be natural to identify such states with sentential attitudes, accepting sentences. The meaning of s is then given, as on Ramsey's theory, by specifying what z would be *believing* by accepting s, what $n + 1$th order state z would be in by being in the nth order state that thus involves s. This order of explication eliminates the independent 's means p' which is needed if sentential attitudes are the basis of propositional attitudes.

9.4 COMMUNICATION THEORIES OF SEMANTIC PROPERTIES

The question I turn to now is whether a communication theory of semantic properties can adequately cover the whole topic of natural language meaning – whether, in other words, semantic properties in the broad sense of the previous section are exhausted by those properties of sentences which are a function of their use in communication. I should say at the outset that, while possibly wrong, I do not think the thesis obviously wrong, or rather, obviously far from being right. And while the communication-related properties of language that are most naturally thought of in this connection are Gricean, I am not implying that Grice, or others who have developed the analysis of those properties, have subscribed to the strong thesis that they exhaust the semantic properties of natural language.[1] For there is the more modest but still important thesis that Gricean constructions suffice to explicate all the concepts of the semantics of language in communication – of sentence meaning, illocutionary force, what makes L the language of p, and so on, presupposing an independent, more foundational, account of the language of thought. That weaker thesis is the topic of chapter 10.

Gricean theories of sentence meaning proceed in two stages. First there is the explication of speaker's meaning, what a person means by a certain utterance. This has been illuminatingly and extensively discussed by Grice (1957, 1969) and Schiffer (1972). The key concepts are intention and belief; nothing about *conventional* meaning is invoked. A speaker's meaning consists in a complex intention, the core of which is the intention to affect a hearer's beliefs, intentions or actions in certain ways. The second stage is to explicate the conventional semantic properties of sentences, etc., as deriving from conventional regularities that associate sentence-types with communicative intentions.

Now I am going to raise a difficulty for the theory that such

[1] Perhaps Strawson has (Strawson, 1971).

properties exhaust the semantic properties of natural language. But the problem is not the often alleged one of a vicious explanatory circle, out of which the functionalist theory of propositional attitudes points the way; nothing irreducibly semantical is presupposed in the explication of '*x* intends that *y* should believe that...'.

Nor is the problem exactly that complex intentions are impossible without language: the functionalist theory shows that objection to depend on a deficiency of imagination; there are many ways in which a complex functional organization can be realized. Moreover, the strong thesis under consideration (that Gricean properties exhaust the semantic properties of natural language) is compatible with its being *empirically* necessary for complex propositional attitudes that one has undergone language learning processes.

The problem is the account of language learning or understanding that is implied by the strong Gricean theory; it does not appear to fit plausible assumptions about conceptual development. If meaning consists in complex social–psychological facts, understanding a language presumably must be identified with knowing such facts. This does not mean that understanding would require knowing a semantic theory for a language, but rather that, for each sentence, up to the limits of one's understanding, one would, if presented with it, judge it correctly to have a certain social–psychological role. It is difficult to think of a different model of understanding on the strong Gricean account.

But consider a child's learning a first language. There is a time, surely, when a child understands (some) language but does not yet possess the sophisticated concepts of communicative intentions. If what the child learns is counted as meaning, according to the earlier demarcation of that topic, it then follows that Gricean properties are not necessary for meaning. Now there are (at least) two strategies for accounting for language learning, on which propositional attitudes are basic and which accommodate conceptual innocence. They have quite different consequences for the strong communication thesis of semantic properties; only one enables it to be preserved roughly intact. I shall call them the non-cognitive and the cognitive accounts of understanding.

9.5 NON-COGNITIVE MODELS OF LANGUAGE LEARNING

Suppose that monolingual speakers of English do have a language of thought and that it can, moreover, be identified with English. Learning a language would then involve first, acquiring the capacity to be in states that are (somehow) internalizations of English sentences, and second, those states' acquiring the functional roles of beliefs and desires. That means, for instance, that a certain internalization of 'rats eat cheese' would acquire the functional role of the belief that rats eat cheese. This is not to say that one thereby acquires the belief that rats eat cheese, but rather that a certain state-*type* comes to have those functional second-order properties that define that belief-type.

This is not supposed to exhaust ordinary language learning, but to be part of it. Learning a language would be in part the acquiring of concepts, capacities to have certain beliefs (cf. Harman, 1975). This is a *non-cognitive* model of learning in this sense: learning a language would be a matter of acquiring not (only) knowledge *about* language, but (also) the capacity to think *in* language. The upshot would be a level of the semantic description of English – the theory of meaning for English as the language of thought – that is independent of Gricean properties.

What might "thinking in English" amount to? Earlier I denied that word–word/structure–structure isomorphism between English and the language of thought is enough to justify that locution in any interesting sense; it could obtain between distinct natural languages. A stronger requirement is this. A psycholinguistic theory could introduce inner states which are *language-specific* and *sententially individuated*. Suppose the theory has a component that describes a hearer's phonological syntactic analysis of heard speech, and implies that, corresponding (roughly) to each sentence of the overt language, there is a possible inner state which is the potential output of that interpretive component. Such states could be language-specific: the theory may imply they cannot be the output, of that phonological syntactic component, for heard sentences of other languages. They would be internal *representations* of English sentences (but not in any sense that implies *beliefs* about syntax, etc.). Such a syntactic–phonological component of a psycholinguistic theory would presumably be a *functional* theory.

Now suppose those syntactic–phonological representational states also have the functional roles of beliefs. In other words, the syntactic–phonological component specifies them intrinsically as nth order functional states, and as it happens, they have $n + 1$th order functional roles that make them beliefs. Or suppose the psycholinguistic theory says certain distinct nth order states have such and such functional relations to those syntactic–phonological representations, relations which, according to the theory, they could not have to representations of sentences of *other* languages (they are thus language specific), that those states have a suitable nth order structure, and that they have the $n + 1$th order functional roles of beliefs.

On either possibility it would be natural to say we think in English. If learning English were in part a matter of those syntactic–phonological states (types) acquiring the functional roles of beliefs, the semantic theory of English would not be exhausted by the theory of its role in communication. This speculation is not meant to cover all ways in which English could be counted as our language of thought; no doubt there are other models on which states with the functional roles of beliefs may be suitably language specific. The point is that the truth or falsity of such models affects the scope of natural language meaning; whether communication-theoretic properties might exhaust natural language meaning must wait upon psycholinguistic theorizing.

There is another way in which learning a language could be "non-cognitive", one in which the idea of a language of thought does not play a role. Imagine creatures who are perfectly *credulous* – they believe whatever they are told. (We may imagine mechanisms for avoiding large-scale inconsistencies.) Suppose they do not form such beliefs by reasoning or inference from premises, especially not ones that involve semantic propositions, like: 'he said s, s means p, he is a truth-speaker; hence, p is true'. The picture is rather that a non-inferential process leads from hearing to believing, the only belief being the terminal one. *Learning* a language would then be acquiring a disposition to form certain beliefs in response to certain sounds. It need not involve acquiring propositional knowledge *about* language. If that disposition associated belief-types with sentences in a language-like way, the corresponding belief-types would determine *meanings* for those sentences.

This mechanical and uncritical believer is not being suggested as a component of ordinary language acquisition. The point is that non-cognitive models of language learning could differ greatly. What is important about both possibilities is that they fit nicely into a framework in which propositional attitudes are basic. Semantic description of the language acquired is straightforward; naturally it would involve some generative or recursive framework for associating sentences with belief-types. Notice, finally, that on any non-cognitive model of language learning, the idea of *correct* learning can be captured, not as the acquiring of true beliefs, but as the acquiring of that dispositional association of sentences and belief-types which holds for the language group from which the learner learns.

With these observations about language learning in hand, let us consider a certain radical position of Jerry Fodor's about language learning, in his important book *The Language of Thought* (1975). Learning one's first natural language, he claims, presupposes already being in possession of a language, in which the meanings of the sentences to be learned can be represented. This assumes that learning a language is the acquiring of knowledge *about* the meanings of its expressons, and therefore presupposes already having concepts adequate to those meanings. It of course also assumes a strong language of thought hypothesis, for which Fodor has argued independently. (With the assumption that thought requires a language of thought I shall not take issue here.) Given that learning any language presupposes already having a language of thought, Fodor embraces the obvious consequence that one's language of thought is not one's natural language, and is innate.

Now two related assumptions here can be doubted. The first is that learning a language is a *cognitive* matter, in other words, involves acquiring knowledge about the language. The second is that one cannot *acquire* a system of concepts (which, on the language of thought hypothesis, means – learn a language of thought). We have seen that there is a non-cognitive sense of understanding and of learning language; and if this turned out to apply to natural language learning, Fodor's argument would directly fail. But there is a deeper point to be made. It *may* be true that learning a natural language is a cognitive matter, for the non-cognitive model depends on a psycholinguistic hypothesis that may be false. Suppose it is; would Fodor's argument then force us to an innate language of thought? Not a bit. Regardless of whether a background system of concepts is a language (in the sense of 9.1), there is no reason to suppose that a system of concepts cannot be learned. Having certain concepts is having a certain functional organization; acquiring a system of concepts, or a language of thought, is a matter of one's inner states *coming to have* such a functional organization. And what is so impossible about that? Naturally there must be something genetic that explains our capacity for acquiring a given functional organization in response to a given environment; but it is odd to suppose *a priori* that that functional organization – that set of concepts – *must* itself be innate, that different environments could not interact with the genetic factors to produce different conceptual functional organizations.

If meaning consisted entirely in communication-theoretic properties, then understanding, grasping meanings correctly, would consist in knowledge of those properties. But it seems it can't if the language learning child lacks the necessary concepts. Earlier I mentioned that first language learning might involve acquiring propositional knowledge of properties of language that are *weaker* than, entailed by but not entailing, communication-theoretic properties. This possibility is important for several reasons. First, if the non-trivial thesis that we think in English were not correct, the strong Gricean thesis about meaning could still be largely vindicated. Second, even if a thinking-in-English hypothesis were correct (which, doubtless on insufficient evidence, appears likely to me), adding a certain further simple cognitive level to language learning illuminates and vindicates (as against recent tendencies) the intuition that language learning involves, in part at least, acquiring knowledge of truth conditions.

The account has two components. First, when children learn language, they do acquire knowledge, but not of complex psychological and social facts; they learn that there is a certain systematic correlation between words and things, a correlation that is somehow strikingly and uniquely important, by which 'dog' is thereby associated with that thing, 'it is barking' with the possibility that that thing is barking, and so on. The child learns an *abstraction* from what the adult knows – as though one were to learn the extension of a relational expression ('means', 'refers') and not its meaning. The child acquires parallel, attenuated conceptions of reference and truth conditions. This is not to say that the child learns a truth *theory* for the language; the knowledge is sentence by sentence, and in a way merely potential. A disposition is somehow systematically acquired to judge, when presented with certain expressions, 'this denotes that', 'this is true iff such and such'. The important thing here is that what is acquired involves propositional knowledge about language.

This might seem to run afoul of a major consideration for the non-cognitive model of language learning. While it avoids ascribing to the child advanced concepts, the new model does presuppose the possession of the concepts required for thinking the relevant truth conditions. One can't judge that 'it barks' is true iff that thing barks, unless one has the concept of barking. It seems, moreover, very plausible that at least sometimes learning words is thereby acquiring the relevant concepts. Taking language learning to be cognitive then appears self-defeating; it presupposes possession of the concepts thereby acquired. This apparent difficulty brings us to the second component of the simple cognitive model.

It is perfectly coherent to suppose that at the same time a child acquires the concept dog *and* learns that 'dog' denotes dogs, these being distinct states of affairs. The non-cognitive model of learning is not self-evidently correct for it is not self-evident that we think in the language we speak; so suppose it turns out to be false. Then, if learning language involves acquiring concepts, it may have to be described thus: the child thereby both acquires the concept dog (the capacity to be in certain functional states, to have beliefs about dogs) and learns that 'dog' denotes dogs. The distinct achievements are somehow tied. (Why learning language and acquiring concepts go together would then need a substantive explanation, which is not so on the non-cognitive model.)

Now it is plausible indeed that the simple cognitive model should be at least part of any account of language learning. For when a child learns a word like 'dog' it does learn *that* a certain fact obtains which involves both a certain vocable and certain things; similarly for sentences and truth conditions. This leads us to a further, more rounded possible picture of language learning, an amalgam of the non-cognitive and simple cognitive models. When one both acquires a concept and learns a bit of language, perhaps what happens is this. An internalized word acquires the functional role of a certain concept (internalized sentences involving that word acquire the functional roles of certain beliefs). Such a non-cognitive mastery of 'dog' enables the child to think-the-English-sentence ''dog' means dogs'; and that mastery is a component of the broader capacity to think internalized sentences of the form '*s* is true iff...', where 'dog' occurs on the right hand side. On that two-level model, the intuition that learning a first language is learning how to think, and the intuition that it is learning truth conditions, are both accommodated.

I hope it is clear that learning denotations and truth conditions is, on that model, not trivial. It might seem to be, if one thought that sentences like '*W* denotes...' and '*s* is true iff...' merely provide translations of what is mentioned on the left into what occurs on the right. But naturally I am not suggesting that the child learns that a certain expression translates that very expression. The idea rather is that the child acquires propositional knowledge that the vocable 'dog' stands in a certain strikingly salient relation to dogs, not to expressions.

Similarly for truth conditions. On any functional or conceptual-role account of belief, the belief that 'dog' is R to dogs ought to count as different from the belief that 'dog' is $R^\star$ to 'dogs', regardless of whether the belief is in the natural language or not.

Notice that if the thinking-in-English hypothesis turned out to be false, then (provided no other non-cognitive model were correct) the strong Gricean position, that Gricean communication-theoretic properties exhaust the semantic properties of natural language, would be considerably promoted. For one could say that what children learn about English is a truth-theoretic abstraction from such properties, which sets them on the path to the full mastery of language in communication. Naturally the question arises how learning truth conditions might do that. How might learning word–thing correlations contribute to that mastery of correlations of sentences and types of communicative intention which the communication-theoretic model requires? This is especially important given the thesis that what individuates propositional attitudes, and hence communicative intentions, is functional role and not truth conditions. Perhaps this simple model will help. First, the sentences the child has mastered *somehow* acquire a secondary use in ascribing beliefs, etc., to others: the sentence 'dogs bark' comes to index others' beliefs that dogs bark. Secondly, the child's learning truth conditions for sentences, the abstract correlation that is independent of their indexing role, thereby generates a general conception of the truth conditions of beliefs, given the use of sentences as belief indices. Thirdly, because of the intimate connection between truth and fulfillment conditions and the ascription of propositional attitudes (cf. 8.4), the child's learning truth conditions is an indispensable component of learning that association of sentences and communicative intentions which, on the communication-theoretic model, constitutes meaning. Learning truth conditions is then a substantive step towards mastering meaning in the Gricean sense.

9.7 LANGUAGES AND TRUTH THEORIES

Certain questions about the pragmatic underpinnings of semantics are clarified if we have on hand the concept of a *language*, something that abstractly associates sentences with meanings.[2] The most obvious one is what makes L (abstractly described) the language of a population P or a person z. Posing questions about sentence meaning in that way

[2] The influence of David Lewis should be evident here (cf. Lewis, 1975).

has the advantage of allowing us to express in summary form that conventional association of sentences with types of propositional attitudes which a theory of linguistic meaning must explicate. So, a language is a function from sentences to meanings. What are meanings?

Suppose all sentences were indicative, unambiguous, and contained no indexical expressions, so that each sentence, in abstraction from context, expressed exactly one definite belief. So far we have seen two relations between a sentence s and a belief b which, given that assumption, could constitute the former's meaning: s's internalization has the functional role of b, or s is a conventional device for expressing b. In either case, s's meaning would be the content of b, and to specify it is just to give that *sentence* of the content language which indexes b. So if we want entities to serve as meanings, sentences of the content language serve nicely, given an account of the relation between sentence-type and belief-type that constitutes the former's meaning.

The initial paradox of taking a sentence's meaning to be a sentence must at first increase when one reflects that, if s is in English, then s's meaning is s itself! The paradox quickly evaporates when one takes into account the role that s has *qua* meaning. It indexes a belief, relative to our standard English speaking scheme, which associates that-clauses with beliefs. It is against the background both of that system of indexing, and of the relation between beliefs and sentences that constitutes meaning, that s can count as the meaning of s. *Qua* belief index, it captures the details of its own meaning in English.

Identifying meanings with sentential indices of beliefs makes sense of the classical intuition that meaning determines truth conditions. If the meaning of s, for person z or population P, is our content sentence s', then we have:

> s is true in the language of z or P iff Ts' (i.e. iff the belief that s' is true).

The meaning of '*la neige est blanche*' in French consists in a certain relation to the belief that we index with 'snow is white'; hence it is true in French iff T ('snow is white'), that is, iff snow is white. In this way the *non-relativized* Tarskian truth predicate serves as the basis for the interlinguistic, relativized, notion of truth in the language of z or P, *via* the mediating non-relativized notion of truth for beliefs.

Let us turn to the question what a language is, and its relation to the correct *truth theory* for a given person or population. In the restricted case (indicative, non-indexical, etc., sentences) a language is a function from sentences of the object language to sentences of the content language of our belief–desire theory. It is simple then to say what would make L the person z's language of thought:

L is z's language of thought at t just in case, for any s and s', if $L(s) = s'$ then z's internalization of s at $t = z$'s belief that s' at t.

The question what makes L the *public* language of a certain population P is of course more complicated, and will be discussed in 10.4.

Naturally we should expect a language to determine *truth conditions* for its sentences; and indeed that is secured on my account, simply because the meaning of a sentence determines its truth conditions in the sense just explained.

We then have a straightforward criterion for what makes T the *correct truth theory* for the language of P or z: T must imply, for each sentence s of P's language, that s is true in P iff q just in case s *is* true in P iff q – a suitably banal result. This is worth pointing out, for it means that the notion 'correct truth theory for z's or P's language' presupposes an *independent* status for 'true in z's or P's language', rather than the other way around, which has been a tendency in some recent (as I see it, anti-semantic realist) theorizing about truth. This is in keeping with my account's realism about semantic properties. A correct truth theory reports truth conditions and does not constitute them.

Further constraints on how a truth theory should assign truth conditions to sentences, e.g. by recursive clauses that associate iterable contributions to truth conditions with iterable syntactic features, are not constraints on the correctness of a theory of truth conditions, but on the correctness of the *grammar* for the language (the subject of 9.9). There could be some merely verbal issues about what to count as a "truth theory". For even among realists (cf. Field, 1972), '*theory of truth for L*' may mean something that shows how truth conditions of sentences depend on the references of their parts. My point is simply that, in a more basic sense, a "truth theory for L" is a theory that purports to capture the truth conditions of the sentences of L. It is a further matter how truth conditions depend on sentential structure, etc. This distinction is not pedantic; for the matter of objective and determinate reference is something over and above objective and determinate truth conditions (cf. 9.9).

The restriction to indicative, unambiguous and non-indexical sentences may be lifted. Consider an indicative sentence with indexicals, say, 'she beat him handily'. No specific belief is associated with it *qua* sentence of English, but rather a class of beliefs, roughly those of the form 'θ_1 beat θ_2 handily' (where θ_1 and θ_2 are descriptions) or those whose indices have the form '$\langle$'x beat y handily', $\langle \alpha, \beta \rangle \rangle$' (sentential analogues of singular propositions). The meaning of that indexical sentence is given by the open sentence 'x beat y handily' of the content language, together with something that represents the contributions of 'she' and 'him' (cf. Loar, 1976a, pp. 153–5, and Loar, 1976b, p. 375). The details are not my point here; but the "meaning" of that sentence will contain at least the predicates 'male', 'female' of the content language. This "meaning" is an ordered n-tuple of these and other appropriate elements. The language assigns such sentences satisfaction conditions rather than fully determinate truth conditions; this again is by virtue of the special status of T, and its related satisfaction predicate, in connection with the content language.

Moods other than the indicative are represented in "meanings" by something that represents propositional attitudes other than belief. The meaning then is, say, an n-tuple, of a marker of mood, the relevant open or closed sentence of the content language, and so on. What it is about the pragmatics of conventional language use these "meanings" capture will, I hope, become clearer in 10.4.

Finally, information about a sentence's *grammatical structure* is not part of its meaning in the current sense (for a different view, see D. Lewis, 1972a). That is represented in the *grammar* of the language, which says how sentential structure and constituents contribute to meaning and truth conditions. As regards the intuition that a sentence's meaning is a *holistic* fact about it – i.e. a matter of its place in the whole language, rather than its direct connection to something like a propositional attitude – that intuition has in effect been accommodated on my account at a more basic level, namely (1) in the determination of a propositional attitude's content by its place in the overall belief–desire functional organization, and (2) in the implicit holistic considerations inevitably appealed to in determining truth conditions for beliefs on the basis of reliability.

9.8 WHAT IS A THEORY OF MEANING?

While an answer is close to the surface in the foregoing, it may be useful to present it as such. I mean a theory of meaning for a specific language, as spoken by a certain population, or as thought in by a certain person – that is, a comprehensive systematic description of the semantic properties of the language, relative to that person or population. Here 'language' means 'such and such set of sentences', and not 'such and such association of meanings with sentences'; a theory of meaning for the language (first sense) of a population is in part an identification of the language (second sense) they speak or think in. A theory of meaning would also include a *grammar* for the language (cf. 9.9; 10.4).

This abstract characterization is hardly enough; for a theory of meaning must also say what empirical connections with propositional attitudes are captured by a language, that is, by that function from sentences to meanings. Thus a theory of meaning for z's language of thought associates sentences with the functional roles of their internalizations, while one for a public language associates sentences with classes of complex communicative intentions that they are conventional devices for expressing.

John McDowell writes: "a theory of meaning for a language should be a systematic portrayal of the *capacity* possessed by someone who *understands* it [my italics]" (McDowell, 1980). My reaction to this is mixed. It fits quite well a theory of meaning for a language of thought. For the non-cognitive understanding of a sentence is just a matter of that sentence's having acquired the right functional role; hence a theory that mapped sentences onto those functional roles would indeed be "a systematic portrayal of the capacity possessed by someone who understands" those sentences. Also, the other non-cognitive model of language learning (described on p. 215) on which it consists in acquiring a disposition to produce certain beliefs in response to certain sounds, would also make that characterization apt. (That model in fact resembles McDowell's account of that nexus between sentence and belief which is constitutive of meaning (1980, ibid.).)

If "meaning" is a matter of sentences being conventional devices for making known communicative intentions, a theory of meaning for a (public) language simply says which sentences are conventionally associated with which intentions. "Understanding" that language then consists in *knowing* of each sentence what it means, and so the correct theory of meaning will indeed capture what one understands. But, in that sense, any theory of a subject X is a theory of what one knows in knowing the facts about X: a theory of nitrogen-fixing bacteria is in effect a theory of what one knows if one knows the facts about nitrogen-fixing bacteria. If, in other words, understanding consists in "propositional knowledge" of meanings, it is misleading to bring it into an account of a theory of meaning. So, rather than characterize theories of meaning in general as theories of understanding, it is better to characterize them as theories of certain possible connections of sentences with propositional attitudes. This covers the possibility (depending on, e.g., the "thinking-in-English" hypothesis) that understanding is not otiose, i.e., that the obtaining of those connections is tantamount to understanding.

It would be well, finally, to clarify the connection between theory of meaning and theory of truth. Let us revert to the simplified language whose sentences are indicative, unambiguous and non-indexical. A theory of meaning for it associates each sentence s with something, say, of the form 'x believes that...', or, to accommodate an undiscussed possibility (McDowell, 1980), something of the form 'x says that...'. McDowell has suggested that a truth theory has the function of associating sentences s with statement-contents '...', by virtue of implying things of the form 's is true iff...'. The truth theory is a systematic way of associating sentences with what they say.

But there is a problem. I assume 'x says that...' is relational: 'that...' denotes something. But then what captures the association of sentences with contents is a *function*, and 's is true iff...' does not express a function, or any relation; 'true' is a one-place predicate, and '...' is occupied by sentences and not names.

Perhaps we should move up a linguistic level, so that what associates sentences with contents does so by relating sentences s to equivalences of the form 's is true iff...', via the meta-truth-theoretic statement that for all s and p, s is relevantly associated with saying (believing) that p just in case T implies that s is true iff p. But that is rather baroque. What is wanted is a function that maps each s onto the right p. While the meta-truth-theoretic statement does express such a function, to say it involves 'true' or any predicate of sentences is beside the point. It is better simply to take a theory of meaning for L to incorporate that function-in-extension, that language, which maps each s onto (in our simplified language) the sentence '...' which indexes the belief s expresses.

What then is the relation between a theory of meaning and a theory of truth? The answer has already in effect been given. A correct theory of meaning for P or z says which language, which function of that kind, is the language of z or P. A language determines its own truth conditions, not by mapping sentences onto truth conditions, but by mapping sentences onto the sentential indices for beliefs. Sentential indices, relative to Bel, determine truth conditions: for, in the sense explained in 7.3, it is trivial that the belief that s is true iff Ts, (although by no means trivial that the truth theory captures something interesting). So a theory of meaning for a language determines a theory of truth for that language, and, it goes without saying, is not exhausted by it.

9.9 THE DETERMINACY OF REFERENCE

Nothing so far has been said about the meaning and reference of terms or subsentential expressions, or the logical form or semantic structure of sentences. Indeed as regards *referential* semantics, those matters are largely underdetermined by considerations about truth conditions and sentence meaning; the references of names and predicates are not determined by the truth conditions of the sentences they occur in. That observation (which I shall explain in more detail) is the basis of Quine's thesis of the *inscrutability of reference* (1969). Quine's thesis, though, is far stronger than the underdetermination of references by truth conditions; for he also holds that there are no *further* aspects of physical fact and theory that determine reference. If that were true, then, given the physicalist premise, there would be no "fact of the matter" about whether the English word 'dog' refers to dogs, etc. Let us then take the claim that reference is inscrutable to be this: the references of the terms of L are underdetermined by the conjunction of physical fact and theory and any assignment of truth conditions to the sentences of L.

Now I shall be arguing that the claim of inscrutability is basically not true. The qualification is due to a vagueness in the main issue, about what is required for a discourse, which is not explicitly physicalist (e.g. the semantic) to be *determined* by physical fact and theory.

Before turning to reference, it may be of interest to note a level of linguistic description that deserves to be called semantic, involves the characterization of subsentential expressions and of sentential structure, is determinate with respect to properties of linguistic meaning that have already been introduced, and is (then) not about reference. There is a distinction between *functional semantics* and *referential semantics*. For, a certain sentence's conventionally expressing a certain belief in P, or having the internal functional role for z of a certain belief, does not presuppose anything about truth conditions or reference, given how beliefs are individuated by functional role. Now, their fine-grained functional roles are a physically determinate fact about beliefs (cf. 6.1).

Now it is pretty clear, without going into the details, that if the sentence '*les rats mangent le fromage*' and '*les chats mangent le fromage*' have the functional roles, in the language of thought of French speakers, of the beliefs that rats eat cheese and that cats eat cheese, then we could assign well-defined distinct functional properties to the internal phrases '*les rats*' and '*les chats*', properties derivative from the functional roles of all sentences in which those phrases occur. The form of such a functional semantics is roughly this: the functional "meaning" of a certain word, syntactic structure, etc., E of a given object language will be captured simply by that word, syntactic structure, etc., of our content language common to the indices of all beliefs in whose object language realizations or expressions E occurs. The functional–semantic grammar of L is then a function from words, structures, etc., of L to words, structures, etc., of our content language, in the ideal case of perfect isomorphism, and, otherwise, some more roundabout characterization of their contributions to functional role.

Considerations of reliability and simplicity motivate at most a restriction of suitable truth predicates for beliefs to those strongly equivalent to T. But this leaves great leeway in how a truth predicate assigns references and satisfaction conditions. Quine's well known examples (in Quine, 1969) illustrate the point well. If in writing out a truth theory, we stipulate that 'x is a rabbit' is satisfied by y iff y is a time-slice of a rabbit, and make suitable adjustments in the satisfaction conditions of all other predicates (e.g. so that 'x is one year old' is satisfied by y iff y is a time-slice of something that is one year old), as well as in the satisfaction conditions for identity (so that '$x_1 = x_2$' is satisfied by $\langle y_1, y_2 \rangle$ iff y_1 and y_2 are time-slices of the same four-dimensional rabbit), then given standard assignments to the logical connectives, etc., beliefs will have truth conditions, under that truth theory, strongly equivalent to those they have under T. There being two one-year-old rabbits behind that bush is the same thing as there being two time-slices of one-year-old rabbits behind that time-slice of a bush.

Let us call any assignment of satisfaction conditions that has this feature a *truth-conditionally adequate reference scheme*. Now some such reference schemes assign even more surprising references to the predicates of the English language than the foregoing. So, to take an example that has figured in some interesting discussions of these matters (Wallace, 1977; Field, 1975; Davidson, 1979), let φ be any permutation of the universe, a one–one function that maps every object or space–time region onto some other. Then let 'φ-satisfaction' be defined so that, e.g. 'x is a rabbit' is φ-satisfied by y iff $\varphi(y)$ is a rabbit; and, in general, $\ulcorner Fx_1, \ldots, x_n \urcorner$ is φ-satisfied by $\langle y_1, \ldots, y_n \rangle$ iff $\langle \varphi_{(y_1)}, \ldots, \varphi_{(y_n)} \rangle$ satisfies, on our standard reference scheme, $\ulcorner Fx_1, \ldots, x_n \urcorner$. Given a few refinements, the resultant truth predicate will be strongly equivalent to T: for example, the φ-truth conditions of 'every rabbit hops' will be 'for every x, if $\varphi(x)$ is a rabbit, $\varphi(x)$ hops'. But the references of 'rabbit', on the φ-scheme, can include things otherwise quite unconnected with rabbits – e.g. a locomotive and a cloud.

Our topic is the determinacy of reference for discrete, subsentential, expressions. If *beliefs* have reference that would be because they are in some language whose expressions have references; if there is a language of thought which is not a natural language, it will do. If we are to speak of the belief that rats eat cheese as referring to rats in a way that suitably parallels saying that the English sentence 'rats eat cheese' refers to rats, the belief would have to have a subsidiary repeatable feature which specifically has that reference and contributes it to every other belief in which it occurs, like the word 'rats'. But, as I argued in 9.1, it is not guaranteed by the belief–desire theory that beliefs have linguistic structure. But I shall discuss the problem of reference within the artificial assumption that beliefs themselves are in fact linguistic in the sense of 9.1. We may then take the question to be whether reference in English, *qua* language of thought, is inscrutable, or would be if English were our language of thought. This permits establishing a straightforward connection between reliability motivations for ascribing truth conditions to beliefs and considerations about reference, and it is natural to suppose there is an intimate connection between motivations for ascribing truth conditions and for ascribing references. The theory of reference for public-language expressions, independent of the language of thought hypothesis, will then be much easier, given an account in these terms.

As I characterized inscrutability, whether reference is *determined* by physical fact and theory is central. But what does that mean? The question whether statements like 'x refers to y', which are not explicitly in physicalist language, are "determined by physical fact and theory" I shall interpret as concerning whether there is a correct *explication* of those statements in a physicalist language. As regards 'refers', there is no problem in constructing a physicalist explication that gets its *extension* right. Simply use the Tarski technique of enumerative definition, thus: 't refers to y' = def. 't = 'cat' and y is a cat, or t = 'dog' and y is a dog, or...', through the lexicon. Of course, this is physicalist in a minimal sense, for no chunky, non-trivial, physical relation between terms and things is thereby defined (cf. Field, 1972);

but it is physicalist in the sense of being expressible in a physicalist language.

Naturally that is not enough to eliminate inscrutability. For what has been claimed in support of Quine is that singling out that relation for special attention, christening it 'refers', is *arbitrary*, "a matter of convention". To say our reference scheme is arbitrary is at least to say there is no non-trivial relation, independent of whatever constitutes our conventional decisions, that is an appropriate candidate for explicating "refers". That would mean, in other words, that there is no relation which exactly determines our preferred extension for 'refers', and which is so uniquely empirically salient that it is unsurprising that we have a special term for it. This characterization does not eliminate all vagueness, and the question whether reference is determinate is ultimately vague. But I shall try to show that the truth lies more on the side of determinacy than indeterminacy. There is a plausible candidate for the explication of 'refers' that is no more arbitrary than reductive explications in non-semantic subjects.

That empirically salient relation is evidently not determined solely by the considerations that determine truth conditions. But it would beg the question against the determinacy of reference to presuppose that the *only* considerations that could be relevant are those that motivate the assignment of truth conditions. That an adequate theory of reference must be *compatible* with an adequate theory of truth conditions goes without saying; moreover, one ought to expect a theory of reference to explain that requirement of compatibility.

The structure of my account is as follows. (1) I suggest a *causal* condition (not surprisingly) that eliminates most truth-conditionally adequate "φ-reference" schemes, but does not determine a unique reference scheme. (2) Then I consider an argument of Davidson's to the effect that even the foregoing degree of referential determinacy is illusory. (3) Finally I turn to the difficult question of the objective *uniqueness* of our preferred reference scheme.

While *reliability* considerations do not discriminate among truth-conditionally adequate reference schemes, something connected with reliability is quite promising. Human contacts with rabbits are relevant to the reliability under T of beliefs in whose indices 'rabbit' occurs, while contacts with other objects (for which the values of φ are rabbits) are not in general thus connected with the reliability of those beliefs. An *explanation* of that reliability will mention rabbits, but not arbitrarily chosen φ-related items. My basic suggestion about reference is this: *referential relations are causal relations that figure in the explanation of the reliability of our beliefs under T.* Even for non-observational beliefs, the explanation of their tendency towards reliability under T will contain something about such causal connections. That the references of beliefs count intuitively as constituents of their truth conditions is then some function of how they must do the explaining.

Bringing in the explanation of reliability advances us further than hitherto within the general causal theory of reference; for it imposes a condition on which causal relations are referential, without saying what they are intrinsically. The advantage of this in an *explication* of reference is evident. Apart from a general relevance of perception, memory and language learning, psychological theory gives no account of referential relations. In any case the details might vary among persons. Moreover, it is not explicatively elegant to tie reference too closely to the human situation; a condition that covers non-human language-using creatures, unlikely though it is that we shall discover any, has a distinct appeal. In short, the suggestion has the same advantages as functionalism: reference is explicated in terms of a *higher-order* property of causal relations.

It is difficult to see how causal relations could be successfully invoked here without reference to something like *properties*. Not everything which satisfies a predicate is causally related to occurrences of the predicate. Snakes we have never known satisfy 'x is a snake'; they belong to the set denoted by 'snake'; they are among its references. Evidently it is not enough to require of the set denoted by a predicate that *some* of its members are causally related in the relevant way to some of the predicate's occurrences. That radically underdetermines the denotation of 'snake': $\{x:x$ is a reptile$\}$ and $\{x:x$ is cold-blooded$\}$ would qualify. Something like *being a snake* must be invoked in explaining the reliability of beliefs indexed by 'snake', as *being a reptile* or *being a boa* are not. I say "something like" properties, because intensions need not be invoked.[3]

An indirect consequence is that the reference of our words is in part a *social* fact. The reliability of beliefs under T is a fact about a whole population, and it is explanations of *that* property that I suggest determine reference. This does not mean that my word 'snake' can't differ in reference from yours, for it may differ in its functional role.

---

[3] For these "properties", expressions of our basic physicalist language will serve non-circularly, with Tarskian satisfaction imitating platonist instantiation. Pure Tarskian satisfaction is not in its turn a causal notion.

But given sameness of functional role, sameness of reference would be secured, subject to the Twin Earth provisos (cf. 7.4).

The explanation of reliability under T evidently does not determine our preferred reference scheme; although necessary, it is not a sufficient condition. For example, there are doubtless causal relations between internal occurrences of 'snake', and certain neural events, that figure in explaining the reliability of our beliefs about snakes; but 'snake' denotes no neural events. Before turning to the question of further refinements, let me turn to an argument of Davidson's that *no* causal condition, however refined, could contribute to eliminating radical inscrutability of reference.

In a recent discussion of inscrutability Davidson (1979) offers what seems to be two arguments for inscrutability. The first depends on assuming that the only possible evidence for a theory of reference for L is whatever there is for a theory of truth for L. Davidson takes a theory of truth to be determinable only by its role in explaining behavior, while on my account the assignment of truth conditions is radically underdetermined by considerations that are simply about the explanation of behavior, reliability involving, as it does, far broader connections with the world than those required to explain behavior. But Davidson's point is more abstract than his account of what determines truth conditions; whatever that may be, it exhausts considerations for assigning reference. Clearly enough, if that were true, reference would indeed be radically inscrutable. But of course I am suggesting that, while a theory of reference must *fit* a theory of truth conditions, it may be motivated by further considerations. The fact that our beliefs are reliable under T is one thing; that such and such explains that fact is a further thing.

But Davidson offers what is really a further argument, as follows (with the examples changed). Suppose a theory of reference T_1 says 'snake' refers to x iff causal relation C relates certain occurrences of 'snake' and x.[4] Then consider the theory T_2 which says that 'snake' refers to $\varphi(x)$ iff causal relation C relates relevant occurrences of 'snake' and $\varphi(x)$. The second theory comes out right if 'C' is suitably re-interpreted: let C_1 be its interpretation on T_1; then let C_2 hold between a term and $\varphi(x)$ iff C_1 holds between that term and x. If C_2 interprets 'C' on T_2, T_2 is an equally adequate theory of reference.

Let me restate the argument in what seem equivalent terms; if I have

---

[4] This does not mean that x itself causes those occurrences of 'snake'; the "causal relation" might be indirect: x belongs to a natural kind K such that causal connections between those occurrences and members of K explain the reliability, etc.

misunderstood Davidson, there is still an important general point to be made. In the semantic metalanguage L_m, in which we talk about the truth and reference of expressions of L_o, we have the terms 'refers' and 'C'. But the reference of those terms (it is being said) *is itself inscrutable*; we can interpret C as C_1 or as C_2 – on the former, our standard reference scheme is determined by the causal criterion; on the latter, the φ-reference scheme is determined by the "same" criterion. Unless we have nailed down reference for the metalanguage, it is not thereby nailed down for the object language. But there is then an indeterminacy all the way up, which no causal criterion can eliminate.

This argument begs the question. The proponent of the causal explication of 'refers' is naturally going to hold that it also captures what determines reference for the metalanguage L_m. The foregoing argument *presupposes* that there is no objectively determinate reference scheme for the metalanguage, which, as a premise in an argument that is supposed to show there are no objective reference schemes for languages in general, presupposes a negative judgment on the point at issue. Rather than yield to the indeterminacy of reference all the way up the metalinguistic hierarchy, we ought, when presented with an otherwise satisfactory explication of 'refers', to find determinacy all the way up.

In diagnosis of what has gone on here, let us return to what inscrutability means. The indeterminacy of reference with respect to physical fact and theory, I suggested, means that there is no otherwise adequate non-arbitrary explication of 'refers' that determines our preferred extension for it. What else could indeterminacy be? If there does exist such an explication (which remains to be seen), then 'x refers to y' is as determinate, with respect to physical fact and theory, as any predicate that is not initially in an explicitly physicalist language could possibly be. To accept such an explication for 'refers' would then be to accept reference as an objectively determinate relation between words and things.

Let us return to the problem of specifying the causal condition. There may be causal relations of words to features of the world that are not referential but still figure in the explanation of reliability, for example, to a neural state common to all English speakers and causally essential to the well-behaved formation of beliefs involving 'dog'. Why do such relations not count as reference?

A striking property of our truth predicate T is that it assigns conditions that are on the whole about *external* states of affairs. Similarly with our standard reference scheme. When it does otherwise, as with 'pain', there simply is no single feature of the external environment causally involved in explaining the reliability under T of beliefs that have 'pain' in their indices. This suggests a further interesting feature of our standard reference scheme: it looks outward when it can, to features of the T-conditions themselves. The reason, I suggest, is that our preferred referents are the *terminal* elements of the relevant explanations. Even if there were unified causally intervening features, say of light or sound, which could rival dogs themselves as common external factors in explaining the reliability of beliefs involving 'dog', connections with dogs themselves are essential to the explanation (not of the beliefs, but of their reliability under T). What about external factors which in their turn explain why such things as dogs are in a position to be thus causally related to us? Perhaps the idea is this. Any further such factors are not essential to explanations of the reliability of beliefs about dogs in the manner of dogs themselves. For if we eliminate relations to those further factors from the picture (across suitably similar possible worlds) and leave the relations to dogs intact, the explanation of the reliability of our beliefs about dogs survives, whereas, if we eliminate our relations to dogs from the explanation, the explanation perishes.

This suggests a certain general question about the relation between reference and truth conditions. The classical notion contains the Fregean idea that references determine truth conditions; this is related to Russell's idea that references are constituents of truth conditions. If they differ, it is because the Fregean idea suggests an interpretive *process*; one may proceed in regular ways from the references of parts outward to the truth conditions of the whole. (φ-reference schemes show that not just any way of setting up this process leading to the right truth conditions captures the right references.) Now the current suggestion as to what determines reference, something causal, is not on the face of it about *computing truth conditions* at all. Why then should determining causally related items be a step in computing truth conditions?

The first part of the answer is this: among the truth-conditionally adequate reference schemes, i.e. those computationally adequate assignments, there are some (including the time-slice schemes, etc.) that also capture salient explanatory connections. But why should this be possible? The second part of the answer is this: it is difficult to see *how* our beliefs could be systematically reliable under T *unless* there were

232

such causal connections between features of the beliefs and features of the relevant states of affairs, T's assignment of those features being the basis for the generative procedures whereby T assigns conditions to complexes on the basis of their constituents. Wouldn't reliability otherwise be inexplicable?

There are still those Quinean reference schemes that assign to 'dog' time-slices of dogs, undetached dog parts, or dogginess. They are all rather ineliminably present when dogs are, and are the terms of causal relations that may be just as explanatory of reliability under T as a causal relations to dogs themselves. Now, I see no prospects for a non-arbitrary further refinement of the causal relation itself that would rule out undetached dog parts, etc., and rule in only dogs.

What else could yield complete determinacy of reference? It may be tempting to accept whatever indeterminacy remains, content with the result that on all surviving reference schemes 'rabbit' refers to something very intimately connected with rabbits. But there is a paradox in this. It is extremely natural to think that, when one says 'that rabbit, etc.', in the normal way, an objective relation is thereby created between one's utterance and a certain rabbit, one that does not hold between the utterance and any of the rabbit's undetached parts, etc. How can we account for this if we give up trying to resolve indeterminacy of reference beyond the point we reached? Is the intuition simply wrong?

Let me mention a strategy that doesn't work. Four-dimensional rabbits are very specially involved in the T-conditions of beliefs whose indices contain 'rabbit'. For, truth theories which distinguish, say, 'there is a fat white rabbit' from 'there is a white rabbit and there is a fat rabbit', must somehow bring in the individuating conditions of four-dimensional rabbits. This much is obvious. Even φ-reference schemes, which may imply that 'rabbit' denotes some locomotive, are going to have to bring in rabbit-individuating conditions, if only by using the word 'rabbit' in the metalanguage when the scheme says 'rabbit' refers to γ iff $\varphi(\gamma)$ is a rabbit. So the thought occurs that what makes 'rabbit' refer to rabbits is that their individuation conditions are the *common factor* in the truth conditions of sentences containing 'rabbit'.

This suggestion simply misses the point. The problem is about the determinacy of *referential grammar* – about whether there is some empirically salient feature of our preferred way of assigning references to *parts* of sentences that makes it unique among all the others that are equally good at capturing the right truth conditions. All truth-conditionally adequate grammars in their way also associate correct rabbit-individuating conditions with sentences involving 'rabbit'. What the successful non-standard grammars show is that the other devices in a sentence can be reinterpreted to provide some of the machinery for rabbit individuation when that is not encapsulated, in the usual way, by the entities assigned to 'rabbit' itself (cf. the non-standard interpretation of '$x = y$' on p. 226).

Indeterminacy of *reference* is not the same as indeterminacy of *ontology*, that is, indeterminacy in the entities that must exist if a sentence is to be true. For under any truth predicate strongly equivalent to T, 'there exist rabbits' turns out to be true iff there exist rabbits, however one writes out those truth conditions, e.g. in the form 'rabbithood is instantiated'. Naturally some adequate reference schemes may quantify over abstract entities while others that are strongly equivalent do not. The foregoing point about individuation conditions might be taken to show that determinacy of truth conditions would secure determinacy of ontology, except for abstract entities. But nothing about the determinacy of reference, of referential grammar, follows.

The basic idea of what follows is that the remaining "indeterminacy" is not special to reference or to the realm of the semantic; once one sees it in the appropriate broader setting, there appears to be no interesting sense in which reference is indeterminate with respect to physical fact and theory.

Consider this attempt to solve the problem by stipulation. Suppose the considerations advanced so far determine a causal relation C such that, for each expression such as 'snake', 'rabbit', etc., the items to which it has C are connected with each other in the manner of snakes, the time-slices of snakes, snakehood, undetached snake parts. Call them the expression's 'broad reference class'. Then define 'refers' so that, for such expressions F (of a certain functional class), the four-dimensional objects in F's broad reference class, which are not proper parts of other members, are the references of F.[5] The idea, in short, is simply to add to C, for predicates of certain sorts, conditions that select

[5] This assumes two things. (1) A suitable set of predicates (like 'rabbit', etc.) can be demarcated functionally. Once standard references are determined for enough predicates, the rest of the standard reference scheme will be determined, given truth-conditional adequacy. (2) That the broad reference class of some of these predicates might contain objects of which their standard references are themselves proper parts is taken care of in the initial selection.

from among their broad reference classes the objects we naturally favor.

This stipulative solution is not enough to dispel the appearance of indeterminacy. But it has two interesting features. (1) Evidently such an explication of 'refers' is in a broad sense physicalist; for the condition 'y is a such and such four-dimensional object, etc.', is all that has been added to the causal condition. (2) Moreover it yields an *interlinguistically* ascribable relation of reference, for the causal relations between 'rabbit', '*coniglio*', '*lapin*', on the one hand, and rabbits, rabbit time-slices, etc., on the other, are not language-specific; nor is the new restriction. The extension of 'refers' is determined, for any language, by taking into account the functional roles of certain words, their broad reference classes as picked out by C, and the further conditions appropriate to their functional role.

There is still a real arbitrariness in the selection of references, and thus, it seems, no final resolution of the indeterminacy of reference. For what makes it appropriate that the four-dimensional object, rather than the time-slice, is chosen? It is of course compatible with Quine's point that, in our semantic metalanguage, we naturally *favor* talk of four-dimensional objects over talk of time-slices; pointing that out does not reduce the arbitrariness or conventionality that motivated that diagnosis of inscrutability. It does not help to say that, given the causal facts, it follows from what we *mean* by 'refers' that 'rabbit' refers to rabbits and not to rabbit time-slices, for that should no more reduce the arbitrariness than the parallel move with regard to truth (saying that it is just what we mean by 'true' that beliefs are true iff they are T).

But consider *non-semantic* locutions which express causal relations in whose range we count certain four-dimensional objects and not time-slices of them, etc. For example, consider 'a mammal's blood is pumped by its heart'. That involves a causal relation; but if there is arbitrariness in the reference case, i.e. in regarding the terms of causal relations as the most comprehensive relevant four-dimensional objects, we ought to detect a similar arbitrariness here. It is hard to see what the difference might be, since the point in the reference case has nothing to do with the *kinds* of causal relation involved. Suppose it is said that it is simply false that certain undetached parts of hearts do any pumping. But then so could we have replied in the reference case: "but it is just false that 'rabbit' refers to any undetached rabbit parts". If that is beside the point in the case of reference, so in the case of pumping. The upshot is that if there is an indeterminacy of reference, it is an instance of a general feature of causal relations to objects, one that has nothing specifically to do with *semantic* concepts.

What does this "indeterminacy" amount to? Do we really want to say that the truth of 'blood is pumped by the heart' is *underdetermined by*, or *indeterminate with respect to*, physical fact and theory? I do not think so, at least not in any interesting sense from which we should be prepared to conclude that "physiological facts are second-class facts". But if not in physiology, why in semantics? I have seen nothing that distinguishes the cases. In both, the explication couples a causal connection with a condition that requires the *relata* to be comprehensive four-dimensional objects, and that successfully determines our preferred extensions for 'x is pumped by y' and 'x refers to y'. In both cases the condition is in a broadly physicalist language, and thus determinate with respect to physical fact and theory.

But something here needs explaining. For have we *eliminated* the arbitrariness that seems to be present in the selection of four-dimensional objects over their proper parts? We have shown it to be a wider phenomenon that we previously thought; but why then is there not an indeterminacy in *all* such cases? I suggest that, while certain kinds of arbitrariness do warrant speaking of a real indeterminacy with respect to physical fact and theory, others do not. The difference has to do with the nature of explication.

As I argued in 7.3, the Tarski predicate T on our usual indices for beliefs provides, in its way, an adequate explication of the truth of beliefs. But the selection of T does nevertheless appear arbitrary, in such a way that were there nothing more to be said, e.g. about reliability, it would appear that in an important sense the truth conditions of beliefs are indeterminate with respect to physical fact and theory, because nothing in the latter would warrant that selection over others.

One way of looking at what was going on there is this. Before such issues of determinacy were raised, our commonsense philosophical semantic theories implied that there is a substantial non-trivial property of beliefs that constitutes their truth conditions. The Tarski predicate of course cannot on its own capture this. If no natural, substantive, property of beliefs had been forthcoming, a physicalist would have had to conclude that the commonsense–philosophical theory was wrong. The indeterminacy of 'the belief that s is true iff p' would have consisted then in this: on that theory 'true iff p' was supposed to capture a substantive property of beliefs, but given physicalism and the unavailability of a physicalist account of such a property, it does not. The point is this: any such arbitrariness would mean an interesting indeterminacy, for there would not then have been a fact of the matter *when pre-explicatively there was supposed to be one.*

Whether a certain concept, e.g., 'pumps', is "indeterminate with respect to physical fact and theory" depends on what that concept could pre-explicatively and plausibly be supposed to imply. If it was not committed to anything not expressible in a physicalist language the concept could thus hardly be said to be indeterminate. Semantic concepts of truth conditions and translation did purport, on certain theories at least, to correspond to substantive features of the world which pick out our preferred extensions for them uniquely; thus, if Quine's claim were correct, the upshot would be an interesting indeterminacy indeed.

But there is simply no reason to take our preanalytic concept of 'refers' as purporting to be any less arbitrary than non-semantic causal relations like 'pumps'. There is no reason to take our choice of hearts, rather than time-slices of hearts, as the terms of the pumping relation, as due to anything other than what is reflected in the extra stipulation about four-dimensional objects. The explication does not leave out any non-arbitrary determination of four-dimensional objects that preanalytically purported to be there; hence there is no feeling that 'pumps' cannot conservatively and determinately be explicated within a physicalist framework.

Similarly for reference. The sort of arbitrariness that remains is unlike the arbitrariness of selecting an extension for a term when that extension is not uniquely determined by the term's best conservative explication in a physicalist language. The appearance of indeterminacy of reference beyond the establishment of the causal condition is an illusion, due to the fact that not everything that determines our references is, in some intrinsic sense, part of the causal relation.

This is not to deny that there is something important in Quine's inscrutability thesis. We see here something of a piece with the under-determination of truth conditions by functional roles. One lesson to be drawn from Quine's work is that naturalizing semantic concepts destroys the Platonic–Cartesian–Brentanian theory of something *entirely mental* which determines unique projections of thought onto the world. But that is compatible with the availability, within a naturalistic framework, of ingredients adequate for conservative explications of those semantic concepts, which then make them physically determinate.

10

Public language semantics

Perhaps we think in English; but the most salient level of semantic description is quite independent of that hypothesis. I mean the description of what we say, ask, command, mean, refer to in interpersonal speech, as well as what sentences and words mean in a public language. I shall use '*public language semantics*' for the theory of such concepts – *locutionary* concepts (what *x* says), *illocutionary* concepts (what *x* requests, asks, promises, etc.), *sentence and word meaning* concepts (what they mean in a population in abstraction from particular utterances), and *speaker intention* concepts (what *x* means, implies, implicates).

These all ascribe content. So, in pursuit of my general thesis about meaning and content, I shall in this chapter try to motivate the Gricean hypothesis that all public language semantic concepts can be explicated in terms of communication intentions, that is, certain propositional attitudes. Given a belief-based theory of the language of thought and non-cognitive understanding, that would complete the account of linguistic meaning.

One thesis is that the semantic properties of a public language consist in its being a system of conventional devices for making known and implementing communication intentions, certain intentions to affect others' beliefs and intentions. As we have amply seen, this does not imply that communication intentions are themselves non-linguistic. The point is rather that ascriptions of public language meaning are derivative from ascriptions of content to intentions and beliefs; and the latter *abstract from* whether those states are linguistic. Even if they are linguistic, are in some language of thought, ascription of meaning to them is under the rubric 'belief (desire) that...', and thus there is no circularity.

Suspicion of circularity has been only one source of resistance to the communication intention theory. Another has been this epistemological point: we cannot in general determine a speaker's beliefs and intentions independently of what he says and then determine what he is stating, etc. Of course we cannot; but the communication intention theory in no way implies it. Rather it says that ascriptions of content to locutionary and illocutionary acts are explicable in terms of the intentions with which the utterance was produced, and of the semantic properties of the utterance-type, these being explicable via conventional regularities which associate utterance-types with types of communication intentions. The point is that what we state, promise, command, is *no more directly revealed* by our words than is the combined fact of what we intend and what those words mean. To say "such and such was being asserted on that utterance" is to put a *theoretical construction* on the utterance; the communication intention theory articulates that theoretical construction within the belief–desire theory. Communication intentions are inferentially as close to or distant from the surface of our utterances as the locutionary and illocutionary acts we thereby perform. There is no epistemological reason for resisting their explicative priority.

What other source of resistance to the communication intention theory is there? It is hard to take seriously a mere non-specific distaste for reduction. Spectacular reductive failure, as of phenomenalism and behaviorism, or of descriptive analyses of evaluative discourse, have little bearing on the general possibility of effective reduction. In phenomenalism and behaviorism, evidential conditions are mistaken for truth conditions; in descriptivism, the general function of ethical discourse is misidentified. But Gricean theories hardly confuse evidence for a semantic theory with its theoretical statements. Nor is it apparent how they might be misconstruing the function of ascriptions of meaning, which on any account is closely related to that of ascribing beliefs and intentions – i.e. explanation, understanding, prediction of behavior, inference to independent facts on the basis of reliability.

So those reductive failures indicate little about the current case. Far better analogies are with reductions within mathematics, or explications of knowledge as a kind of true belief, or of free action as action with a certain background of beliefs, desires and abilities. The simplifying, reconcilist motivations of such reductions are evident. There is no *a priori* reason why they should be frustrated, if for no other reason than that reductive success does not have to be total; moderate Procrusteanism may be quite to the point.

But what suggests that communication intentions *are* the basis of public language semantic concepts? Let me first lay out certain intuitive assumptions about meaning and speech acts, and then show how the

Gricean thesis is their most natural, if not absolutely inevitable, interpretation.

(1) The first is this. What sentences mean in a public language is a function of regularities that correlate syntactic and lexical features of utterances, with *purposive* properties that are somehow connected with communication and social interaction.

(2) The conventionality of meaning consists in those correlations, together with the effect that everyone's awareness of them has on their continued existence.

(3) Descriptions of utterances in terms of what is *said*, *stated*, or *asserted* thereby (as well as, perhaps, some illocutionary descriptions like 'pledges', 'bequeaths', 'asks', 'promises', 'commands') imply that what is uttered has meaning in the foregoing sense, and moreover that what is uttered conforms to the relevant conventions. Such notions then *imply conventional conformity*.

(4) Those descriptions, and all illocutionary act descriptions, *imply intentions*. Moreover, those that imply conventional conformity imply that the utterance is made with the intention to do something that conforms to the relevant conventions.

These assumptions, as I shall now explain, lead naturally to the idea that communication intentions are the foundation of public language semantic concepts. There are two sorts of concepts to be accommodated, about what sentences mean, and about speech acts such as saying, stating, and promising.

In what might meaning-generating regularities of usage consist? They somehow associate specific meanings with utterance-types, not by virtue of all such types having already been uttered but by some extrapolation from what has been uttered. Candidates for what utterance-types are correlated *with* are these. (A) Truth conditions, perhaps as possible states of affairs of which linguistic utterances are reliable indicators. So the regularities would (by extrapolation) associate 'maples shed their leaves in autumn' with the possible state of affairs that maples shed their leaves in autumn. (B) Relations between utterer and utterance, which, since they must determine specific meanings, presumably have the form 'the utterer thereby φ's that p'. What other possibilities are there apart from these two?

Assumption (1) about the regularities, that they involve purposive aspects of speech, eliminates (A) directly; I shall return to why this is reasonable. But, in pursuit of (B), what candidates are there for φ? Obviously they cannot be convention-implying speech acts, like stating, for that would introduce a vicious circle into the specification of the conventional regularities. The only apparent candidates are non-convention-implying illocutionary act types, an unexplicated non-convention-implying type of speaker's meaning, and propositional attitudes. I am aware of no theory on which non-convention-implying illocutionary act types or speaker's meaning are not also supposed to be reducible to propositional attitudes. While there could be such a theory, it is not clear what its motivation might be. So we are left with propositional attitudes as the relevant φ's. If the regularities involve *purposive* aspects of speech having to do with communication, that rather strongly suggests that the relevant propositional attitudes are *intentions* to affect others' thoughts, actions and intentions.

Why should the regularities not be a matter of correlations with truth conditions? Imperatives might then be explained in terms of correlations with hearers' reactive behavior. Without doubt, there are interesting systematic correlations between utterances and the obtaining of states of affairs we count as their truth conditions. But such correlations would also be explained by communication intention regularities; while to leave the latter out of the picture simply fails to account for our seemingly fundamental conception of public language meaning as involving the goal-directed use of language in communication.

The foregoing considerations imply that conventional regularities involving communication intentions are central in public language semantics – indeed, that they *constitute* sentential meaning. But there is the further thesis that such regularities and such intentions are adequate for explicating all other public language semantic concepts, e.g. saying, asserting, and convention-implying illocutionary acts. Let us now direct our assumptions to that end.

Stating implies intentional conventional conformity. It seems reasonable that the relevant intentions are not intentions to *state*: that leads *prima facie* to a vicious circle. (While intention-implying action verbs, e.g. 'to murder', can be used correctly to specify the intention with which the action is performed ('x intended to murder y'), there is always another way of specifying what is intended which is not intention-implying – 'to cause y to die'.) Our recent conclusion about the nature of the conventional regularities, together with assumption (3), imply that *necessary* conditions of stating that p are uttering something with a certain communication intention involving p, and uttering something, moreover, correlated by the conventional regularities with that communication intention. That these conditions are also *sufficient* for stating that p is a natural conjecture. For is it not plausible that to state that p is to utter a sentence that conventionally means p (or of whose meaning p is a suitable specification), knowing that that is what it means, and intending it to be taken conventionally?

These considerations are obviously not a theory; but given the explication of propositional attitudes in terms that do not presuppose public language semantic concepts, they provide a reason to think that some construction in terms of communication intentions may yield a reduction of semantics to propositional attitudes. The shape of such a theory might be this. First, a detailed account of communication intentions, or speaker's meaning, of the sort provided by Grice (1957, 1969) and by Schiffer (1972). Second, an account of conventional correlations between utterance-types and types of communication intention, which of course has to accommodate the *compositionality* of sentence meaning. Third, an explanation of locutionary and illocutionary acts in terms of communication intentions and (for some acts) those conventional correlations.

Communication intention theories of meaning have appeared to some not to give a properly central role to language and to the compositionality and conventionality of meaning. But that is a false impression. Communication intentions are invoked to explain what the conventional regularities *are* that constitute L as the language of P, the compositionality of meaning being a matter of the *system* in the correlation of utterance-types with the purposive aspects of discourse. That communication intentions do not presuppose anything semantic conflicts in no way with intuitions about the extreme dependence of communication on conventional regularities. Instead, they provide a non-circular way of saying what those regularities are, and thereby a way of explaining the intuition that conventional regularities are central to communication.

10.2 UNCOVERING THE STRUCTURE OF COMMUNICATION INTENTIONS

The recent career of the idea that communication intentions are the foundation of public language semantics was launched by H. P. Grice in his famous article 'Meaning' (Grice, 1957). There we find the idea of communication intentions whose specifications involve nothing about linguistic or conventional meaning, and of then accounting for linguistic meaning via regularities involving those intentions. Grice's original proposals have been elaborately enlarged upon by him (1968, 1969) and by Schiffer in *Meaning* (1972). Those accounts of communication intentions are conceived as *explications* of locutions involving '*means*': 'the speaker *x* means that *p* by his utterance *u*', 'the speaker *x* means that the hearer is to do *A*', etc.

Both Grice's and Schiffer's explications are elaborate; to present them here as such, without the extensive motivation they meticulously present, would not be helpful. But some idea of their structure is essential to what follows. The general idea might be conveyed by considering '*x* means that *p* by uttering *u*'. Its explication has three components. (1) A specification of the relevant intended effect: *x* intends some audience actively to believe that *p* is true. Schiffer gives interesting reasons for requiring that the belief be intended to be held for "truth-supporting" (as opposed to prudential) reasons, to distinguish 'meaning that *p*' from 'meaning that one's hearer ought to believe that *p*' (cf. Schiffer, 1972, pp. 57–8). (2) How the belief is intended to be brought about is essential. For Grice that was by means of the hearer's recognition of the speaker's intention to produce it. Schiffer is more liberal, requiring merely that a certain connection between the utterance and *p* is intended to be recognized by the hearer. (3) The speaker intends his relevant intentions to be recognized; there are various ways in which they may be, in cases which are thereby unlike ordinary communication (1972, pp. 17–30). Schiffer requires that the speaker intends the foregoing intentions to be completely out in the open between speaker and hearer, a notion he explicates as the speaker and hearer "*mutually knowing*★" the speaker's intentions. Two persons mutually know★ that *p* iff each knows that *p*, knows that the other knows, knows that the other knows that the other knows, etc. (I shall discuss whether this is too strong.)

I want to raise two sorts of questions. (1) Should we conceive of the project as the explication of various locutions involving 'means'? (2) Do Grice's and Schiffer's analyses, involving as they do complex intentions, over-intellectualize ordinary communication and understanding? Do we as speakers normally have such complex intentions and mutual knowledge★ and, as hearers, make the required complex inferences? I shall take up (2) in the following section.

In Grice's and Schiffer's explications of speaker's meaning, part of the point is not to *require* the utterance to have conventional or linguistic properties. If the project is construed as explicating '*x* means that *p* by uttering *u*', certain contrary intuitions about "meaning" may be triggered straightaway, *e.g.* '*that isn't meaning*; meaning is *conventional*, a matter of *rules*'; 'that isn't meaning; meaning is *compositional*'; 'that isn't meaning; it implies that the gibberish of a madman may have meaning, since it could be produced with the relevant intentions'. As those sympathetic to the communication intention theory have amply discovered, discussions involving points like the foregoing can be irresolvable. The fact is that they are completely beside the point.

The theoretical utility of Gricean intentions has little to do with non-linguistic or non-conventional communication, and of course nothing at all to do with ignoring the compositionality of linguistic meaning. It is true that humans sometimes engage in performances whose purposes are interpersonal, which do not involve the use of language or of anything with conventional meaning, and which bear strong analogies to linguisitic performances. It is an interesting and satisfying feature of Gricean theories that they enable us to capture the analogies. But the focus of the communication intention theory is *linguistic* meaning: what conventional regularities establish meaning, how compositionality is explained – i.e. what sentence meaning is compositional with respect to; what kinds of conventional act saying, stating, promising are; how truth conditions are associated systematically with sentences. And while the communication intention theory offers *explications*, they are not of such locutions as 'the speaker x means that p', but rather of 'says', 'states', 'promises', 'asks', 'this sentence means such and such', 'this is an approximately accurate translation of that', and so through the full array of convention-implying semantic concepts. This is not to deny that non-convention-implying speaker's meaning is important. On the contrary, it is an enormously useful notion in semantics, and perhaps in broader areas of interpersonal psychology. But it is *not* best presented as something initially given which the theory of meaning is to explicate independently of an antecedent conception of its theoretical role. What then are the constraints on a theory of speaker's meaning?

The general motivation I offered for a communication intention theory provides an answer. The relevant communication intentions are those whose correlation with the sentences are L are what constitute L as the language of a given population. Also, consider 'x asserts that p'. The communication intention theory implies that it is true of x only if x uttered something with communication intentions that are not intrinsically convention-implying and what is uttered is a conventional way of making known such intentions. The analysis of speaker's meaning, then, is simply the *abstraction* of whatever communication intentions play those and similar roles. This may help to place certain disputes about 'means' in perspective. If a critic denies an utterance can have "meaning" if it does not mean something in some language, the communication-intention theorist simply replies 'What you mean by 'means' is what I mean and/or that something with an appropriate conventional or linguistic meaning is uttered. I have independently accounted for the latter in terms of regularities that correlate utterance-types and meaning in *my* sense.'

This suggests how to go about isolating communication intentions. The procedure resembles Grice's and Schiffer's procedure, *as if* in explication of a locution such as 'the speaker x means that p'. Consider all speech acts, such as telling, objecting, asserting, reminding, that conventionally may be performed by uttering straightforwardly indicative sentences ('the cat is on the mat', and not 'I hereby promise to give you a hundred dollars'). Let us capture what such acts have in common, when expressed by conventionally appropriate sentences, under the term 'stating'. Then list all *necessary* conditions of x's stating that p which do not imply conventional semantic properties of x, thereby getting *sufficient* conditions for an utterance to be as similar to stating that p as possible without uttering something with conventional semantic meaning. In our "explication" of 'speaker's meaning that p', then, we reject as not necessary any condition that is not true of all central cases of stating that p and is convention-implying; and we reject as not sufficient any set of conditions not *maximal* with respect to those constraints. Grice's and Schiffer's extensive consideration of cases, and the intuitions that prompt acceptance and rejection of proposed conditions for x's meaning that p, may be seen in this light.

This technique also provides the key to the explication of *illocutionary* act concepts in a way that sidesteps the issue whether certain illocutionary acts are convention-implying, as Austin and Searle maintain, or not convention-implying, as Strawson and Schiffer maintain (Austin, 1962; Searle, 1969; Strawson, 1964; Schiffer, 1972). Schiffer's theory of illocutionary acts (1972, pp. 92–104) provides an excellent basis; it goes like this. A type of illocutionary act, like requesting or objecting, is defined in terms of two variable components, namely (1) the type of speaker's meaning involved, i.e. x's meaning that p, or x's meaning that the hearer is to do A; and (2) further aspects of the intentions involved, having to do with (one or both of) two factors: (a) the *reasons* the hearer is intended to have for the intended response; (b) some further specification of the (primary) intended response. (The basis for this approach is to be found in Strawson, 1964.)

Let us consider how 'orders' and 'objects' fit the scheme. If x orders y to do A, x means that y is to do A and x intends that y's recognition of x's power or authority over y shall be y's reason for doing A. The important factors are the imperative classification ('x means that y is to do A') and the intended reason. As regards objecting, x objects that p, to a certain proposition q advanced by y, if x means that p and that p is a reason for y's doubting that q. Here x means two things – namely, p, and something additional which determines the type of illocutionary act x performs (objecting).

This scheme is illuminating and explanatorily fruitful. Schiffer gives lists of illocutionary acts thus classified (1972, p. 99), and it is impressive how well the theory appears to accommodate them. Schiffer's scheme, moreover, vindicates Austin's proposal that there is a unified class of speech acts to be labelled 'illocutionary', although it does not exactly coincide with Austin's on the fringes.

This divergence is due to the fact that on Austin's theory conventionality is essential, whereas on the Strawson–Schiffer model it is the intentions that are essential. (Cf. Strawson, 1964, for an excellent account of the issues involved here.) Now I want to point out how little it matters whether some, or even all, illocutionary act types are convention-implying. Suppose on one's intuition about an illocutionary description, 'promises' say, it does not apply unless a conventional device for performing that illocutionary act, e.g. 'I promise', has been uttered. Schiffer's method is then to be supplemented as follows. Define a notion $I^\star$ (promising*) in terms of intentions, whose specification involves intended reasons, intended response, or both, and nothing about the conventional properties of what is uttered. Then the convention-implying illocutionary description 'I' is explicated thus:

> 'x I's that p iff x $I^\star$'s that p by uttering a conventional device for $I^\star$-ing that p.'

The phrase 'conventional device' alludes to whatever conventional regularities relevantly associate utterance-types with communication intentions, and thus convention-implying illocutionary acts are quite accommodated within the Gricean framework. Then questions about whether it is possible to promise or to command without uttering conventional devices for promising or commanding quite lose their interest. This is not to deny that there are excellent pragmatic reasons to build conditions of formality, of using conventional devices, into certain classifications of speech acts. For it may be desirable that utterances with certain intentions should have certain institutional consequences only when those intentions are made known conventionally, and thus desirable to have a verb to capture that.

This strategy for explicating an illocutionary act type I parallels the procedure for uncovering speaker's meaning. Find necessary conditions (following Schiffer's recipe for the intentions) which conjointly are sufficient for a speech act's resembling I-ing as closely as possible apart from whether a conventional device for I-ing has been uttered. If it is then thought that I-ing should be counted as convention-implying, let those conditions define $I^\star$-ing, and define I-ing as '$I^\star$-ing by uttering a conventional device for $I^\star$-ing'. ('Speaker's meaning' and 'stating' are thus related.)

10.3 THE REALITY AND RELEVANCE OF THE ALLEGED INTENTIONS

Grice's and Schiffer's theories are not unlikely to occasion the sceptical reaction: 'Do I then have such complex intentions when I speak?' Scepticism may also seem appropriate regarding the correlative account of the hearer; for understanding in the Gricean framework is often construed as an *inference* to the speaker's complex intentions. One may be inclined to suppose that the minds of speaker and hearer are usually less cluttered than the Gricean theory seems to require (so uncluttered, even, that the proper mental focus of meaning and understanding is just the information communicated, cf. McDowell, 1980).

Is it possible that those complex intentions are fictions, arising from the over-intellectualizing tendency generously present in traditional epistemology and action theory? I shall try to make it plausible that something very much like the alleged intentions are there and are essential to capturing public language semantic concepts.

Let us begin with the alleged *primary* intention in communication, the intention to produce an effect in the hearer which is the core of all other relevant intentions. On Schiffer's account, (1972, p. 63), imperative utterances are made with the primary intention to get the hearer to do A. Obviously that intention is present in normal cases; when it is not present, that is because the speaker is planning something more indirect – say, that the hearer intend to do A, or think that the speaker intends him to do A. In other words, deviations from the simple intention occur when the way to describe things realistically is to ascribe a more complex conscious intention.

On Schiffer's account, an indicative utterance is made with the primary intention of activating in the hearer a belief that p. And that intention is clearly present when a speaker intends to *inform* the hearer that p, to *remind* the hearer that p, to get the hearer to *conclude* that p. Deviations from that model occur again when more indirect intentions are present; thus, the speaker intends the hearer to believe that the speaker believes that p; or when the speaker expects mistrust the intention may be that the hearer recognize something like this: the speaker has *gone on record that* p. (This concept is intriguing. It seems to imply uttering something that literally means p, and is then parasitic upon conventional regularities involving the more usual intentions. It also implies further audience direction intentions; what they are it is not altogether easy to say. But *some* effect on the audience is intended; for the speaker doesn't simply focus attention on the proposition being asserted; he is trying *to get something across*, perhaps a refusal to acknowledge either that not p or that he does not believe that p).[1]

The complexity of Schiffer's analyses of indicative and imperative speaker's meaning lies in the *subsidiary* intentions, that the hearer recognize the speaker's intentions, that the hearer's intended response be produced in a certain way, etc. One may doubt that one usually has such intentions. To a query about the time one replies 'it's three forty-five'; one's thoughts are not cluttered with complex communication intentions.

That is correct, but beside the point. Let us begin with an observation about belief. Not everything one believes is something one actively or consciously thinks, not even things one has just begun to believe. Many beliefs are implicit, even for their entire careers. Now, some implicit beliefs are expectations. So, when one addresses a sentence in normal circumstances to a person who is attentive, a speaker of one's language, etc., one has many implicit expectations about that person's impending psychological states, about how they come about, their content, and so on. More directly to the point, there is nothing in Schiffer's theory, among the required intentions for meaning that p, which it is unrealistic

---

[1] There has been a tendency to assume that, for 'the speaker x means that p', some single primary intended response must be settled on (say, the belief that p or the belief that the hearer should believe that p). But if the enterprise is to isolate the communication intentions with which the relevant regularities correlate utterance-types, that assumption appears unnecessarily restrictive. It should not be difficult to explain why one type of sentence, say the indicative, is associated with a certain range of primary intended responses.

to count among normal speakers' implicit expectations. Not all expectations, of course, are intentions; but let us first be sure of the expectations.

In Schiffer's final account of a speaker's meaning that p (1972, p. 63), the speaker intends the hearer's activated belief to arise from his believing that the utterance is related to the belief that p in a certain way R. Now R may be the utterance's conventionally meaning p; or a semi-conventional relation – thus, if the sentence uttered contains demonstratives and p fits the sentence's literal meaning, and p is specially relevant to current conversational concerns; or a non-conventional relation: you round your hands in response to "What did you have for breakfast?" and mean you had a grapefruit, similarity in shape being one part of R, and relevance another. Can it be doubted that, ordinarily, speakers do *implicitly expect* that the, perhaps implicit, registering of such relations by hearers contributes to activating the intended beliefs? Such implicit expectations about the psychological states of others are automatic, except when the speaker is explicitly unsure, or is dealing with an infant, idiot, or *enfant sauvage*.

Schiffer's account requires the speaker to intend those intentions which constitute his meaning to be completely *out in the open* between speaker and hearer. That ordinary communication is transparent in this way is made clear by cases in which the intentions are not fully out in the open, and which intuitively are quite unlike ordinary communication. Schiffer proposes this account of mutually transparent knowledge:

x and y mutually know★ that p
    iff
x knows that p;
y knows that p;
x knows that y knows that p
y knows that x knows that p
    ⋮
ad infinitum

But there is a problem which concerns the psychological reality of the construction. For having such mutual knowledge★ requires *knowing* things ordinary mortals cannot consciously *think*, because of their complexity. (Each further stage involves a distinct proposition.) Although a person knows many things without consciously thinking them, it seems counterintuitive that a person knows things he is *incapable* of thinking consciously.

However, the intuitive idea of mutually transparent knowledge can be captured without knowledge of unthinkable propositions. Often one has *sufficient grounds for thinking* things one does not think, which may even be too complex to think. We can use this notion iteratively to capture knowledge that is "out in the open":

x knows that p

y knows that p

$$\vdots$$

x has sufficient grounds for thinking that y knows that p

y has sufficient grounds for thinking that x knows that p

$$\vdots$$

ad infinitum

Capturing this recursively, in a finite set of conditions, is of course quite a simple matter. So the idea is that knowledge of overly complex propositions is not required, while the absence of a block to transparent mutual awareness is captured.

If Schiffer's account is interpreted along these lines, there is nothing in what is supposed to be intended that normal speakers do not implicitly expect. (This is true of certain details I have not mentioned, as well.) But are these implicit expectations *intentions*? The concept of an intention one has *in* doing an action, but which is not the primary intention, is not altogether clear to me. But perhaps we need no general account here, for something about the relevant implicit expectations justifies Grice and Schiffer in counting them as more than mere concomitant expectations. Consider again Schiffer's idea that the hearer is intended to recognize a relation R between utterance and meant proposition; normally if the speaker *had not (implicitly) believed* that his hearer would believe that the utterance u stood in the relevant R to p, and that that belief of the hearer's would or might activate the belief that p, the speaker would *not* have produced u. Consider Grice's condition that the hearer's belief is intended to be brought about by means of recognition of the speaker's intention to induce that belief. When that expectation is present, e.g. in cases of telling, normally if the speaker had not had it, he would not have produced the utterance with the relevant primary intention. Again, consider the intention that the other intentions be mutually known by speaker and hearer. Usually, if the circumstances *had not been* such as to secure the relevant mutual knowledge, the hearer characteristically would not have known what to make of the utterance; so the speaker's expectation of the mutual knowledge is normally necessary for his having the intention to produce *that* belief, by *that* utterance, in *those* circumstances. (A big exception to this lies in cases of *reminding*. Then the "intention" that the mutual knowledge obtain may be a mere idle expectation.)

The general point, then, is that the subsidiary "*intentions*" of Grice's and Schiffer's accounts can be realistically acknowledged in the form of operative implicit expectations without which the utterance would not have occurred. Unless speakers were able to have those expectations about aspects of the hearer's response other than what is primarily intended, they would not be able to intend, normally, to produce the primary intended response by the usual utterances in the usual circumstances.

Philosophers of language generally sympathetic to communication intention theories of meaning have sometimes found the panoply of alleged subsidiary intentions too much, and have thought it possible to make do with simpler intentions (cf. Bennett, 1976). But not only is that economy not necessary for a realistic theory; to eliminate the alleged intentions eliminates something that seems fundamental to communication once one notices it. That the intentions, expectations and beliefs of ordinary communication and personal relations are simple appears so improbable that it puzzles me why it should be thought to be the more realistic view.

Consider again Schiffer's theory of illocutionary acts, which classifies them according to details of speakers' intentions. The satisfyingly unified structure that theory imposes can be counted a further reason for regarding those complex expectations, which correspond to Gricean and Schifferian subsidiary intentions, to be ineliminable accompaniments of primary communication intentions; their fundamental role in the theory of illocutionary acts makes it fitting that they appear in the basic account of speaker's meaning. Moreover, try to imagine what communication would be *like* if one lacked all those implicit expectations about hearers' reactions – different, clearly, from what we ordinarily experience. The core intentions are not enough.

Let us turn to the hearer's point of view. A caricature of the Gricean interpreter is of a creative diagnostician, who notices what is uttered, computes how it fits the conventional regularities, takes into account what he knows about what the speaker knows including what the speaker knows about him, registers the speaker's immediate concerns and interests, surveys the local scene, and then, after a complicated calculation, neatly deduces that the speaker has asked him if he would like another drink. The credit is not only the hearer's, for the speaker has foreseen the whole remarkable performance. What makes this a caricature is that it takes Gricean theories to imply that understanding involves conscious inferential processes. They are committed to much less.

First, and most obviously, nothing in the Gricean framework requires a hearer to know a semantic theory of the speaker's language in any ordinary sense of 'know'. What is perhaps not implausible is that knowing a language involves the capacity to know *of* each sentence (within limits) what its semantic properties are.

Second, the implicitness of beliefs is relevant. Many of the premises the caricature ascribes to the hearer's reasoning are in fact among an ordinary hearer's implicit beliefs.

Third, these implicit beliefs are such that without them the hearer would not ascribe the meaning he does ascribe. As has become a commonplace in epistemology, one sense of 'inferring p from q' is 'believing p because* one believes q', where 'because*' captures some suitably restricted causal connection. So, ascribing an *implicit inference* to the hearer does not seem unrealistic.

Fourth, the following could seem a problem for a Gricean theory: one's (conscious) judgment about what speech act some utterer is performing is not usually about some set of complex intentions. This may be granted. But the point is not inconsistent with communication intention *explications* of meaning and speech acts, in the sense of 2.5. To explicate a concept W as XYZ does not commit one to construing 'z believes... W...' as 'z believes... XYZ...'. Explication is *replacement*, however conservative it may be; hence, to propose an explication is not thereby to propose something interchangeable in psychological contexts with the concept being explicated. *Explicans* and *explicandum* will not be equivalent in functional or conceptual role. (Thus there is no paradox of analysis.)

It has been suggested by McDowell (1980) that understanding is like perception, that is, perception on a non-inferential model. One somehow comes to judge that x has asked one to pass the salt on the basis of what one hears, just as, in visual perception, one somehow comes to judge that the salt cellar is before one on the basis of what one sees. However, that does not seem as well motivated for understanding as for perception, precisely because it appears realistic to ascribe to ordinary hearers complex, implicit, operative, states, corresponding to the speaker's implicit expectations, which fit the (implicit) inferential model. (This is consistent with the preceding point that the *terminal* judgment that constitutes understanding is not about complex intentions.) But this does not imply the initial caricature of the Gricean interpreter. What Gricean intentions require of the hearer is more modest than the caricature, but more elaborate than McDowell's perceptual model.

10.4 LITERAL MEANING: SEMANTICS FOR A PUBLIC LANGUAGE

There is a classical model of language which, although quite intuitive, is nowadays subject to heavy scepticism in many quarters. It is that sentences have *literal* meanings, by virtue of conventional regularities of usage and/or facts about the psychology of interpretation and performance. The literal meaning of an utterance is supposed somehow to interact with context in determining specific communication intentions, truth conditions, or whatever; and the manner of that interaction with context is complex. First, even when an utterance is intended literally, not every aspect of what is meant is determined by the language. For its references and specific illocutionary force are often quite dependent on contextual features: the identity of the speaker, the time of utterance, and virtually anything the speaker may take the hearer to believe about the speaker's background beliefs, anything relevant to determining the speaker's intentions which goes beyond the literal meaning. Second, there is the matter of non-literal utterance – e.g. metaphor. Here communication intentions do not directly correspond to literal meaning, but, virtually always, knowledge of the literal meaning is essential to inferring the non-literal intentions.

Certain other basic intuitions in semantics depend upon that model. So, the ambiguity of a lexical item like 'bank' is perceived as quite different from what has sometimes been called the "ambiguity" of an indexical – e.g. 'this'. In both cases, the element may make different contributions to different utterances; and in both cases the result may be pragmatic ambiguity, when the hearer lacks the information to assign a specific meaning or reference. But in the former case the multiple potential is seen as equivocity in literal meaning, while in the latter case not. The explanation of this distinction in a literal meaning/context model could be roughly this: (a) the two or more contributions of 'bank' are themselves entrenched in past usage, but, with 'this', what is entrenched is not what it variously refers to but how it refers; and (b) mastery of 'bank' requires storing two pieces of information, which is not true of 'this'.

Certain models in linguistics distinguish a *semantic component* of the theory of a language, and that depends on an objective distinction between literal meaning and context, if, that is, the semantic component's task is to assign meanings to sentences and is not meant to include *everything* relevant to interpretation, which is to say, all knowledge.

Let us put the question in terms of a language L, that is, a function from sentences to meanings, which somehow encapsulate literal meanings. The question in effect is whether there are objective facts about a population which motivate selecting a given L as *the* language it speaks. Are there objective generalities about the communication practices of a group and their mastery of them which a "language" comprehensively captures? Is there an objective basis for the idea of literal meaning?

It will help to have some idea of what information a sentence's literal meaning might contain. Let us speak of the communication intentions involved in meaning that p as intentions to *express the belief that p*. Now consider a sentence which is indicative, contains no indexicals, and is not ambiguous. All you need to know about its literal meaning is what belief a literal utterer would be expressing, and that is captured by some sentence in the content language of our theory of belief. In that simplest case, a literal meaning is a sentence of the content language paired with a marker for the class of indicative illocutionary acts: it determines a class of communication intentions, via a relation whose definition is in our general background theory, which we might call *fitting*. Thus, suppose our marker for indicative illocutionary acts is the number 1. Then $\langle 1,$ 'snow is white'$\rangle$ is the "meaning" of the French sentence '*la neige est blanche*'; and the general definition of 'fits' will secure that if s has that meaning in P, z's communication intentions, on an utterance of s, fit s's meaning in P if and only if z intends thereby to express the belief that snow is white.

The *truth conditions* of such a sentence are, of course, the truth conditions of the belief it literally expresses; in what follows about sentences that contain indexicals, it should be clear how their truth conditions (or fulfillment conditions) are determined by the satisfaction conditions of certain elements in their "meanings" – certain sentences or open sentences of the content language.

What communication intentions speakers have on literal utterances of sentences that contain demonstratives (etc.) is controversial – whether they express beliefs that contain descriptions or that are irreducibly *de re*, etc. (cf. Schiffer, 1981). The question is how the "meanings" of demonstratives constrain the communication intentions behind literal utterances of the sentences they occur in. So, the sentence 'Hand me that hammer' might be assigned a meaning according to which the literal speaker intends a hearer to recognize a certain object y by virtue of its being (or appearing to be, etc.) a hammer, and to take the speaker to mean that the hearer is to hand y to him. The "meaning" could then be this object: $\langle 2, \langle \text{'hammer'}, \text{'me'} \rangle, \text{'}x \text{ hands } y \text{ to } z\text{'} \rangle$, where '2' is the imperative marker, and 'hammer' and 'me' as expressions of the content language determine constraints on how the hearer is to identify the referents, and the rest determines what the speaker intends the hearer to do. Naturally, ordering is important. The real work would be accomplished by the appropriate definition of 'fits'; it is really this language-independent relation between meanings and communication intentions that allows us to use the notion of a language in what follows (that is, a function from sentences to (sets of) meanings). There are other ultimately equivalent ways of explaining how sentences constrain communication intentions (e.g. taking a semantic theory to define a language-specific 'fit' relation), but it is convenient to be able to quantify over languages.

To say that a sentence's literal meaning determines a class of communication intentions is not thereby to say *which* generalizations in usage constitute L as the language of P – it is not to say, e.g. that sentences of L are almost always uttered by members of P with such and such communication intentions. The point is simply that the classical idea of the literal meaning of s is of a range of intentions within which those of a literal utterer of s would lie. It is another question altogether which generalizations about usage, etc., determine who is a "literal" speaker, and whether there are objective facts about usage in P from which literal meanings can be regarded as informative and motivated abstractions.

What, then, makes L the literal language of P? I have spoken of conventional regularities, and conventions. David Lewis (1970) and Stephen Schiffer (1972) have given helpful accounts of conventions, their common core being roughly this: 'a convention in P is a regularity in action in P (a correlation between actions and something else) which is mutually known among members of P to obtain and which continues to obtain because members of P expect it to'. Are there, then, *conventions* of meaning whereby L is the language of P?

The obvious first thought is that L sums up a simple correlation between sentences and communication intentions:

(A) There is in P the convention that if $L(s) = \{M_1,, \ldots, M_n\}$ and z is a member of P, then z utters s only if z has communication intentions that fit one of $M_1, \ldots, M_n$.

Now there are two respects in which this is apparently too strong. First, conventions require knowledge, and L is within the scope of 'convention that'; so it seems members of P have to have knowledge about L (as a whole). It also appears that the only non-circular way they could have this (i.e. apart from knowledge of L as 'the language of P') would be via an abstract description of how L recursively maps sentences onto meanings. Speakers would then have to know the semantic rules of their language, a rather strong requirement. To weaken the convention in this respect I have elsewhere suggested (1976b, p. 158) that speakers should instead have potential knowledge of the sentences of L one by one – which is to say, for each s, if $L(s) = \{M_1, \ldots, M_n\}$ members of P know that the communication intentions of s's utterer would fit one of $M_1, \ldots, M_n$.

On the face of it, this also requires too much knowledge, if L is an infinite language like English; for we do not understand very complex sentences of English, given limited capacity for processing embeddings, etc. Two things could be done here. On the one hand, give up the idea that any infinite language is a language of *ours*, which rules out making full sense of classical literal meaning. On the other, introduce the idea of our finite *effective* language, each of whose sentences we understand, and then let the full literal language be an unlimited extension of our effective language via the grammar that explains mastery of our effective language. I shall return to this.

Second, convention (A) is also too strong in not allowing for *widespread non-literal utterance*. I have suggested elsewhere a way of meeting this difficulty (1976b): the idea is to require the correlation to hold only when it is not improbable, for reasons *independent* of the existence of the convention, that the speaker's intentions fit the literal meaning. These reasons might be the hearer's having a better explanation of the utterance, or the unlikelihood of the speaker's meaning the relevant thing by any utterance, in the circumstances. Let us say that if such improbabilities do *not* hold with regard to a meaning M (it is not thus improbable that the speaker's intentions fit M), 'the speaker's utterance is *free* for M-ing'.

We then have this convention:

(B) There is in P the convention that if L $(s) = \{M_1, \ldots, M_n\}$, z utter s in circumstances in which z is free for M_i-ing, only if z's intentions fit M_i.

This has to be understood to require only sentence by sentence knowledge. (B) has interesting features; for example, it follows that if an utterance of s is pragmatically ambiguous it is at odds with the convention.

Now I think something like that sort of regularity does hold, with fair approximation, in ordinary speech communities. Nevertheless it may still seem unattractive to require something as definite as an actual convention. In any case, as I shall now show, (B) is too weak. And to supplement it successfully requires bringing in the notion of a *grammar* being *entrenched* in a population; but, as I shall explain, if we have that notion we may not also need an actual convention.

The following shows that (B) is too weak. Take a sentence that no member of our community would utter literally, such as 'Apollo has set the evening sky ablaze'. Moreover, suppose we all expect, correctly, that if z were to utter it in circumstances free for certain non-literal intentions M, then z would have M; this might be true, for example, of the intention to express the thought that the evening sky is fiery. Now let L' be like English except that it assigns that meaning to that sentence. Then (B) implies that L' is our *literal* language, whereas evidently it is not.

What is wrong is pretty elementary. Naturally the literal meaning of a sentence is not a matter of what would be meant by it, but of its grammatical and lexical structure, and their contributions to meaning. Let us call a *grammar* for L a generative way of assigning L's meanings to L's sentences on the basis of its repeatable structures and constituents. This idea will now appear obvious: we cannot specify necessary and sufficient conditions for L's being the language of P (in the sense of "literal language") unless we can also specify conditions for G's the correct grammar of P. This would have seemed far from obvious if one had merely reflected that a language can theoretically be generated by distinct grammars, and had consequently concluded that weaker conditions were required to say what makes L the language of P than to say what makes G entrenched (as I shall say) in P.

Within a communication intention theory, a grammar maps syntactic structures and words, roughly, onto structures and constituents of the beliefs sentences express, if we restrict things here (to avoid unnecessary complexity) to indicatives. Given the theory of fine-grained functional structure for beliefs, such a correlation of structures and constituents makes sense. Now what might make such a given correlation of structures and constituents *entrenched* in the usage of a population? Let us not be concerned at first as to what makes a grammar *uniquely* best; the question is how it might capture *empirically salient* correlations within usage.

The structure of the following account of grammar is this: the ground level is patterns of usage, that is, patterns in the structure of utterances and of accompanying intentions; the upper storey is a psychological internalization of those patterns, and its effect on their continuation in the usage of *P*.

Let us pretend that P speaks a simple language *L*, which is unambiguous, lacks indexicals, etc., has only indicative sentences, and is syntactically straightforward in this sense: the principle of syntactic complexity is the simple embedding of (open) sentences or relative clauses, etc., without sophisticated transformations (like "subject raising", etc.). In other words, the surface structure of *L* is very close to its deep structure. Call a syntactic construction *C-dominant* in *s* when *s* has the form $C(s_1)$ or $C(s_2, s_3)$, like 'not' in 'not mauve', and 'if...then...' in 'if snow is mauve then pigs fly'; and call s_1, and s_2 and s_3 the principal constituents of those expressions or sentences. These are purely syntactic notions, relative to the structure of the language of *P*. Now, a grammar for *P*'s language does these two things:

(1) It assigns to each syntactic construction *C* a functional operation *O* (e.g. functional conjunction, which generates the functional role of the belief that *p* & *q* from the functional roles of the beliefs that *p* and *q*; or predicative negation, which generates from the aspect of functional role indexed by a predicate like 'mauve' that aspect of functional role indexed by 'not mauve').

(2) It assigns to each word a meaning, that is, a certain constituent of belief indices.

Such a grammar generates the language *L* by the obvious procedure. You begin with the most embedded words of any sentence *s*, assign belief constituents (aspects of functional role) to them, and work outward by assigning to wider constituents the constituents, or whole beliefs, which you get from applying to the principal constituents the operation the grammar assigns to the dominant construction at each stage. (Naturally in a syntactically complex language like English the generative procedure has to involve complex transformations.)

The effect of *G*'s assignment is an isomorphism of structures – of syntactic structure and the functional structure of intentions to express beliefs. Now the idea of the *entrenchment* of G (not necessarily uniquely) in the usage of a population P is simply this: G's correlations of structure are interestingly widespread in P's utterances. But although there are in usage such correlations of structure, nothing in usage as such determines an objective basis for *extrapolating* correlations – that is, to sentences which haven't been uttered or are uttered with non-literal intentions, apart from simplicity considerations. The only possibility of having the full grammar determined by usage would seem to be *counterfactuals* – the generative procedures of G are extrapolable to an arbitrary sentence s by virtue of its being the case that if s were uttered in circumstances in which s were free for M_i-ing, then the utterer's intentions *would* fit M_i. But the whole point of introducing grammar was that that isn't sufficient. Moreover, many sentences have truth conditions so bizarre or complex that it is hard to say what would be going on if they were uttered. So while a grammar can fit usage, it cannot be determined by it.

I suggest the Chomskyan idea of the internalization of the generative procedures of a grammar has got to be invoked to make sense of the entrenchment of a grammar, and therefore to make sense of literal meaning. The exact force of this can't be spelled out antecedently to a detailed psycholinguistic theory. Consider the earlier idea (in 4.6) that a commonsense concept can be vindicated in terms of a theoretical structure which is not itself part of common sense. Now the ordinary commonsense concept of *knowledge* of the rules of a grammar is not the right idea here. But we do have the idea, at least in a general way, of how a cognitive psychology might contain a generative procedure acquired as a result of the impact of usage, and which plays an appropriate role in the continuation of that usage – that is, in those correlations of syntactic structures and the functional structures of communication intentions. This would vindicate the intuitive idea that *conventional* regularities are at work in language; for the pattern – usage, recognition of usage, and impact of recognition on continued usage – would then correspond to something objective.

Perhaps there is some other way of vindicating the idea that literal meaning is objective. But it seems likely that if the Chomskyan psycholinguistic picture turned out not to be vindicated, literal meaning would have to be counted as an arbitrary extrapolation from structural correlations in usage, one that arises from our simplifying proclivities as theorists. Nothing in the failure of a grammar to be appropriately internalized, however, would diminish the objectivity of the *basis* of the correlations – namely, that certain sentences are uttered with certain communication intentions, and that there is a widespread isomorphism between syntax and functional structure. Whether we are functionally organized according to the requirements of rationality and interpersonally ascribable content is a more general and more important question than whether a psycholinguistic theory of such an adventurous kind is true.

References

Armstrong, D. M. 1973. Acting and trying. *Philosophical Papers* **II**, 1–15.

Austin, J. L. 1950. Truth. *Aristotelian Society Supplementary Volume* **24**, 111–28.

Austin, J. L. 1962. *How to Do Things with Words*. Oxford.

Bennett, Jonathan 1976. *Linguistic Behavior*. Cambridge.

Block Ned 1978. Troubles with functionalism. *Perception and Cognition*, C. Wade Savage, ed. Minneapolis.

Carnap, Rudolf 1947. *Meaning and Necessity*. Chicago.

Church, Alonzo 1950. On Carnap's analysis of statements of assertion and belief. *Analysis* **10**.

Davidson, Donald 1969. On saying that. *Words and Objections*, D. Davidson and J. Hintikka (eds.), pp. 158–74. Dordrecht.

Davidson, Donald 1970. Mental events. *Experience and Theory*, L. Foster and J. W. Swanson (eds.). Amherst.

Davidson, Donald 1973. The material mind. *Logic, Methodology, and Philosophy of Science IV*, P. Suppes *et al.* (eds.). Amsterdam.

Davidson, Donald 1974. Belief and the basis of meaning. *Synthese* **27**, 309–23.

Davidson, Donald 1979. The inscrutability of reference. *The Southwestern Journal of Philosophy* **10**.

Field, Hartry 1972. Tarski's theory of truth. *Journal of Philosophy* **69**, 347–75.

Field, Hartry 1975. Conventionalism and intrumentalism in semantics. *Nous* **9**, 375–406.

Field, Hartry 1977. Logic, meaning and conceptual role. *Journal of Philosophy* **74**, 379–409.

Field, Hartry 1978. Mental representation. *Erkenntnis* **13**, 9–16.

Fodor, Jerry 1975. *The Language of Thought*. New York.

Grice, H. P. 1957. Meaning. *Philosophical Review* **66**, 377–88.

Grice, H. P. 1968. Utterer's meaning, sentence-meaning, and word-meaning. *Foundations of Language* **4**, 225–42.

Grice, H. P. 1969. Utterer's meaning and intentions. *Philosophical Review* **78**, 147–77.

Grice, H. P. 1971. Intention and uncertainty. Lecture to the British Academy.

Grice, H. P. 1975a. Logic and conversation. *The Logic of Grammar*, D. Davidson and G. Harman (eds.). Encino, California.

Grice, H. P. 1975b. Method in philosophical psychology. Presidential address, Pacific Division, American Philosophical Association.

Harman, Gilbert 1973. *Thought*. Princeton.

Harman, Gilbert 1975. Language, thought and communication. *Language, Mind and Knowledge*, K. Gunderson (ed.). Minneapolis.

Kripke, Saul 1972. Naming and necessity. *Semantics of Natural Language*, D. Davidson and G. Harman (eds.). Dordrecht.

Lewis, David 1970. How to define theoretical terms. *Journal of Philosophy* **67**, 427–46.

Lewis, David 1971. An argument for the identity theory. *Materialism and the Mind Body Problem*, D. Rosenthal (ed.). Englewood Cliffs.

Lewis, David 1972a. General semantics. *Semantics of Natural Language*, D. Davidson and G. Harman, (eds.). Dordrecht.

Lewis, David 1972b. Psychophysical and theoretical identification. *Australasian Journal of Philosophy* **50**, 249–58.

Lewis, David 1974. Radical interpretation. *Synthese* **27**, 331–44.

Lewis, David 1975. Languages and language. *Language, Mind and Knowledge* K. Gunderson (ed.). Minneapolis.

Lewis, David 1979. Attitudes de dicto and de se. *Philosophical Review* **88**, 513–43.

Loar, Brian 1976a. The semantics of singular terms. *Philosophical Studies* **30**, 353–77.

Loar, Brian 1976b. Two theories of meaning. *Truth and meaning*. G. Evans and J. McDowell (eds.). Oxford.

Loar, Brian 1980. Ramsey's theory of belief and truth. *Prospects for Pragmatism*, D. H. Mellor (ed.). London.

Lubow, Neil 1977. On defining mental state names. *Theoria*, **XLIII**, 3.

McDowell, John 1980. Meaning, communication, and knowledge. *Philosophical Subjects*, Z. van Straaten (ed.). New York.

Peacocke, Christopher 1979. *Holistic Explanation*. Oxford.

Putnam, Hilary 1973. Meaning and reference. *Journal of Philosophy* **LXX**, 699–711.

Putnam, Hilary 1975. On properties. *Philosophical Papers Vol I*. Cambridge University Press.

Putnam, Hilary 1978. Realism and reason. *Meaning and the Moral Sciences*. London.

Quine, W. V. O. 1960. *Word and Object*. Cambridge, Mass.

Quine, W. V. O. 1969. Ontological relativity. *Ontological Relativity*. New York.

Quine, W. V. O. 1970a. On the reasons for indeterminacy of translation. *Journal of Philosophy* **LXVII**. 178–83.

Quine, W. V. O. 1970b. *Philosophy of Logic*. Englewood Cliffs, N.J.

Ramsey, F. P. 1927. Facts and propositions. *Foundations*, D. H. Mellor (ed.). London.

Ramsey, F. P. 1929. Theories. *Foundations*, D. H. Mellor (ed.). London.

Russell, Bertrand 1912. *The Problems of Philosophy*. London.

Schiffer, Stephen 1972. *Meaning*. Oxford.

Schiffer, Stephen 1977. Naming and knowing. *Midwest Studies in Philosophy* **2**, P. A. French *et al.* (eds.), pp. 28–41.

Schiffer, Stephen 1978. The basis of reference. *Erkenntnis* **13**, 171–206.

Schiffer, Stephen 1980. Truth and the theory of content. *Meaning and Understanding*, H. Parret and J. Bouveresse (eds). Berlin and New York.

Schiffer, Stephen 1981. Indexicals and the theory of reference. *Synthese* 1981.

Searle, J. R. 1969. *Speech Acts*. Cambridge.

Stalnaker, Robert 1976. Propositions. *Issues in the Philosophy of Language*. A. Mackay and D. Merrill (eds). New Haven.

Stich, Stephen 1978. Autonomous psychology and the belief–desire thesis. *The Monist* **61**, 573–91.

Strawson, P. F. 1950. Truth II. *Aristotelian Society Supplementary Volume* **24**, 129–56.

Strawson, P. F. 1959. *Individuals*. London.

Strawson, P. F. 1964. Intention and convention in speech acts. *Philosophical Review* **73**, 439–60.

Strawson, P. F. 1971. Meaning and truth. *Logico-Linguistic Papers*. London.

Tarski, Alfred 1956. The concept of truth in formalized languages. *Logic, Semantics, Metamathematics* (trans. J. H. Woodger), pp. 152–78. Oxford.

van Fraassen, Bas 1980. *The Scientific Image*. Oxford.

Wallace, John 1977. Only in the context of a sentence do words have any meaning. *Midwest Studies in Philosophy* **2**, P. A. French *et al.* (eds.), pp. 144–64.

Index

ability
 beliefs about, 90
 as functional concept, 90–2
action
 as explained by beliefs and desires, 88,
  90
 truth and the success of, 198–201
anti-reductionism, about beliefs and
 desires, 11–13
Armstrong, D. M., 87
attitude ascriptions
 see propositional attitude-ascriptions
A-type beliefs, 71
Austin, J. L., 169, 245–6

Bel, definition of, 61–3
belief-ascriptions
 see propositional attitude-ascriptions
belief–desire theory, 6–9
 evolution of, 123–4
 interpretations of, 9–15, 78–81, 94–5
 and theoretical psychology, 77
belief–desire–willing condition, 89–90
beliefs
 commonsense generalizations about, 64
 as dispositions, 6, 124
 functional explication of, 57–65
 finite number of, 94–5
 individuation and truth conditions of,
  165–6
 and language, see language of thought
 and linguistic behavior, see linguistic
  behavior
 and meaning, 210–12
 about oneself, 113–17
 about perceived particulars, 98–107
 perceptual or observational, 81–5
 as relations, see propositional
  attitude-ascriptions
 truth conditions and functional roles of,
  65
 uniqueness of systematic roles of, 65,
  71, 74–81

Bennett, Jonathan, 251
Block, Ned, 96n
Brentano, Franz von, 3, 30
B-type beliefs, 71

Carnap, Rudolf, 5, 29, 81
Chomsky, Noam, 259
Church, Alonzo, 29, 30, 152
Church's objections to sentential analysis
 of belief, 29–30, 152
commonsense
 constraints on beliefs, 65, 78
 and scientific psychology, 78–81,
  96n
communication intentions, and meaning,
  212–13, 238–60
conventions, 255
 and illocutionary acts, 246
 and meaning, 240–4, 253–60
contingent principles of
 attitude-ascription, 129–32
conversational maxims, 132n
correspondence theory of truth, 166–70

Davidson, Donald, 8, 20–5, 26, 29, 33,
  38, 91, 127, 138, 172–3, 226
de re belief-ascriptions, 97–8
degrees of belief, 95–6
description theory of beliefs, 98, 99n,
  106–7
 and de re belief-ascriptions, 97
 involving names, 99
 about natural kinds, 159–60
 about perceived particulars, 100, 104–6
 Reichenbach's token reflexive theory as
  a form of, 110–11
desires
 and fulfillment conditions, 196–8
 functional roles of, 86–93
 joint role with beliefs in explaining
  behavior, 6–9
 in the standard scheme of
  attitude-ascription, 129, 132

multiple realization of functional theories,
  50–6
mutual knowledge, 249–50

natural kinds
  and M-constraints, 83–4
  in perceptual input conditions, 68
  and truth conditions, 159–63
  in truth conditions for observational
    beliefs, 185–6

observational–theoretical distinction, 70–1
observational beliefs, uniqueness of truth
  conditions of, 181–7
  see also perceptual input conditions
output of belief–desire theory, 91
  not chauvinistic, 96n

past, beliefs about, 111–13
Peacocke, Christopher, 91, 93
Peirce, C. S., 177
perceived particulars, beliefs about,
  98–107
perceptual input conditions, 65–71, 81
  needed to secure systematic uniqueness,
    9, 65
principle of charity, 8, 130, 133–4, 172–3
propositional attitude-ascriptions
  formal treatment of, 59–63
  meaning of that-clauses in, 164
  propositional interpretation of, 29–31
  relational interpretation of, 26–9, 142–3
  semantic-relation interpretation of,
    31–38
  two functions, 65
propositional attitudes
  earmarks of, 3–5
  meaning and, 1–2, 210–12
propositional field, 94
propositions
  elimination from analysis of belief,
    29–31, 142–52
  fine-grained structure, 58, 74
  as indices of functional roles, 63–5,
    143
  as relata of beliefs, 29–31, 142
  retained for convenience, 58
  two functions, 144
psychophysical correlations, 15–20
psychophysical laws, 20–5
psychophysical reduction, 20–4
public language semantics, 238
Putnam, Hilary, 10, 83, 159, 168n,
  177

Quine, W. V. O., 3–5, 26, 42–3, 118,
  119n, 121–2, 140–1, 148, 153, 170,
  171–2, 187–8, 225–6, 237

Ramsey, F. P., 46–7, 153, 158, 169, 210
rationality
  as constraint on beliefs, 9, 20–1, 24,
    71–4
  and psychophysical reduction, 20–4
realism, 168n
reductionism
  about propositional attitudes and
    meaning, 1–2, 128n, 238–9
  see also anti-reductionism
reduction
  functionalist v. law–law, 23
  constraint on functionalist, 77–8
redundancy theory of truth, 155–6,
  166–70
reference, 225–42
  for beliefs, 227
  causal nature of, 228–30
  social nature of, 229–30
  and truth conditions, 232–3
  see also determinacy of reference,
    grammar (referential)
referential semantics, 225
Reichenbach, Hans, 110–11
reliability and truth conditions, 161–4,
  174–94
Russell, Bertrand, 153, 158, 210

Schiffer, Stephen, ix, 97, 99, 114n, 132,
  210, 212, 242–51, 255
scientific realism, 177
second-order properties and states, 16–17,
  45
Searle, John, 245
self-ascription, see beliefs about oneself
semantic theory
  epistemological status of, 131–2
  of language of thought, 221
  of public language, 253–60
speaker's meaning, 243–5
Stalnaker, Robert, 58, 74, 139–40
standard scheme of attitude-ascription,
  128–32
Stich, Stephen, ix, 124
Strawson, P. F., 106, 169, 212, 245, 246
subjective probability, in psychological
  theory, 79
  see also degrees of belief
systematic roles for belief-ascriptions,
  63–5, 71, 73

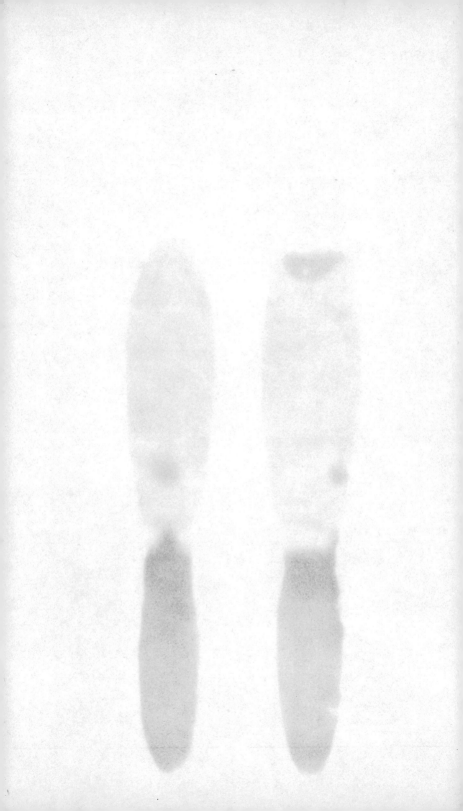